Communication and Instruction

Communication and Instruction

Ronald E. Bassett
University of Texas, Austin

Mary-Jeanette Smythe
University of Missouri, Columbia

HARPER & ROW, PUBLISHERS
New York, Hagerstown, Philadelphia, San Francisco, London

Sponsoring Editor: Alan Spiegel
Project Editor: Rhonda Roth
Production Manager: Marion Palen
Compositor: The Composing Room of Michigan, Inc.
Printer and Binder: Halliday Lithograph Corporation
Art Studio: Danmark & Michaels Inc.
Cartoons by Steven Duquette

Communication and Instruction

Copyright © 1979 by Ronald E. Bassett and Mary-Jeanette Smythe

Library of Congress Cataloging in Publication Data

Bassett, Ronald E., 1946–
    Communication and instruction.

    Includes index.
    1. Interaction analysis in education. 2. Self-perception. 3. Expectation (Psychology) 4. Students—Attitudes. 5. School environment. I. Smythe, Mary-Jeanette, joint author. II. Title.
    LB1115.B277   371.1'02   78-23390
    ISBN 0-06-040526-0

With love and gratitude to our parents—Lambert and Marion Bassett, and Barbara and Earl Hazelip—our first and best teachers

Contents

Preface

This book is about the communication that takes place when students and teachers meet face-to-face in classrooms. We wrote it for prospective teachers, as well as experienced ones, at all levels, teaching all subject matter. Through this text we hope you will gain a better understanding of how and why teachers and students communicate as they do. We believe such understanding is a necessary first step in becoming a more effective communicator and, consequently, a more effective teacher.

In focusing on teacher-student communication, we have drawn together recent theory, research, and practical suggestions from communication, psychology, and education literature with the aim of making our discussion relevant to the classroom situation in which you will (or do) teach. The view of communication we present is intentionally quite broad. We want to provide a perspective appropriate for a variety of instructional settings and subject matter areas. We think we have come close to achieving this goal for several reasons: (1) The principles about communication offered are not limited to any particular type of physical environment in which instruction occurs. The classroom might be a small therapy room in a clinic as well as the traditional setting of "good old P.S. 49." (2) Our view of classroom communication does not assume any particular set of learner characteristics. It applies to the instruction of students with special physical and emotional needs, as well as to nonexceptional students. (3) Our framework is not limited to any particular type of teaching method. Hence its usefulness is not affected whether you employ such traditional strategies as lecture, or newer ones, such as computer-managed instruction. (4) Finally, our perspective on communication is not limited to a particular teaching model or philosophy. Whether you ascribe to the nondirective model of Carl Rogers or to the

xii   PREFACE

operant conditioning model popularized by B. F. Skinner, we hope you will recognize that the principles presented here accommodate both models and many others.

Many people have contributed in important ways to the completion of this book. I (R. E. B.) first thank my wife, Billie. As with all else in the past decade, my part of the manuscript could not have been written without her unflagging patience, understanding, and support. Sherry Everhart-West merits special acknowledgment for her very careful and expert typing of my chapters.

I (M.-J. S.) wish to thank three extraordinary people whose contributions made this effort possible. First, Baboo and Biggie, who endured stolen pencils, bursts of temperament, anxiety attacks, and protracted explanations of the most recently written paragraph with love, good humor, and support. Elaine Wesley faced countless pages of legal pads with almost unflinching equanimity, tried valiantly to impose order on chaos, and kept me supplied with tangerine Lifesavers, an orangutan, and an abundance of help when I needed it most. Others who helped were Marge O'Bryan, with last-minute typing and excellent plant care, and Ron Bassett, who prodded, praised, and probably prayed a lot throughout this project. Final thanks to the student who thought the title of this book was "Communication and Destruction," for the insight.

Finally, we want to acknowledge together the valuable contribution of Ann Staton-Spicer who prepared the instructional activities and other teaching-learning materials in the instructor's manual which accompanies the text. Professor Staton-Spicer, of the University of Washington, has taught a course in classroom communication for several years and has done extensive field testing of the original, experience-based learning activities she has included in the instructor's manual. We want to extend our special appreciation to Robert Hopper, of the University of Texas, Austin, for bringing his knowledge about language to Chapter 4, "The Verbal Symbol System," which he authored. And, we thank Beverly White Spicer for conceiving the ideas for the cartoons appearing throughout the text.

RONALD E. BASSETT
MARY-JEANETTE SMYTHE

Chapter 1
The Communication Process

OBJECTIVES

After reading this chapter you should be able to:

1. explain the importance of effective communication in classrooms.
2. identify four unique characteristics of the classroom group.
3. explain why communication is unavoidable.
4. explain why communication is continuous.
5. create an original example which demonstrates that communication is a process of mutual influence.
6. describe how the psychological conditions of the participants can affect communication.
7. explain how self-concept affects communication.
8. describe how impressions of others affect communication.
9. identify the symbol systems teachers and students use.
10. describe the importance of positive social environments in classrooms.
11. explain the effects of physical environments on communication in classrooms.

Adams and Biddle (1970) tell of a man from Mars who comes to our planet and looks in on a group of earthlings. What does he see? Well, as they describe it:

> He sees people occupied variously. Some sit, some stand, some move about, some talk, some keep silent, some write, draw, point, prod, sing, fidget, cry, laugh, whisper, some even sleep. Among these people, one appears to dominate. This one, apparently, exerts a controlling influence, gives directions which are usually carried out, and makes condemnatory and approving comments.
>
> There is a great deal of communication in this [place]. Some of it is surreptitious, but most of it is public. It takes the form of talking primarily, although much writing is done. It is possible, too, that a peculiar mannerism of the inhabitants, the raising of one arm and agitating it fiercely in the air, is also a means of communication. Messages may be conveyed in other ways in the setting. This individual who dominates the situation may, for instance, frown, raise an admonitory finger, or crash a leather strap on a desk or upon a reluctant hand whereupon the other members become silent. Communication in its many forms appears to be of considerable importance. (p. 8)

The Martian was of course observing a classroom. This book is concerned with the communication which occurs in such places and which our Martian visitor so correctly judged to "be of considerable importance."

Because you have spent so much time in classrooms, though, and have much experience in communicating there, you may ask, "What's new to learn?" We answer by asking, "Are you certain others always interpret your words and actions exactly as you intend? Are you satisfied that you always interpret the words and actions of others exactly as *they* intend?" Unless you can answer "yes" to both questions, there *is* something new to learn about communication. Reading this book, or studying communication in any other way, will not, however, guarantee easy solutions to the communication problems encountered in teaching. We believe, though, that you can acquire some new understanding of the communication transactions in which you and your students participate. By developing new ways of looking at your behavior and that of others, you may be able to become a *more effective* communicator, and effective communication is critical to the process of instruction.

Instruction Is a Process of Assistance

Some ads in popular magazines promise you can "teach yourself" to play the guitar, do magic tricks, hypnotize others, master kung-fu, and so on. Most behaviors humans perform are not, however, literally self-taught. That is, they are learned with the aid of another. Sometimes this assistance is quite indirect, as, for example, in language learning. It is not necessary specifically to teach a child sounds and words for normal language development to occur. It is necessary, though, for a child to *hear* language spoken by *others*. Hence others influence children's language learning simply by talking and thereby providing models for them to imitate.

For other kinds of learning more direct assistance may be required. Consider, for example, learning to read music. It seems unlikely that a person could learn to read music without help from others. For the inexperienced, a sheet of music can be baffling. There are lines that extend horizontally across the page. Tiny circles (some inked in) with vertical lines attached to them are placed on or between, or sometimes a considerable distance from, the horizontal lines. Letters such as *mf, p*, and *ff* are placed at various points on the page. If all the above were not confusing enough, foreign-sounding words such as *lento, allegretto*, and *fortissimo* may be scattered about. Even the most motivated of aspiring musicians might become frustrated in discovering the meaning of this array of symbols without guidance from an experienced person.

To summarize, whether the learner requires minimal or substantial aid, we view the process of instruction as occurring when one person helps another to change his or her behavior. We are able to help others learn simple as well as highly complex behaviors because of our ability to communicate.

To appreciate the importance of effective communication in instruction, we need only consider the goal of the classroom group. Adams and Biddle (1970) have observed that this objective is to change the behavior of the majority (students). Specifically, the goal is to increase knowledge which the larger society has judged valuable, and to promote acceptance of appropriate behavior, norms, attitudes, and values. Now a person can acquire knowledge and attitudes by reading books, watching television, or simply observing others. In the classroom, however, the assumption is that students learn through *interaction* with the classroom group.

Learning, however, is only one of the possible outcomes of this interaction. Despite a teacher's attempts to help students learn, the desired changes may not take place. To understand the outcomes of teacher-student transactions, to predict them, and to increase the chances that learning will occur, it is necessary to understand what happens when teacher and student meet face-to-face. What happens? They communicate. It is the quality of this communication, more than any other factor, that determines the success of instruction. Teaching is, after all, professional communication.

The remainder of this chapter presents a perspective for viewing communication, which should be valuable for you as a teacher. To understand this perspective fully, you must first know about some of the unique features of the classroom group which influence communication. In the following section the most important of these features are identified.

THE CLASSROOM GROUP

A teacher and his or her students constitute a social unit we may refer to as the classroom group. Because this organization of teacher and students functions as a group, principles of human communication observed in other groups may be expected also to apply to the classroom group.

Certain characteristics of classroom group members and the relation of members to the group and to each other *are* unique, however, in important ways. Frank (1973) has identified four of these unique characteristics.

First, in most groups the members have a substantial amount of control over membership. By comparison, membership in the classroom group is determined almost completely by nonmembers (i.e., the school administration). Hence neither teacher nor students have much say about who is admitted or permitted to remain.

Second, people retain membership in most groups because they value the goals of the group or derive pleasure from relationships with other members. In essence, group membership is maintained because membership satisfies some need. In the classroom group, however, some, many, or all of the students may be there involuntarily because of parental demands, state laws, or degree plans. Furthermore, some of those physically present may not even consider themselves members, because they have rejected the educational objectives, classroom norms, teacher, or fellow students.

Third, members of most social groups usually share a number of personal characteristics. Students, on the other hand, frequently differ in such characteristics as sex, race, physical and emotional maturity, socioeconomic background, career goals, achievement levels, and basic values and objectives regarding the educational process. In addition, the teacher is likely to differ greatly from the students. Teachers are adults (usually female) and, most importantly, are perceived by students as agents of authority.

Finally, while many types of groups contain subgroups, the classroom group is unique in both the number and nature of the subgroups likely to exist. The most basic subgroup is composed of the teacher and a single student who competes with other students for rewards controlled by the teacher. The typical classroom, then, might be described as containing as many as 30 subgroups. In addition, some classroom groups may contain students with memberships in groups outside the school (e.g., a social fraternity). Frequently, students have greater allegiance to such groups than to the classroom group, making the social unit of the classroom even more complex and unstable. Combined with these somewhat formal subgroups, there is a great number of informal ones which may range from two students (or a teacher and a student, as seen above) to a number of combinations of teacher and/or students.

The implication of these differences between classroom groups and other social organizations is that, over a semester, a class becomes an exceptionally complex group. Despite the unique characteristics we have identified, however, *the process of communication* is essentially the same in classroom groups as in a variety of other organizations. It is artificial, then, to talk of classroom communication as if it were a distinct form of communication. Rather, we should say that the classroom is a unique context for communication. This fact suggests that teachers wishing to function effectively within this specific context must possess specialized skills and knowledge about the process of communication. In our view, such skills and knowledge can best be acquired when the study of communication focuses on the particular types of transactions frequently observed within the classroom.

Having considered briefly the unique features of classroom groups, we proceed with the task of defining communication. A number of principles may be stated about communication. Three which are most important to your understanding of classroom transactions are examined in the following section.

PRINCIPLES OF COMMUNICATION

What happens when student and teacher meet face-to-face? Communication takes place. What is communication? It is an event. *It occurs whenever people assign meaning to each other's behavior.* The first thing you must realize is that it is impossible for them to do otherwise.

Communication Is Unavoidable

We said that it is possible for student and teacher to interact without learning occurring. When either is aware of the other's presence, however, *it is impossible for communication not to occur.* If you believe communication occurs only when people talk to one another, the previous sentence may not make much sense. The explanation which follows may help clarify our point.

We all have an uncontrollable need to interpret events we experience. By the term "events" we would include the behavior of others around us. If you are in the presence of someone, stop and look. Is the person talking, staring at you, sleeping, scratching, or reading? No matter what the individual is doing, he or she is *behaving*, and you cannot be aware of the behavior and fail to interpret it in some way.

Some times we want people to be aware of us and interpret what we say and do in particular ways. At other times we do not seek attention and do not want meaning attached to our acts. It is important to realize, however, that, regardless of our intentions, we cannot keep people from attributing meaning to our behavior.

The mere absence of talking does not mean that communication is not occurring. You learned long ago how to indicate to teachers that you didn't know the answer to a question. You simply stared at your desk top and avoided their gaze. Even in such periods of silence, there are few teachers who do not "get the message." There are numerous other non-talking behaviors students perform regularly, which may provide the teacher with a wealth of information. Students frown or smile. They sit rigidly or slump. They squirm in their seats. They run around the room. They tap their feet and drum their fingers, or move neither. They stand or sit close to their teacher or at a distance. They gaze out the windows or look at their teacher. The teacher who is sensitive to these and other nonverbal behaviors knows they can indicate whether students are interested or bored, friendly or hostile, attentive or inattentive.

We have seen that it is impossible for students to keep their teacher from assigning meaning to their behavior. You, as a teacher, should also realize that with a class of 30 students your behavior may be interpreted in 30 different ways. Students react not only to the words you speak, but also to the tone of your voice and whether you speak softly or loudly. They also attach meaning to the formality of your clothing (a dress or a suit versus jeans), facial expressions, posture, gestures, hair length and style, touching, and way of walking.

A teacher and a student do not have to talk for communication to occur. If one is aware of the other's presence, he or she will assign meaning to the person's behavior. Communication is unavoidable.

Communication Is Continuous

When two people meet face-to-face, communication is nonstop. Both are *simultaneously* behaving and attributing meaning to the behavior of the other. At one moment the teacher may be talking. While the student is interpreting what he or she is hearing, as well as what the teacher is doing, the teacher is attributing meaning to the student's eye movements, body tension, facial expressions, and other responses. This interpretation of behavior is continuous when people are aware of one another, and it may even continue when they are no longer in each other's presence.

For our purposes, we consider that communication begins when

FIGURE 1.1 COMMUNICATION CAN OCCUR WITHOUT TALK.

teacher and student meet for the first time. It does not follow, however, that because we can identify a beginning we can identify an ending. Communication *cannot* be said to end when teacher and student part company at the close of the school day. If teachers review the events of the day, they will certainly continue to attribute meaning to the behavior of students. Students, in remembering and perhaps describing their day's activities to friends or parents, continue to interpret the behavior of their teacher as well as that of their classmates. To specify when communication ends, we would have to identify the moment at which people stop attributing meaning to the behaviors of others. Since it isn't possible to look directly into people's heads, you can appreciate the difficulty of the task. Therefore we suggest you think of communication as a continuous process.

Communication Is a Process of Mutual Influence

When two people meet face-to-face, each influences the other. This simply means that neither person behaves independently. As we have seen, when two people interact, each continuously attributes meaning to what the other is saying or doing (or not saying or not doing). The meaning you attribute to another's behavior influences the way you respond. Likewise, the way in which another person interprets your actions influences the way in which he or she responds to you. Thus the process of communication binds people together in a unique manner. Your response at any moment has been influenced by your interpretation of the previous actions of the other person. Your response in turn is interpreted by the other and influences his or her response. And the process continues, on and on.

Perhaps an example from the classroom will help to clarify this principle of mutual influence. No matter at what level you teach, there will doubtless be numerous times when you talk to the entire class. Your talking might range from an off-the-cuff description of an upcoming assignment to a prepared, somewhat formal, lecture.

Imagine that it is Monday morning and, rested from the weekend, you are well prepared to deliver your favorite lecture to your eight o'clock class. Your students, however, are not nearly as eager to hear the lecture as you are to deliver it. You notice immediately that several heads nod, most bodies slump, and few eyes are visible. Observing these responses you say to yourself, "I'm bombing. The students are bored. In a few minutes they will all be asleep."

You respond by developing a bad case of stage fright. Beads of sweat pop out on your forehead. You look at your students less frequently. You begin to lick your lips rapidly. You mispronounce words and lose your train of thought. Students interpret these responses as signs that you are poorly prepared. In response, they indicate by their behavior they are even less interested in listening now than when you began.

What we have here, to use a well-worn cliché, is a vicious circle. If left unchecked, conditions will only deteriorate further. With each additional student response you interpret as indicating boredom, you are likely to become more undone. The result is that students react even more negatively. Perhaps you will be saved by the bell. A more desirable alternative is for you to take direct action to break the cycle. We have found that simply laying down one's notes and walking slowly to the side of the room to tell a humorous anecdote can recapture attention. Obviously there are many other tactics. In any event, if you are like us, you will find that, when the students appear to start listening again, you will regain composure and become more effective in making the presentation. In turn, the students will become more attentive.

The purpose of this example has not been to suggest ways of capturing and maintaining attention. Rather, we have sought to illustrate how each participant in the communication process is affected by the behavior of the other. These effects may not always be so intense as those in our example, but you may be certain they will occur.

In this section we have examined some unique features of the classroom group and three important principles of communication. A set of additional principles follows, which summarizes the most important points made thus far.

PRINCIPLES 1.1

1. Effective communication is important in the classroom because the instructional process is based on the assumption that students learn through interaction with the classroom group.
2. Classroom groups are unique because (1) the members don't determine the membership, (2) membership is often involuntary, (3) members are frequently highly dissimilar, and (4) many subgroups exist.
3. Communication is unavoidable because one person cannot be aware of another and fail to assign meaning to the other's behavior.
4. Communication continues for as long as one person assigns meaning to the behavior of another.
5. Communication is a process of mutual influence in that, when two people interact, each affects the other.

BECOMING A BETTER PARTICIPANT IN COMMUNICATION

As stated earlier, our purpose is to help you gain a better understanding of communication and become a more effective participant in the classroom group. In our view, teachers are truly effective participants when they interpret students' behavior in the way students intend, and when they

FIGURE 1.2 EFFECTIVE COMMUNICATION OCCURS WHEN MEANING IS SHARED.

behave so that they convey their intended meaning. Granted, it is difficult to achieve these two conditions. This is the case because the meaning one person attributes to the behavior of another is highly personal. No other person in the world would make *exactly the same* interpretation, and it is impossible for you to perceive the exact interpretation intended by another. Why not? Because no two people have the same set of experiences, and it is through our experiences that we filter the words and actions of others to arrive at their meaning.

It *is* possible to become a more effective participant. To do so, however, requires that you develop a better understanding of *why* people interpret the behavior of others as they do. To predict accurately a student's interpretation of what you say or do, you must have an understanding of his or her (1) psychological state, (2) self-concept, (3) perception of you, (4) symbol systems, (5) perception of the social environment, and (6) perception of the physical environment. Likewise, to understand why *you* attribute some particular meaning to a student's behavior, you must understand *your* psychological state, self-concept, perception of the student, symbol systems, and perception of the social and physical environments.

In the remainder of this chapter we briefly introduce you to these six concepts. Subsequent chapters examine these factors, as well as others of importance to the process of communication and instruction, in greater detail.

Psychological State

When we interact with a person who is blind or deaf, we are acutely aware of the limitations the person may have in responding to *all* of our behavior. When senses are impaired, there exists the possibility that the person will simply not be able to detect our words and actions. Obviously, if a person has difficulty hearing or seeing, the probability that he or she won't interpret our behavior as intended is also greatly increased. But all of us are partially blind and deaf when it comes to the accurate interpretation of another's behavior. The nature of human perception makes this inevitable.

We are constantly immersed in a sea of stimuli. Even when face-to-face with only one person, countless stimuli compete for our attention in addition to the facial expression, voice, words, posture, scent, and body movements of the other. These competing stimuli include all objects, sounds, light, and movement external to us, as well as our own thoughts and feelings. If a student is having an anxiety attack because she fears she will fail the chemistry test to be given next period, it will be difficult for her to attend closely to your detailed explanation of the Battle of Bull Run. If a student is daydreaming about baseball on a spring afternoon, he may be unaware of events in the classroom. Thus simply because students are in your presence does not ensure that they are attending to you. Only by carefully observing responses can you hope to know whether you have their attention and whether you are creating the meaning you intended. And only by closely attending to your own thoughts can you know whether you are giving full attention to students. Most of us, teachers as well as students, have become quite skilled at pretending we are paying attention, while actually we are hearing and seeing little of what the other person is saying or doing.

Self-Concept

Your self-concept is composed of a vast number of ideas you have about how you appear, your abilities, your history, and your value. The development of a person's self-concept is affected in large part by the ways others respond to him or her. In turn, a person's self-concept affects the meaning he or she attributes to others' behavior and his or her own subsequent responses. As you have seen, your responses to others influence the way they respond to you. Others' responses in turn affect your self-concept. Let's briefly consider one example of how a student's self-concept can affect his or her interpretation of a teacher's behavior.

Gergen (1971) has observed that children who receive many negative responses from parents, brothers and sisters, and playmates may come to dislike themselves. When they meet a teacher, it may be with the expectation the teacher will also treat them badly. As a result, they may interpret the teacher's behavior in a way that satisfies their expectations. Psychologists call this phenomenon *biased scanning*. When we engage in biased scanning we are searching for cues which confirm the self-view we hold. Hence students who dislike themselves may look for the smallest clue to support their belief that the teacher also dislikes them. Conversely, children who have been well treated and have come to view themselves as valued and loved may selectively scan the behavior of others to support these beliefs.

Self-concept influences not only our interpretation of another's acts, but also the goals we set and our motivation for achieving them. Possession of a favorable self-concept is very important to students' success in school. We devote considerable attention to examining how teachers can have the most effect in helping students develop positive self-concepts.

It is also important for teachers to have positive self-concepts. Problems that teachers have in being effective participants in communication often result from the ways in which they view themselves. If you think about yourself in a certain way, you are likely to behave that way. Hence if you view yourself as ineffective, you are likely to *become* ineffective. Effective teachers, in contrast, have high self-regard and see themselves as competent, accepted, and needed by others. One of the first steps in becoming more effective is to gain a better understanding of *how* you view yourself and recognize the potential you have for becoming more effective.

Perception of the Other

It is impossible to interact with people and not form impressions of them. Your students probably have images of you which differ a lot from your own self-view. What a particular student thinks of you may be entirely different from what others think or from what you really are. No matter, a student's impressions are accurate as far as *he or she* is concerned. Likewise, the impressions you have of any student are likely to be accurate as far as *you* are concerned.

When you first meet a class, your physical characteristics (height, weight, age, sex, racial or ethnic origin, and physical attractiveness) are the primary factors contributing to the impression students form, and vice versa. It is frustrating to acknowledge that these aspects over which we have the least control are critical factors in initial impression formation. From the early school years onward, however, good looks are sometimes equated with goodness and talent in students as well as teachers.

We also form impressions of others on the basis of their actions. By the end of the first hour of the first class meeting, both students and teacher have formed impressions of liking and disliking. These first impressions may not be accurate, but they influence how each perceives the other's future actions.

We cannot overemphasize how important it is that students have positive images of their teachers. As stated earlier, a teacher's mission is to help students change. Furthermore, we believe that teachers facilitate student learning through interpersonal influence. To be effective in promoting student learning, teachers must frequently *persuade* students that the learning goals (or methods of learning) they advocate are worthwhile. Investigations of the process of interpersonal influence have shown that, to be successful, persuaders must be perceived in positive ways by those whom they wish to persuade.

Symbol Systems

Symbols are representations of objects, feelings, people, and events. Symbols can be used to represent *anything*, and *anything* can be a symbol. Symbols come into use when people agree to let a word, facial expression, gesture, movement, or whatever stand for something else. Even though you could create your own set of symbols for everything from aardvarks to zebras, they would be worthless unless at least one other person agreed on their meaning. Humans have invented and continued to perfect symbols because they facilitate ability to convey meaning. When students and teachers interact, one way meaning is conveyed is by verbal (language) symbols.

It is possible there are students in your classes who speak a variety of English different from the variety you speak. Varieties in spoken English differ primarily in the *sounds* used to make words, rather than in the meanings of words. These differences in sounds probably cause little *actual* difficulty for you in understanding what your students say. Sometimes, however, we let our attitudes about people who sound different from ourselves interfere with our understanding. When you speak with people from a foreign country, you realize that their language is different, but it is unlikely that you believe yours to be better. When we say that you must understand the language a student is using, we don't mean only that you must be fluent in English. We also mean that it is necessary for you to recognize that the student's variety of English may be different from the one you speak, but that "different" is not equivalent to "deficient." The teacher who seeks to be an effective participant in communication must be on the lookout for such differences, so that they will not be taken for signs of ignorance or defective speech.

A second way in which meaning is conveyed is by nonverbal symbols. You attach meaning to the way students look, move, and dress, and they do the same with respect to you. Even though you may share a common culture and similar experiences, there is no guarantee that you will accurately interpret each other's nonverbal behavior. For example, each person engages in a variety of actions that are random and not intended to convey meaning. As we saw earlier, however, it is impossible to keep from assigning meaning to others' behavior or to keep others from attaching meaning to your behavior. Suppose you look out across your classroom and see a student fold her arms across her chest. If you had read one of the "pop" psychology books on the nonverbal code, you might immediately (but erroneously) interpret her actions as meaning that she is "shutting you out." Such nonverbal stereotyping, as you will see in Chapter 5, is often totally inaccurate.

Stereotyping is just one of the problems you must surmount in gaining an understanding of students' nonverbal responses. If you teach young students, for example, you must realize they are less proficient at using words than you are, and that the most important messages may come from their nonverbal behavior. This may cause special problems for teachers fresh from the college environment where so much emphasis is put on what people *say*. It is essential that you realize, however, that many of the most important classroom transactions occur on the nonverbal level.

Still another problem is that most of us are unaware of our nonverbal behavior. We rarely have the opportunity to observe ourselves. Furthermore, people don't often tell us about our actions and the meaning they attach to them. Hence we have little information about the nonverbal messages we convey and others' interpretations of them.

To be more accurate in interpreting students' behavior, and to increase the odds that students will interpret your actions as you intend, you must be aware of the similarities and differences in the symbols you both use. You must also be willing to *learn* to use symbols in ways understandable to students.

Social Environment

The elements of the physical environment of a classroom (e.g., seats, colors, lighting) may remain unchanged for years. In contrast, each class produces a unique *social* environment. Briefly, "social environment" may be defined as the level and quality of moods and feelings experienced by the classroom group. It evolves through teacher-class (group), teacher-student, student-class (group), and student-student interpersonal relationships. Some classes may be formal and serene, while others are chaotic and explosive. In one class participants feel secure, satisfied, and happy, while in another teacher and students alike feel anxious, frustrated, and resentful. Whatever the social environment of a class, it affects the learning and communication outcomes.

There are at least four factors which work against the building of positive social environments in classrooms. The first concerns differences among individuals. Each person brings to the class differing attitudes, expectations, needs, and abilities—all of which lead to an unpredictable mixture. A second factor is the difference in power between teacher and students. The teacher has the authority to determine activities, evaluation criteria and, most importantly, grades. Students, in contrast, have virtually no formal power. Nonvoluntary membership is the third factor. As noted earlier, there are likely to be students who are forced to attend either by law or degree requirements. Teachers, too, may find themselves assigned a subject, group, or meeting time they would prefer to avoid. Resentment resulting from being required to attend (or teach) a class can be expected to have negative effects on the social environment. The fourth factor is competition for rewards. Whether a classroom is oriented toward competition or cooperation makes a critical difference. The anxiety and cutthroat tactics produced by a highly competitive norm create hostility and destructive interpersonal relationships. Some competition is probably desirable, but an optimal level must be attained.

Social environment is obviously not tangible in the way furniture and carpeting are. Social environment is an important variable, nonetheless, because it affects important attributes (e.g., trust versus suspicion, liking versus hostility) characterizing the relationships of members of the classroom group. These attributes can be expected to influence how members behave toward one another and how they interpret the behavior of others.

Physical Environment

Teacher-student meetings occur within some physical setting. The setting may be a traditional classroom with seats bolted to the floor and arranged in rows and columns. Or the structure might be "open," with portable seats and walls. The setting might be a small therapy room in a clinic, or it may even be a swimming pool. Whatever the physical environment, there are features which either promote good interpersonal relationships, effective communication, and learning, or work against their attainment.

The next time you are in a class meeting place, take a close look at it. Is it large enough? The long-term effects of overcrowding are unknown. But overcrowding for short periods of time has a negative impact on how people feel about themselves, the environment, and their purpose for being there. Are the walls and ceilings painted attractive colors? Research indicates that color can influence productivity, achievement, and moods. Is the temperature too high, too low, or just right for you? Little is known about the effects of cold, but when it is too hot, people become irritable. They perceive the entire environment as unpleasant and their reason for being there more negatively. Finally, when you consider the colors, furnishings, and lighting together, is the effect pleasant? People report negative feelings after spending time in unattractive places. Most students are likely to feel better and learn more in attractive surroundings.

Each of the aspects of the physical environment we mentioned can affect people and their communication. Still another important aspect of the classroom setting is the way in which people are arranged within it. There are many ways to position teacher and students in a room. Most teachers, however, arrange students in rows and columns facing the front. The use of this seating arrangement has important consequences for communication. The most important is that pupils in the front-center section interact with the teacher most. Students sitting outside the front-center have little interaction with their teacher. When you consider that the reason for bringing pupils and teachers together is the assumption that learning can best be achieved by interaction, the importance of the seating arrangement becomes apparent.

The physical environment is an important factor in communication. The environment can be expected to affect teachers' as well as students' moods, and momentary feelings influence how each behaves and interprets the behavior of the other. In addition, the positions teachers and students occupy have a significant effect on the interaction which takes place.

PRINCIPLES 1.2

1. To become a more effective participant in communication you must understand why you and others interpret behavior in certain ways.
2. In any interaction our thoughts and feelings compete with the verbal and nonverbal responses of others for our attention.
3. Our self-concepts affect the meaning we attribute to our behavior and that of others.
4. Our impressions of others, whether accurate or inaccurate, influence how we interpret their behavior.
5. Stereotyping of either verbal or nonverbal behavior of students is a significant problem teachers must overcome to be effective participants in communication.
6. The social environment influences how members of the classroom group behave toward, and interpret the behavior of, each other.
7. The physical environment affects teachers' and students' moods as well as interaction in classrooms.

A CONCLUDING NOTE

By now you should be able to appreciate the difficulty students have in interpreting your behavior in the way you intend. You should also appreciate the difficulty you experience in interpreting their behavior. Although it is likely you have responsibility for more than just one student, we believe there is a valid reason for examining the process of communication from the perspective of one teacher and one student. Even though you may have 35 students, each views his or her relationship with you as an interpersonal relationship, one-to-one. Likewise, you are likely to view students not just as a group, but also as individuals. It is obvious of course that, as the number of students increases, you cannot attend to the behavior of each. Similarly, as the number increases, the likelihood that you will interpret any single student's behavior as intended decreases. Furthermore, because of biological limitations on the sheer number of stimuli which can be responded to, your ability to determine if your behavior was interpreted as intended also decreases.

At the outset of this chapter we asked if you believed others always interpreted your words and actions exactly as you intended. We also asked if you were certain that you always interpreted the behavior of others exactly as *they* intended. If you answered "yes" to both questions, you are unusual. If you answered "no," don't feel too badly— you are not alone.

REFERENCES

Adams, R. S., and Biddle, B. J. *Realities of teaching: Explorations with video tape*. New York: Holt, Rinehart and Winston, 1970.

Frank, A. D. Conflict in the classroom. In F. E. Jandt (Ed.), *Conflict resolution through communication*. New York: Harper & Row, 1973, pp. 240-309.

Gergen, K. J. *The concept of self*. New York: Holt, Rinehart, and Winston, 1971.

Chapter 2
Self-Concept

After reading this chapter you should be able to:

1. define self-concept.
2. describe how concepts of self are organized.
3. explain how self-concept is formed.
4. explain why people may have conflicting ideas about self.
5. provide an example of how self-concept facilitates social interaction.
6. explain how self-concept influences behavior as well as meaning assigned to behavior.
7. identify the characteristics of self-concepts held by successful students.
8. identify characteristics of students with negative self-view.
9. explain the importance of self-disclosure.
10. identify variables which affect students' willingness to self-disclose.
11. provide examples of appropriate and inappropriate teacher self-disclosure.

12. explain how observation may be used to draw inferences about students' self-concepts.
13. identify and describe the characteristics of teachers which affect their ability to influence students' self-concepts.
14. identify the characteristics of teachers' evaluations of students which affect students' self-concepts.

Purkey (1970) has retold a fable by H. F. Lowry entitled, "The Mouse and Henry Carson." This little story illustrates quite nicely some points about self-concept formation and its importance. As Purkey relates the story, it was a midsummer's evening when:

> . . . a mouse ran into the office of the Educational Testing Service and accidentally triggered a delicate point in the apparatus just as the College Entrance Examination Board's data on one Henry Carson was being scored.
>
> Henry was an average high-school student who was unsure of himself and his abilities. Had it not been for the mouse, Henry's scores would have been average or less, but the mouse changed all that, for the scores which emerged from the computer were amazing—800's in both the verbal and quantitative areas. When the scores reached Henry's school, the word of his giftedness spread like wildfire. Teachers began to reevaluate their gross underestimation of this fine lad, counselors trembled at the thought of neglecting such a talent, and even college admissions officers began to recruit Henry for their schools.
>
> New worlds opened for Henry, and as they opened he started to grow as a person and as a student. Once he became aware of his potentialities and began to be treated differently by the significant people in his life, a form of self-fulfilling prophecy took place. Henry gained in confidence and began to put his mind in the way of great things. Lowry ends the story of "The Mouse and Henry Carson" by saying that Henry became one of the best men of his generation. (pp. 1–2)

Lowry's story serves as an appropriate introduction to this chapter because it illustrates that the ways in which students view themselves are influenced greatly by the ways in which others respond to them, and that such self-views are very important to success in school. The story is also important because it demonstrates that self-concepts can be changed and that teachers can act in ways to aid students in acquiring more positive self-images.

Our purpose in this chapter is to increase your understanding of self-concept: what it is, how it is formed, and its influence on student success in school and classroom communication. We also want to expand your awareness of the potential you possess to influence the self-concepts of your students and to suggest specific ways in which you can act to have positive effects.

While we devote substantial attention to the self-concepts of students, we also consider the self-concepts of teachers. This is an important concern, because the one factor that has the greatest influence on your communication with students is your self-concept. In the past decade it has become increasingly clear that many problems people have in being effective participants in communication are a function of the ways in which they view themselves. In other words, such problems are not caused by an inability to choose the right ideas, organization of ideas, words, gestures, tone of voice, or facial expression. Rather, they are a consequence of an inability to see oneself as an effective participant and to recognize one's potential for becoming more effective. By acquiring greater sensitivity to your self-concept, you may gain greater insights into its influence on the way you behave and interpret the behavior of others.

DEFINING SELF-CONCEPT

Although we refer to a person's concept of self throughout this chapter, we do not mean that people have a single all-encompassing identity. Rather, it is more accurate to think of self-concept as consisting of a vast number of ideas each of us has about ourselves. For many of these perceptions we seem to step out of our bodies and critically examine the person we see. We have perceptions not only of our height, weight, and skin color, but also of overall attractiveness and the attractiveness of specific body parts such as the nose, abdomen, or teeth. We have perceptions of how we stand, sit, walk, and run, and the sounds we make when talking, laughing, singing, screaming, and whispering. As though watching a videotape, we replay our memories of events to decide if we appear nervous or confident, interesting or dull, fun-loving or serious, friendly or standoffish, and so on. Our self-concept also consists of our conception of our background, talents, and shortcomings. Finally, self-concept consists of the feelings we have about our value, our current status in life, and our general satisfaction or dissatisfaction with ourselves.

Each of us is a unique human being, because each of us has had a different set of experiences which has given rise to the unique set of perceptions we have of ourselves. Moreover, we have organized these perceptions in a distinctive fashion. Each person has a core of beliefs relating to name, age, sex, and race, as well as other perceptions of self which are the very foundation of identity. Core beliefs are distinguished because we have great confidence in their truth and hold them with great conviction. Moving away from the core beliefs, you can organize your other perceptions of self on the basis of their value and your confidence in their accuracy. For example, suppose you believe you are a very poor mathematics student. A series of low grades in math courses over the years has caused you to be very *confident* in this assessment. Yet, if

FIGURE 2·1 SELF-CONCEPT CONSISTS OF MANY PERCEPTIONS.

mathematical aptitude is quite unrelated to your career or life needs, this particular perception of yourself may be of little *importance*. On the other hand, if you wish to be a music teacher, it is important to believe you have musical ability. Your confidence in your ability, however, may go up and down in a see-saw fashion in response to your professors' and others' reactions to your work.

Another way in which perceptions of self might be organized is on the basis of your use of them. As we move through our daily routines we frequently find it necessary to tell others who we are. The ritualized exchange of information in which we engage with strangers, however, includes only a small number of the perceptions we have of ourselves. In addition to these aspects of self which we willingly share with virtually anyone, there are other perceptions which are revealed to only a select trusted few. Still other perceptions of course are not shared with anyone.

Whereas certain perceptions of self, such as core beliefs, are enduring, we engage in a process of learning and relearning other aspects of our identities throughout life. Others are constantly doing the teaching, and in the following section we examine the process by which this learning about self happens.

FORMATION OF THE SELF

As far as we know, newborn children are unaware that they are distinct entities. During the first year of life, however, children learn to distinguish between their bodies and other objects in their environment. In addition to this formation of a concept of physical self, they gradually learn other important notions of their value as persons, which may endure for the remainder of their lives. Argyle (1967) suggests that there are three primary ways in which this process occurs, the first of which is the responses of other people.

For a great many years psychologists have suggested that children learn to view themselves as others view them. During the early part of a child's life, those persons who spend substantial amounts of time with the child can be expected to have a critical influence on his or her self-image. Parents convey that children are loved or unwanted through the amount of time they spend actively engaged with them, as well as attending to their need for food and dry diapers and to be held, cuddled, and stroked. In subtle and not so subtle ways, parents indicate to children their regard for them. Children who are approved of, loved, respected, and esteemed tend to have positive evaluations of themselves. Likewise, children who are ignored, neglected, or mistreated evaluate themselves negatively. A number of researchers have suggested that the level of parental regard in these early years is closely matched by the child's own level of self-regard in later years (Hansen and Maynard, 1973).

It is important to recognize, however, that the child is a part of any relationship. From birth, children differ, even those as similar as identical twins. They differ in appearance, temperament, and their responses to others and events in their environment. Hence it is not accurate to think of others in the child's life as completely responsible for their reactions to the child. Instead, it is important to realize that the characteristics of the infant influence, in part, the way in which others respond to him or her.

A second way in which self-concept is formed is through interaction with peers. If a child's brother and sister are much more attractive, then the child comes to view himself as ugly; if he is more skilled at sports than his playmates, he sees himself as athletic. Because children tend to acquire and maintain a self-image by comparing themselves with others, sending a child to a different school or putting him in a more (or less) advanced class can have an immediate and significant impact upon his self-image.

We once knew an eight-year-old, Karen, who attended a small rural school. Her parents, unlike those of her classmates, were well educated. Coming from a home environment where learning was highly valued, she did not find it difficult to be the brightest child in her class. In fact, Karen appeared so much brighter than her classmates that she was promoted from the third to the fifth grade, skipping the fourth grade entirely. Shortly thereafter her family moved, and Karen was enrolled in a large suburban school. In contrast to her rural school experiences, Karen now found herself struggling simply to keep up. Almost at once she changed from happy and outgoing to sullen and withdrawn. Fortunately, the school psychologist recommended that Karen be put back to the fourth grade, and by the end of the term she appeared to have regained her former positive self-image. In concluding this example, it is important to emphasize that the acquisition of a self-image by comparing oneself to others is not limited only to children. One of the major ways we continue to acquire perceptions about self as adults is by seeing how we "stack up" against co-workers, neighbors, and acquaintances.

The roles you play or have played are a third source of concepts about self. We play roles when we adapt our nonverbal and verbal behavior to meet the requirements of particular social situations. We learn what behavior is appropriate for a given role by observing others perform the role. For example, from observing teachers over a number of years, you know that it would not be acceptable for you as an elementary teacher to wear cutoffs and a T-shirt to meet your class. Neither would it be appropriate for you to smoke cigarettes or swear while teaching. The wearing of exceptionally informal clothing, smoking, and swearing constitute normative role violations. That is, such actions are inconsistent with the expectations we have for the way elementary school teachers should behave, at least in the classroom.

FIGURE 2·2 OTHERS TEACH
US WHO WE ARE.

When you first begin teaching you may be very conscious of your behavior and feel quite awkward about playing the role. After practice, however, you can expect this nervousness to disappear. Furthermore, over time the role may become so familiar to you that you begin to see yourself as really having its characteristics. You may even begin to act "in role" when the actions and words required by the role are neither necessary nor appropriate. Perhaps you have had the experience of observing a stranger at a party, or in a similar setting, and finding that long before learning the person's occupation you had accurately guessed it.

In summary, we learn who we are from the way others act toward us, by comparing ourselves to others, and by viewing ourselves in terms of the roles we play. Through this complex process each person acquires a unique set of images of self which are also unique in the way one organizes and uses them.

Recognizing that a person has multiple ideas about one's identity prompts us to ask if these various concepts are in agreement. Do you think your views of yourself are consistent or do you tend to have conflicting views at different points in time? If you are relatively honest, you will probably admit that some or many of the concepts you have about yourself are conflicting. Does this mean you are schizophrenic? Not at all. It is quite natural for a person to have conflicting ideas and feelings. To better understand why this is so, let's examine why you may view yourself in different ways.

Consider that any person with whom you interact may have a unique image of you. Your roommate may see you as happy-go-lucky, while your biology professor views you as serious and hard-working. Through your interactions with each of these people you have learned something about the image of you which each has formed. After you have learned how a person expects you to act, you may find that simply being in the company of that person causes you to think of yourself in ways consistent with his or her image. For example, several students have related to us the surprise they experienced upon returning home for a visit with their parents after an extended stay at college. Whereas these students had come to view themselves as independent, experienced, and mature while living on their own, they suddenly found themselves feeling dependent, inexperienced, and immature upon returning home. This is not surprising, given that they had thought of themselves as children for much longer than they had viewed themselves as adults. Simply being in the presence of their parents (who continued to view them, at least in some ways, as children) was sufficient for them also to view themselves as children once again. As might be expected, these students reported quickly regaining their views of themselves as adults shortly after returning to college.

The following principles on the section you have just read are intended to give you a framework for examining the way self-concept affects the communication process. We examine this relationship in the next section.

PRINCIPLES 2.1

1. Self-concept consists of a vast number of perceptions an individual has of himself or herself.
2. Perceptions of self can be organized according to their value to the individual, the person's confidence in their accuracy, and the frequency with which they are revealed to others.
3. Individuals acquire concepts of self from the responses of others to them, from comparing themselves with others, and from taking on the characteristics of roles they play.
4. It is natural to have conflicting ideas and feelings about self.

SELF-CONCEPT AND COMMUNICATION

Including a chapter on self-concept in this book can be justified only if self-concept influences teacher-student interaction in important ways. In this section we consider two major ways in which self-view affects communication. First, we see that, if we did not possess concepts of ourselves which can be readily shared with others, the patterns of social interaction to which we are so accustomed would be radically altered. We then consider an even more significant effect of self-concept—the impact it has on how we behave and how we interpret the behavior of others.

The Self and Social Interaction

Gergen (1971) has suggested that self-concept facilitates communication by allowing us to provide information about ourselves to others. When we interact with a stranger we seem to derive some feeling of security from learning about his or her identity. It is not surprising, then, that we spend great amounts of time in initial stages of interaction seeking information about the other person. Although etiquette may keep us from bluntly demanding, "Who are you?," we attempt to achieve the same objective with such requests as, "Tell me something about yourself." It is because we possess concepts of self that we are able to satisfy such requests. The importance of possessing concepts of self which may be readily shared is especially critical in a number of situations frequently encountered. The job interview is one example. On many campuses it is a common practice for personnel supervisors from large school districts to visit briefly for the purpose of conducting job interviews with graduating seniors. Such interviewing sessions demand that prospective teachers be able to provide brief, yet descriptive summaries of themselves. Unfortunate as it may be, those who do not have a set of labels readily available to define themselves are at a distinct disadvantage in such situations.

Self-Fulfilling Prophecy

To understand the second major way in which self-concept affects the communication process, think first of the definition of communication proposed in Chapter 1. Communication was described as an event which occurs when one person assigns meaning to the behavior of another. Your self-concept has such a tremendous impact on communication because it influences your *behavior* as well as the *meaning* you assign to the behavior of others.

In the school setting, as well as in all others, we have to decide how to act. We use the notions we hold about our identities to make these decisions. As Brooks and Emmert (1976) have observed, "Each person behaves in a manner as consistent as possible with his self-concept: he acts like the sort of person he perceives himself to be" (p. 42). Consider the school system in which you teach, for example. It is a formal organization with a hierarchy of power and status. Your concept of self aids you in making a decision whether to be superior or subordinate in any specific relationship with another person in this hierarchy. If you possess a concept of yourself as a teacher, you will know that you are expected to act in certain ways when interacting with students. Likewise, if you possess a concept of yourself as a faculty member, you will realize that quite different behavior may be appropriate when conferring with your principal.

To explore the effect of self-concept on behavior even further, let's consider the case of a student who believes he is disliked by teachers. If a student is already convinced he is disliked by all teachers, it is perfectly consistent for him to respond to you by being unfriendly and uncooperative. You in turn may interpret his bored and hostile appearance as meaning that you are dull and ineffective—hardly a flattering evaluation of one's professional competence. If the student maintains an unlikable self long enough, it will be virtually ensured that most teachers will begin to respond to him in negative ways. He will then have evidence confirming his belief that he is disliked, and his conviction that this concept of self is accurate will be strengthened. Although he has "written his own script," it is doubtful that he will realize that it was his own behavior which was responsible for the outcome.

In short, if we think about ourselves in a certain way, we will behave that way. We relate to others on the basis of our past experiences, and in this fashion shape our futures.

Another way in which self-concept affects communication is by influencing the meaning assigned to the behavior of others. To illustrate how this process works, let's again consider the case of a student who believes teachers dislike her. Typically, students with this belief can't specify *why* teachers feel this way. You can be assured, however, that there is some good reason which motivates the belief. As noted earlier, the child who receives many negative responses from family and peers

FIGURE 2·3 WE INTERPRET OTHERS' BEHAVIOR IN WAYS CONSISTENT WITH OUR SELF-IMAGES.

may come to dislike herself. When she enters into a relationship with a teacher, it may be with the expectation the teacher will also treat her badly. It is also possible that the belief allows the student to avoid responsibility for poor academic work. "After all," she may reason, "if the teachers are out to get me, it isn't my fault I don't do well."

Whatever the origin, once the belief is accepted into the student's concept of self, she can be expected to look for signs that it is correct. Psychologists call this phenomenon biased scanning. When people engage in biased scanning, they look for cues which confirm the self-view they hold. People engage in biased scanning because their images of self provide them with a degree of security, hence they are motivated to seek information which confirms their accuracy. As a general rule, information consistent with self-concept is eagerly accepted; inconsistent information is either ignored, reinterpreted, or rejected.

We have already seen that the student can confirm his belief that he is disliked by behaving in "unlikable" ways. He can also engage in biased scanning to interpret the teacher's behavior to conform to his expectations. So, when the teacher smiles, it isn't a sign of friendliness and warmth, but rather an indication that she is laughing at him. When the teacher attempts to include the student in a class discussion by calling on him, he perceives the real motive is to humiliate him publicly. By remembering that meaning is in people, and not in words and gestures, it is possible to understand how the student can interpret the teacher's greatest efforts to be accepting as indications of rejection.

In summary, self-concept affects communication because we behave in ways consistent with our self-views and because we interpret the behavior of others in ways consistent with our self-images. Hence self-concept is at the very core of the communication process, and the importance of possessing positive self-concepts cannot be overstated.

EFFECTS OF SELF-CONCEPT ON SUCCESS IN SCHOOL

From the preceding discussion of the effects of self-concept on communication, you might predict that students who view themselves in positive ways will do well in school, and that those who have negative views of themselves will do poorly. This was Purkey's (1970) conclusion after reviewing a large number of research studies concerned with self-concept and academic performance. In the investigations upon which Purkey based his conclusion, measures of self-concept were typically obtained through self-reports by students. The grade point average (GPA) was the measure of academic achievement most often used. From his review, Purkey suggested this composite view of students who demonstrate high academic achievement:

1. They have a high regard of themselves.
2. They are optimistic about their potential for success in the future.

3. They possess confidence in their competence as persons and students.
4. They believe they are hard workers.
5. They believe other students like them.

Fitts (1972) is another psychologist who has reviewed the evidence of the relationship between self-concept and school performance. He concludes that many important variables which affect academic performance are related to self-concept. Specifically, in Fitts' view, students with low self-esteem are likely to be characterized in the following way:

1. They have unfavorable attitudes toward school and teachers.
2. They do not assume responsibility for learning.
3. They have low motivation.
4. They have low morale and are dissatisfied with school experiences.
5. They have low class participation rates.
6. They act in ways to create discipline problems.
7. They have high dropout rates.
8. They have poor personal and social adjustment.

Before you conclude that a positive self-view directly produces a high GPA, or that negative self-esteem is the direct cause of a low GPA, we must offer a word of caution. While a substantial number of research findings indicates that self-concept *influences* academic achievement, achievement can also influence self-view. Hence a repeated number of high grades on math tests, science projects, and English themes can cause students to regard themselves more positively, while a series of low grades can have the opposite effect. This conclusion is perfectly consistent with the earlier observation that people acquire views of self from the evaluations of others and by comparing themselves to others. Although we can't say precisely how self-concept and academic achievement affect each other, research evidence "does stress a strong reciprocal relationship and gives us reason to assume that enhancing the self-concept is a vital influence in improving academic performance" (Purkey, 1970, p. 27).

Given the effects of self-view on communication and academic performance, it is obvious that teachers should attempt to help students acquire positive self-images. It is necessary first, however, that they obtain an accurate understanding of the self-concepts students hold, and in the next section we suggest how this can be accomplished.

PRINCIPLES 2.2

1. Self-concept facilitates communication by allowing us to provide information about ourselves to others.
2. Self-concept influences communication because we tend to act in ways consistent with self-views.

3. Self-concept affects communication because we tend to interpret the behavior of others in ways consistent with our self-images.
4. Students who view themselves in positive ways tend to do well in school, while those who have negative self-views tend to do poorly.

DISCOVERING THE SELF-CONCEPTS OF STUDENTS

Teachers can acquire an understanding of students' self-concepts in two ways. The first is through self-disclosure, the process of learning about another from the information the person voluntarily provides about oneself. The second is observation, the process of drawing inferences about a person's self-concept on the basis of his or her behavior. We first examine the process of self-disclosure as a means of increasing mutual understanding between teachers and students and improving the effectiveness of their communication.

Self-Disclosure

One of the most important assumptions about interpersonal communication is that, the more each of us knows about the other, the more likely each is to interpret the words and actions of the other as intended. We find out about each other through the information we involuntarily and voluntarily reveal. You saw in Chapter 1 that it is impossible for communication not to occur. So also is it impossible for you to not reveal information about yourself. The words chosen, the way they are spoken, and your body movement disclose information not only about the feelings you are experiencing but also about their intensity. In addition to this information, which we have little or no control over disclosing to others, is the information about us which others are unlikely to find out unless we give it to them. Others form images of us by combining both types of information. Keltner (1973, p. 49) expressed particularly well the consequences of this image-forming process when he stated that "no one really talks or communicates with the total other or even with the real other person. What we actually do as we speak with and to each other is talk to ourselves." He adds that the images others have of us may be quite different from how we really are. As a result, when others talk to us, they may be quite incapable of knowing how we view the world. How can we overcome this obstacle to effective communication? Each of us must learn more about the other, so that our self-image and the images others have of us become very similar.

Facilitating Student Self-Disclosure

While current knowledge about the process of self-disclosure is far from complete, research findings permit some general suggestions regarding how a teacher may facilitate self-disclosing by students.

Most people feel uncomfortable in revealing confidential information in public. You can easily confirm this by considering occasions when professors have required students to make introductory speeches about themselves. The information shared in such speeches rarely provides a basis for relating to the speaker as a distinct individual. Devito (1976) has suggested several reasons to explain our preference for making disclosures in dyads (two-person groupings) rather than in large groups. He observes that, when you disclose information to just one other person, you can monitor closely the responses of that person to what you are saying. If the other reacts in an accepting way, you can continue; if not, you can stop at once. When two, three, or several other persons are present, however, problems arise. It becomes more difficult to attend closely to the responses of all present. More importantly, the acceptance by listeners of what you are saying is likely to vary, and the decision to continue or stop disclosing becomes more difficult to make. Finally, many people feel that disclosing to a group of people makes an individual appear to be an exhibitionist.

The implication is obvious: Students are most likely to share important information about themselves in private conversations. If you wish to know students, you must be available for these private meetings. Being available means, however, more than simply spending an extra half-hour in the classroom at the end of the day. It also means being ready to accept, *without evaluation*, whatever a student may choose to share. Being available also means having a genuine interest in knowing your students as distinctive human beings.

Students' self-disclosure can be expected to occur in small amounts which increase as their relationships with you develop in positive ways. An important element in a positive relationship is *trust*. We are unlikely to share personal information with people who will then repeat it indiscriminantly to others. Hence, to build trust, you must keep secret any information given in confidentiality.

There are at least two other variables which can be expected to influence students' self-disclosure quite independently of your behavior. The first is age. You can expect younger children to be more self-disclosing than older ones. Jourard (1964) has explained that young children are relatively unconcerned about revealing their thoughts and feelings to those around them. They say what they think and tell what they have done. As children grow, however, they learn the consequences of disclosing. To some statements, adults respond approvingly; to others, reactions are disapproving. As a result, children gradually learn to censor the information they reveal about themselves.

The second variable affecting self-disclosure is sex. Wenburg and Wilmot (1973) observed that norms in our society represent the ideal male as a stoic individual. Males who honestly express their feelings, particularly feelings of insecurity, run the risk of being labeled as weak and unmasculine. Little boys soon learn that "big" boys act tough, and that self-disclosing is *not* part of the role.

Teacher Self-Disclosure

Although you may readily agree that it is important for you to facilitate self-disclosure *by* your students, you may be quite reluctant to disclose yourself *to* your students. Be assured that this reaction is quite normal: We are all reluctant to some degree to disclose ourselves. There seem to be two major reasons for this feeling. First, people may believe their true identities are not very attractive and that, if they are revealed, others will find them unacceptable and reject them. A common fear also is that, if we reveal ourselves to others, they will have some degree of control over us. If you are reluctant to disclose yourself for either of these reasons (or others), consider what the consequences may be. The first is strain. As the teacher, you are constantly on display in the classroom. Being in this fishbowl can be incredibly exhausting if you are continually on guard, screening your behavior to avoid slips which would reveal yourself to your students. The second consequence is the impression you convey about your regard for your students. When you disclose yourself, you indicate that you trust them, that you care about your relationship with them, and that they are significant enough for you to want them to understand you.

Self-disclosure seems to be a reciprocal process. The teacher who demonstrates trust by taking the initiative in sharing information is likely to find that students respond in the same way. Likewise, the teacher who holds students at a distance, not permitting them to understand her and indicating that they are not trusted, respected, or cared about, should not be surprised if students respond in a similar fashion.

Appropriate Teacher Self-Disclosure

We have found that most teachers readily accept the notion that their self-disclosing will increase the effectiveness of their communication with students. The problem they frequently report as difficult to resolve, however, concerns what is appropriate to disclose. Regrettably, the question is much too complex to allow a neat, tidy answer. What and how much to reveal is an individual decision for the teacher, but a desirable goal is to strike a median point between what has been termed *overdisclosure* and *underdisclosure*.

You may have known overdisclosing teachers. They relate intimate details of family and personal problems, financial position, and so on. Teachers who reveal innermost thoughts and feelings to their classes are likely to make students feel uncomfortable and embarrassed, even though they may have made such disclosures with the best of intentions. Over-

FIGURE 2.4 OVERDISCLOSURES MAKE US FEEL UNCOMFORTABLE.

disclosers have a problem in not distinguishing what is appropriate to reveal in a given situation, with the result that they reveal virtually anything to anyone. At the other extreme is the underdiscloser. You may also have known this type of teacher, who from our experience seems particularly prevalent at the university level. Underdisclosers appear to be little more than robots. They arrive at class, take roll, lecture, and leave. Even though many hours of watching and listening to them may have gone by, we feel at the end of the semester that we know little more about them than we did before the course began.

In striking a middle ground between these two extreme types of disclosers, three factors should be considered. The first concerns *norms* for teacher behavior. Traditional norms do not encourage teachers to disclose themselves to students. Consequently, when students are confronted with an overdisclosing teacher, their expectations are violated and they may be confused as to how to respond. Ironically, because the norm is for teachers *not* to disclose, students probably feel more comfortable with underdisclosing, rather than overdisclosing, teachers.

The second factor concerns the *context* in which self-disclosure occurs. As noted before, self-disclosure typically takes place in two-person interactions. Hence for a teacher to do extensive revealing to an entire class again violates student expectations for self-disclosure to be a relatively private event. Finally, the third factor concerns the *reciprocal nature* of self-disclosure. When one person discloses, the other may feel some obligation to indicate that the trust is shared by also self-disclosing. The overdisclosing teacher, then, may make students uncomfortable if they believe they are also expected to engage in extensive self-disclosure before the class.

In searching for the ideal amount of self-disclosure we suggest you ask yourself two questions: First, "What can I reveal about myself which would help students to understand who I am and how I view the world?" But, also, ask the question, "Will revealing this information cause discomfort on my part or on the part of my students?" Unless you are quite certain that the answer to the second question is "no," then simply avoid (for the moment at least) sharing that particular information.

Observations

While the self-reports of students are an invaluable way to increase your understanding of them, they have one major limitation: They are dependent upon what students are willing to reveal. If students have learned that some self-views they hold are unacceptable to others, or if they believe that teachers cannot be trusted, then they may reveal only what they believe will be acceptable, or nothing at all. Because of these limitations, we recommend that you also use systematic observation to gain an understanding of students. Such observations may be most profitable if the following suggestions regarding *how* and *what* to observe are considered (Purkey, 1970):

1. Recognize at the outset that you cannot be totally objective in observing and drawing inferences about another person. Examine your own feelings about the student to identify the biases you bring to the observation task. You may not be able to suspend these prejudices (positive or negative), but you can be aware of how they can influence how you interpret the behavior you see.

2. Before drawing conclusions, observe the student in as many different situations as possible. It would not be unusual, for example, to discover that a student behaved much differently on the playground than in your classroom, and related to peers in a pattern quite different from that followed when interacting with either adults or younger children.

3. Because self-concept may be manifested in a number of ways in a student's behavior, look closely at, and listen attentively to, the individual. It might be profitable, for instance, to ask yourself how often the individual smiles and what events seem to produce smiles. A person who seldom smiles is often greatly dissatisfied with his or herself and life. Listen to the student's vocal cues. A voice that is continuously whining or filled with sarcasm may indicate low self-esteem.

4. Finally, the manner in which a person presents oneself in interactions with others can be especially revealing. For example, low self-concept may be indicated by the following:
   (a) frequent statements of self-criticism
      ("I've never been able to do this");
   (b) negative expectations toward competition
      ("What's the use, I haven't got a chance");
   (c) criticism of the achievements of others
      ("He's really stupid, but he just got a lucky break");
   (d) unwillingness to accept blame
      ("It's not my fault");
   (e) readiness to point out the failures of others
      ("Her problem is... "); and
   (f) inability to accept praise
      ("I don't believe you really mean that").

After interacting with students over time, you may be able to combine the information they have volunteered about themselves with your observations to determine whether their overall self-concepts are positive or negative, as well as the specific beliefs they hold about themselves and the strength of these beliefs. On this basis you may be able to tell if students have particular problems which are likely to affect their school performance. When you have this information, you may be better able to look at the world through the students' eyes and have greater understanding of their responses to you, their classmates, and the process of instruction.

PRINCIPLES 2.3

1. It is important to self-disclose, because the more teachers and students know about one another, the more effective classroom communication is likely to be.
2. Students are most likely to share important information about themselves in private conversations with teachers.
3. Self-disclosure increases in small amounts as trust develops in the relationship.
4. Age influences self-disclosure in that younger children are more disclosing than older ones.
5. Sex influences self-disclosure in that social norms tend to discourage self-disclosing by males.
6. Being reluctant to self-disclose is quite normal.
7. Self-disclosure is a reciprocal process.
8. To determine what is appropriate to disclose, teachers must consider students' expectations and the context for communication.
9. Teachers may obtain the greatest understanding of students' self-concepts if they combine information students disclose with inferences drawn from systematic observation.

INFLUENCING STUDENTS' SELF-CONCEPTS

You have seen that children come to school for the first time with expectations for how others will treat them and for their own success. The script is not completely written, however, for, next to the home, the school is the most important setting where experiences affecting self-image occur. Furthermore, just as parents can be expected to have the most significant impact on childrens' attitudes toward self learned in the home, teachers have the potential to be the most significant shapers of childrens' self-images in the school environment.

Despite the potential they possess, it is apparent that many teachers have little or no positive effect on their students' self-concepts. Yet you can probably think of one (or perhaps several) teachers who had significant positive effects on your self-image. There seem to be two factors which account for such influence. The first is the *characteristics* of the teacher. The second factor concerns *what* the teacher tells students about themselves (Gergen, 1971).

The Teacher's View of Self

A basic assumption derived from self-theory is that persons behave in ways consistent with their beliefs. If this assumption is true, then it follows that what teachers believe about themselves is a critical factor in their effectiveness. What are the self-views influential teachers have about themselves? In summarizing research findings, Lembo (1971) suggests these two:

1. *He sees himself as being competent to cope with life's challenges and problems.* He believes that he is capable of accepting each phase of living, of rolling with the punches. He does not view himself as having major failings.
2. *He sees himself as being accepted, needed, and wanted by others.* He believes that his judgment and skills are valued and that others see him as being a worthy person. (p. 82)

In short, the influential teacher has high self-esteem. A number of research studies suggest that such persons are very willing to try to influence others. Furthermore, they tend to be more *successful* in influencing others than those with low self-esteem. As might be expected, persons who have negative views of self and experience dissatisfaction with self are unwilling to try to influence others. The explanation for these differing patterns of behavior is unclear. It may be, however, that persons with low self-esteem are eager to win the approval of others. Such persons may believe that approval can be won by readily complying with others' wishes. Of course, persons with low self-esteem may also refrain from attempting to influence others simply because they have no confidence in their ability to do so.

It should be apparent that before a teacher can help students build more positive self-views he or she must possess positive attitudes toward self. We are aware of course that, if you have low self-esteem, simply telling you that you need high self-esteem won't be of much help. We hope you recognize, however, that the development of self-concept has been described in this chapter as a learning process. Just as existing concepts you hold have been learned, so can new concepts also be learned. Self-concept is flexible, adaptable, and capable of change throughout one's lifetime.

Credibility

The second characteristic which determines your ability to influence the self-concepts of students is credibility. Essentially, credibility refers to what students think of you. McCroskey, Larson, and Knapp (1971) suggest that the attitudes others have toward us consist of several dimensions including perceptions of competence, character, and intention. When students evaluate the competence of a teacher, they ask if she is qualified by experience and ability to "know what she is talking about." When they evaluate the character of a teacher, they wish to know if she is basically honest and fair. They also wish to know her intentions and may ask, "Is she concerned about my welfare, or her own selfish interests?"

We cannot overemphasize the importance of students' positive attitudes toward their teachers on these dimensions. To be effective in helping students develop more positive self-concepts teachers must *persuade* students to view themselves in new ways. Research into the process of persuasion has revealed that a would-be persuader must be perceived in positive ways by those she wishes to persuade. Your own experiences should confirm this. Think again about the teacher who had the most positive effect on your self-concept? Don't you perceive that person as very qualified, honest, and unmanipulative? We devote substantially more attention to credibility in Chapter 7. For the moment, recognize that it is the most important characteristic you must possess if you wish to influence the self-concepts of students.

Personalism

During our days as students, one of the most hated events of the college year was registration for classes. Registration was unpleasant in part because it required us to fill out a seemingly endless number of forms and then to stand in line for hours. Thinking back, however, we realize that the most frustrating part of the experience was the impersonal way in which faculty and staff members often communicated with us. After being asked the same question for the one-hundredth time, it is understandable that the harried adviser's response might begin to sound like a recording. This realization, however, didn't help us accept the fact that the adviser was responding to us as objects, not as individuals. We may label such communication "impersonal."

A teacher is impersonal when he doesn't take into account the details about you which make you a unique human being. The teacher who can't remember your name, or in which of his courses you are a student, conveys that he attaches little significance to your existence. Evaluations from such impersonalistic teachers, even very positive ones, are likely to have little impact on a student's self-concept. "After all," the student is likely to ask, "Why should I believe this teacher's evaluation of me is accurate when he doesn't even begin to know who I am?" A personalistic teacher, by contrast, convinces us that he is genuinely interested. The personalistic teacher remembers details about us, and in interactions is sensitive to our moods and feelings. In short, when we are convinced that a teacher has a sincere concern for us, and an accurate picture of who we are, we are greatly influenced by that teacher's appraisals. An experimental study by Gergen (1965) has demonstrated this principle vividly.

In Gergen's research, young women were interviewed individually by a slightly older female. The interviewer smiled and gave other signs of approval whenever the person being interviewed made a positive statement about herself, and signs of disagreement when the interviewee made negative self-references. One-half of the women had been led to believe that the interviewer was simply practicing interviewing techniques and that she was responding in prescribed ways (the impersonalistic condition). The other half was told that the interviewer was trying to respond honestly during the interview (the personalistic condition). Women in both groups completed a measure of self-esteem prior to and after the interview.

Before reading on, make some guesses about the outcomes of the study. Were there any changes in ratings of self-esteem as a result of the interview? If so, which group had a positive gain? You guessed correctly if you predicted that the women in the personalistic condition had significant increases in self-esteem. In summary, this study suggests that a teacher can have the greatest effect in building a student's self-concept if he or she is perceived as sincere and understanding of the student as a unique individual.

Difference between Student Self-View and Teacher Evaluation

We have seen that to influence students' self-views it is important for you to possess a positive self-concept and to be viewed as highly credible and personalistic. Hence the first important factor is your characteristics. Of equal importance, however, are the characteristics of the evaluations you make of students. The success of your attempts to influence is a function of the interaction between these two variables. If, on the one hand, you are not regarded highly, then, no matter what you tell students about themselves, you are likely to have little impact. On the other hand, even if you do possess high credibility, the types of evaluations you make will affect the kind and amount of influence you have on the self-views they hold.

One very important aspect of teacher evaluations is the extent to which they differ from students' self-views. At least three major conditions may be identified. The first is really a no-difference state. This occurs when the teacher has exactly the same view of the student which the student has of himself. For example, the student views himself as very intelligent, and the teacher also views him as very intelligent. In the second condition, however, there is a minor difference between the student's self-perception and that of the teacher (e.g., very intelligent versus intelligent). Finally, a third condition exists when there is a major difference between the student's self-view and the view of the teacher (e.g., very intelligent versus very stupid). Under which condition would you expect the student's self-view to be most likely to change? Well, under the first condition, where the teacher's view confirms the student's, no change in the student's view would be expected, although the strength with which the student holds the view might increase. Likewise, when only minor differences exist, little pressure is exerted on the student to revise the self-view. Where the difference is large, however, the greatest change in the self-view would be expected. In short, as the difference between the self-view and the other's view increases, there is greater pressure to change the self-view.

Some time ago in one of our classes, a student related an experience in her life which vividly illustrates the effect of teacher evaluations which are greatly discrepant from self-view. This young woman told of coming to a large university from a relatively small-town environment. Her career aspiration was to be an artist. Throughout the earlier years of her life, public school art teachers, parents, and friends had convinced her that she possessed substantial artistic talent. Her first university art class, however, provided a different set of evaluations. The professor disliked her work and upon several occasions observed that she had no discernible potential as an artist. The effect of these negative appraisals was devastating and permanent. Brushes and paints were stored away, not to be retrieved during the four years of her undergraduate education.

At this moment you may be thinking of a similar instance in your own life in which your self-view remained intact despite the drastically discrepant view of another. How can such instances be explained? An answer may be found by considering what is likely to happen when a person receives a discrepant evaluation from another. Gergen (1971) explains that, while the pressure to change one's self-view increases as the discrepancy between self-view and another's view increases, another tendency also comes into play. That tendency is to question the accuracy of the other's view: "How," you might ask, "could just one art professor in a single semester cancel out the effects of positive evaluations of other teachers, parents, and friends over a period of years? Why didn't the student simply ignore the negative evaluation?" The explanation may rest with the credibility of the person making the evaluation. If we view the source as incompetent, then we can cope with the potential pressure created by a discrepant appraisal by simply rejecting it. If the source is perceived to be highly qualified to make the evaluation, however, we will attach more weight to his or her opinion. The art student in our example happened to be strongly influenced by the professor's university position and reputation. Because she attributed high credibility to him, it was difficult to question the accuracy of his judgment.

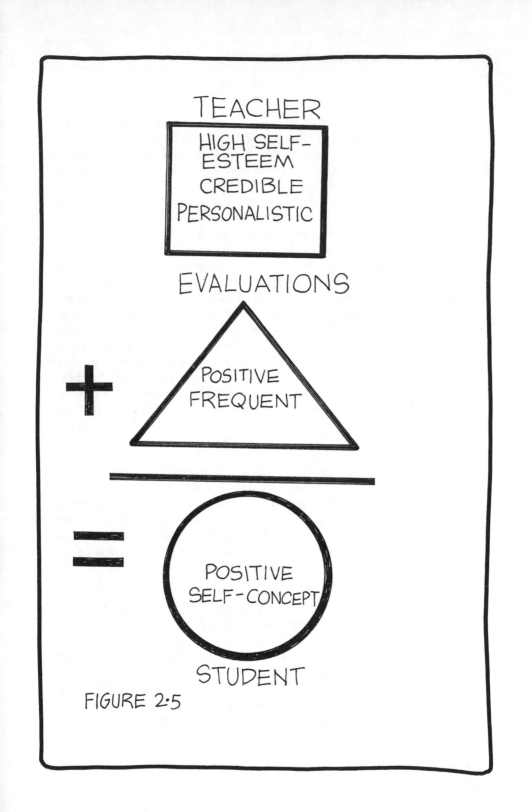

TEACHER

HIGH SELF-
ESTEEM
CREDIBLE
PERSONALISTIC

EVALUATIONS

+

POSITIVE
FREQUENT

=

POSITIVE
SELF-CONCEPT

STUDENT

FIGURE 2·5

Number and Consistency of Appraisals

Gergen (1971) maintains that the sheer number of times an individual receives a certain appraisal strongly influences the impact of the evaluation on the person's self-concept. The general principle is that, the more frequently a person receives a certain evaluation, the more likely he or she is to believe that it is true. Consider that children and adolescents spend years in school and that teachers make formal evaluations of students continually. Is it surprising then that the evaluations a student receives day after day from teachers remain part of their self-image for many years after, perhaps for the remainder of their lives?

Gergen also indicates that, in order to understand the impact of appraisals, it is necessary to consider not only the frequency of a given evaluation, but also its consistency with other evaluations students receive about themselves. For example, although a teacher tells a student on numerous occasions that he is bright, the effect of this positive evaluation may be offset if the student is told on other occasions that he is stupid. You might argue here that only a heartless and cruel teacher would ever tell a student he was stupid. We agree, but because teachers must evaluate student performance it is likely that inconsistent appraisals occur quite frequently. The "A" earned for an oral book report on Monday, for example, may be negated by the "D" received on Tuesday's spelling test. While it is impossible to predict which of the two evaluations will be incorporated into the student's self-concept, it seems likely that the student with an existing negative self-view will accept the "D" as support for his beliefs. It also seems reasonable that the conflicting evaluations will be a source of confusion for any student with less than a very positive self-view. The implication of course is that, to develop positive self-concepts in students, teachers should provide positive evaluations as often as possible and avoid negative evaluations as much as possible.

A CONCLUDING NOTE

We have placed this chapter on self-concept at the beginning with good reason. All communication begins with the self, and the self is the most critical factor affecting the outcomes of student-teacher interactions. One purpose of this chapter is to increase your understanding of the role of self-concept in communication and student achievement.

It is also our intent that there will be other consequences. We hope that you will carefully consider your own self-concept and examine how it influences the way you express yourself and relate to others. We hope you will try to gain greater understanding of the self-views your students hold and that you will be more willing to share your self-view with them. Finally, we hope you will *act* to help students gain positive views of themselves.

PRINCIPLES 2.4

1. Teachers who have high self-esteem are more likely to try to influence students' self-concepts and to be more successful in doing so than teachers with low self-regard.
2. Teachers perceived by students to have high credibility are more successful in influencing students' self-concepts than those with low credibility.
3. Personalistic teachers have a greater impact on students' self-concepts than impersonalistic teachers.
4. Pressure to change the self-view increases as the discrepancy between the student's self-view and the teacher's evaluation increases.
5. The more often a student receives a certain appraisal from teachers, the more likely that this evaluation will be incorporated into his or her self-concept.
6. Conflicting evaluations from teachers may cause students to become confused about self-views.

REFERENCES

Argyle, M. *The psychology of interpersonal behavior.* Baltimore: Penguin Books, 1967.

Brooks, W. D., and Emmert, P. *Interpersonal communication.* Dubuque, Iowa: Brown, 1976.

DeVito, J. A. *The interpersonal communication book.* New York: Harper & Row, 1976.

Fitts, W. H. *The self-concept and performance.* Nashville, Tenn.: Dede Wallace Center, 1972.

Gergen, K. J. Interaction goals and personalistic feedback as factors affecting the presentation of self. *Journal of Personality and Social Psychology,* 1965, 1, 413–424.

Gergen, K. J. *The concept of self.* New York: Holt, Rinehart and Winston, 1971.

Hansen, J. C., and Maynard, P. E. *Youth: Self-concept and behavior.* Columbus, Ohio: Merrill, 1973.

Jourard, S. *The transparent self.* New York: Van Nostrand Insight, 1964.

Keltner, J. W. *Elements of interpersonal communication.* Belmont, Calif.: Wadsworth, 1973.

Lembo, J. M. *Why teachers fail.* Columbus, Ohio: Merrill, 1971.

McCroskey, J. C., Larson, C. E., and Knapp, M. L. *An introduction to interpersonal communication.* Englewood Cliffs, N. J.: Prentice-Hall, 1971.

Purkey, W. W. *Self-concept and school achievement.* Englewood Cliffs, N. J.: Prentice-Hall, 1970.

Wenburg, J. R., and Wilmot, W. W. *The personal communication process.* New York: Wiley, 1973.

Chapter 3
Expectations: Beliefs About People and Events

OBJECTIVES

After reading this chapter, you should be able to:

1. define expectations.
2. explain the relationship between expectations and communication.
3. describe human perception as individual experience.
4. describe human perception as information processing.
5. identify the stages of information processing.
6. define, verbally and by example, each of the four perceptual selectivity processes.
7. explain the role of the perceptual selectivity process in shaping expectations.
8. define, and distinguish among, the three elements of cognitive organization (beliefs, attitudes, and values).
9. explain the role of belief formation in the development of expectations.
10. identify types of beliefs teachers form about students.
11. provide examples of halo and pitchfork effects.

12. distinguish among different types of beliefs on the basis of their importance in shaping expectations.
13. discuss the implications of belief formation for expectations.
14. explain the difference between the concept of a self-fulfilling prophecy and the concept of expectations.
15. describe the origin of the Pygmalion effect as it relates to teacher-student relationships.
16. identify the conditions necessary for Pygmalion effects to occur.
17. describe characteristics of teacher behavior which contribute to the formation of expectations.
18. distinguish among overreactive, reactive, and proactive teacher behavior with regard to the formation of expectations.
19. identify verbal and nonverbal signals through which teachers convey performance expectations to students.
20. distinguish between student characteristics on which teachers base performance expectations and those on which they do not.
21. describe the characteristics of expectations teachers form for pupil performance.
22. identify strategies teachers may use to offset the development of Pygmalion effects.

The lounge was quiet. Three teachers sat quietly sipping coffee and sharing impressions. "Jill," intoned Ms. Barks, "is really awfully bright, but too aggressive for any good reason." Mr. Hardesty puffed on his pipe and inclined his head knowingly while Ms. Richards raised her eyebrows and murmured "Oh-oh." Thus encouraged, Ms. Barks elaborated, "It's very subtle but you can detect that kind of attitude from the way she does things. Bright but erratic. Likes the abstract ideas but hates the detail work—that kind of thing... would you look at the time? My next class is in five minutes!"

Scenarios like the one just described are played countless numbers of times by teachers, for, whenever they meet, the topic sooner or later shifts to students and classes. In fact, there is nothing unusual at all about the conversation except the timing. It is the beginning of the new school year at Morris County Community College, and Ms. Barks is describing a student in a class that has met for only the second time. We came into the conversation near its end. The student named Jill had done nothing unusual in class and was only one of several students Ms. Barks had discussed. For that matter, Ms. Barks' readiness and confidence in predicting Jill's behavior is not unusual. She is merely doing what each of us does every time we encounter new people: We form expectations for their future actions based on our initial impressions. Expectations are not uniquely educational phenomena. Their effects on teachers and students, however, make them very significant in the classroom setting. The principles we discussed in Chapter 1 with regard to communication illustrate their importance. Like communication, expectations occur continuously. Because they shape and limit our perceptions of one another, they become a process of mutual influence. Most importantly, expectations are inevitable.

Communication would be functionally impossible without expectations. From our earliest days, we begin to acquire an ever-increasing set of experiences with the stimuli that surround us. We learn quickly from these experiences that certain of these stimuli behave in predictable ways. One, for example, brings us nourishment, cuddles us, and makes a variety of peculiar sounds whenever it comes near us. Long before we have babbled our first "Mama," we have developed a remarkably extensive list of characteristics associated with this individual. We have also already learned that, when we behave in a certain way (e.g., kick and scream), she responds as we anticipate (i.e., picks us up). This sequence of events, or one similar to it, represents our discovery of a means of understanding and controlling our environment that we will use throughout life.

By the day we enter a classroom for the first time we are quite proficient in the use of expectations. Our communication experiences have taught us that certain patterns of behavior have predictable, specific outcomes. For example, pouring syrup in your hair instead of on your pancakes leads to a spanking. Reciting verses well earns praise. Saying goodbye to grandma means having the breath squeezed out of you. Whether your personal experiences in the formative years matched ours or not is not important. The point is that you developed a set of beliefs which helped you predict the behavior of others. This set of beliefs constituted your expectations which, along with your brand-new schoolbag, you carried into your first classroom.

Most of us can recall our first experiences with formal education fairly vividly. For some the initial encounter was doubtless positive. Others, like Scout in *To Kill a Mockingbird*, decided that they'd just as soon skip going to school for a while. One of us (M.-J. S.) had an experience early in the first grade which illustrates the point we're moving toward. After waiting impatiently to be old enough for school, I set off brimming with excitement and anticipation. On the first day, the teacher instructed us to take out our tablets and pencils. She wanted to see, she said cheerfully, how many of us could make the letters that spelled our names. Was I ready! You see, my brothers had already taught me how to read and write, and I had learned that grown people thought that made me rather special. In fact, I had become notorious for asking anyone who came to our home if they'd like to see me write, or select one of my books for me to read aloud. Flushed with expectations of praise, I marched up, presented my scrawled signature to my teacher and stood back, awaiting my first compliment. What I received was something else altogether. The remarks my teacher made I no longer recall. I never will forget though, the humiliation I felt at having to hold my paper aloft as an example of the wrong way to write your name. My brothers had neglected to teach me the fine and ancient art of printing, and that of course was what the teacher had expected. Throughout the rest of first grade, I took some pains to hide the fact that I could read and stumbled through the saga of Dick and Jane as ineptly as I judged any self-respecting first grader should.

This piece of nostalgia demonstrates the reason we have included a chapter on expectations in this text. As you already learned in Chapter 2, teachers can have a profound effect on the development of their students' self-concepts. One of the ways this influence operates is through the teacher's expectations for a student's performance. Only recently have the full implications of such expectations for student achievement and adjustment become apparent. They are staggering! Desirable as it might be, we cannot make you an expectation-free teacher through reading this chapter. We can, however, alert you to this dimension of teacher-student communication and the ways in which it shapes your interactions with students and the outcomes of your instruction. To this end, we first establish the bases of expectations in terms of perception and communication processes. Then, we trace the development and consequences of teacher expectations for pupil performance.

THE NATURE OF HUMAN PERCEPTION

Perception as Individual Experience

What you see is what you get . . . almost. This variation on a familiar colloquialism expresses a basic truth about the way we select, process, retain, and retrieve information from our environment. As our earlier example of the baby illustrates, each of us learns to perceive and process information from our environment in basically the same way. But each of us *interprets* the information in a unique way. We do this for two reasons. The first deals with individual differences in physiological capabilities. All of us vary somewhat in our sensory equipment and preferences. Thus some people have a particularly keen sense of smell, while others might be unable to detect a skunk at five paces. Our preferences for one sense over another also determines our ability to process messages from our environment accurately. Some teachers, for example, require every idea be presented in writing, while others seem able to grasp a half-formed idea simply from listening. Such preferences indicate the sensory

FIGURE 3·1 SOME UNPLEASANT MESSAGES ARE UNAVOIDABLE.

modality either teacher feels most comfortable in when dealing with abstract concepts.

A second reason for the idiosyncratic nature of perception lies in the principle of hedonism. The hedonic principle (Fishbein and Azjen, 1975) states that our use of information is governed by the extent to which we find the information useful or reinforcing. The assumption is that we prefer to have pleasurable experiences and avoid those which are negative or painful to us. It is precisely this aspect of perception that enables us to say, "What you see is what you get," because we tend to "see" only what we want to get. The "almost" addition is necessary, however, because some unpleasant messages are unavoidable. We cannot escape the unpleasant information that someone thinks ill of us while he or she is raining blows upon our person. Similarly, you cannot avoid the message that a teacher finds your work inadequate when your paper is marked with a big, red "F."

We may conclude that perception relies on sensory information we gather from the environment. In this sense it is an innate process. We may also characterize perception as a learned process, in that the meanings we attach to stimuli are influenced by our culture and language. The characteristics of physical beauty, for instance, illustrate this cultural contribution to perception. Finally, perceptual processes are idiosyncratic, reflecting differences in our physiological abilities and preferences for certain types of information attributable to our personal needs, desires, and motives.

Perception as Information Processing

All of us are information processors, and people are included within the realm of information. Beliefs we form about the behaviors of others we observe and the meaning we assign to these behaviors is influenced by the operation of our perceptual selectivities. McCroskey and Wheeless (1976) suggest a four-stage sequence of perception: (1) acquisition of messages from the environment, (2) identification of the message codes, (3) interpretation of coded information to determine meaning, and (4) storage of the acquired meanings within our memories for subsequent use. The process is equally applicable to sizing up a new teacher or a used car or to reading this book. In each case, the same sequence of steps is involved.

An example may help clarify the concept. Assume you are standing in the middle of a crowded gymnasium during the class registration period. You have to select an elective course and have no idea what to take. You are standing near the philosophy department's location at the table. The line of students waiting there looks shorter than any of the others, so you wander over to see what courses are available. (Notice how your behavior thus far has reflected your hedonic impulse to avoid the pain of a long wait in line?) You step up to the table and find yourself facing a woman whose name tag identifies her as Dr. Glowson. She smiles and asks which course you are interested in. You recount your dilemma, and she describes two courses which have openings. Neither sounds interesting, so you thank her and leave.

Let's focus on one of the many pieces of information you processed in that brief exchange: Dr. Glowson. The initial message is composed of your visual impression quickly supplemented by the sound of her voice. The relevant codes are verbal, her name tag, the words she used in speaking to you, and nonverbal, her physical appearance, age, clothing, jewelry, and so on. You interpret this information based on your previous experiences with female professors during indecisive moments at registration and conclude that Dr. Glowson is a woman who is friendly and cooperative. As you walk away, you make a mental note to check the schedule of classes to see what she teaches for future reference. Just that quickly you have processed information and probably also formed some expectations about the type of person or teacher Dr. Glowson is. The same information, though, could have led to an entirely different outcome, based on the operation of perceptual selectivities. For each of the four stages of the information-processing sequence, there is a related selectivity which shapes and modifies the information as you perceive it. To facilitate your understanding of these mechanisms we consider each separately.

Selective Exposure

All of us make choices about which of the available stimuli we allow to enter our perceptual world. For most messages, this involves placing yourself in physical proximity to a given message source, whether this source is another person, a magazine, or whatever. If you happen to be biased against graduate teaching assistants as instructors, you are not likely to enroll in a course you know is taught by a graduate student. Or, if you discover your instructor is a graduate student, you may drop the course or change sections. In somewhat the same way, teachers may avoid teaching courses they know regularly enroll students of a particular type. Some of our colleagues reflect this tendency in their studied avoidance of courses that enroll large numbers of undergraduate nonmajors. These examples illustrate the conscious exercise of selective exposure in information processing. It's important to note that the process occurs most often on an unconscious level. Decisions are made and acted upon without conscious thought processes like those in our examples. When selecting a place to eat dinner, for instance, the possibility of dining at the most popular student hangout does not occur to a teacher.

Selective Attention

The process of attending to a stimulus involves the adaptation of your sensory mechanisms to facilitate reception of a specific message. It's a bit like deciding to focus only on a single stimulus and adjusting your senses to focus on that stimulus alone. When dealing with people, we may selectively attend to only certain aspects of their appearance or behavior in making a judgment about them. Until fairly recently teachers often selectively attended to certain appearance cues, such as hair length or dress cues, to acquire insights about their students. Today, these distinctions are considerably less useful. Attention requires a sort of "fine-tuning" of your physiological senses. Hence it is susceptible to many internal influences. These include your physical state at the moment, your ability to concentrate, and the nature of the stimulus itself or the context in which it appears.

We attend to stimuli in short bursts averaging about 17 seconds. We are likely to attend more frequently and for longer time periods to people or events we like, even though we are unconscious of the process as it is happening. Similarly, if a student or teacher has a trait or behavior we find offensive, it is sometimes difficult to stop attending to that irritant and focus on the individual as a whole. Distortions resulting from either of these operations have obvious classroom implications. One teacher we know turned the information she gained from one course in speech pathology into a virtual obsession in the classroom and elsewhere. She selectively attended to vocal cues so thoroughly that in searching out slurred syllables she often lost much of the meaning of a conversation.

Selective Perception

Once behaviors, events, or individuals have captured our attention, we begin at once to apply meanings. The specific meanings we attach may have little in common with the meanings others assign to an identical stimulus. Moreover, there may be no relationship between the meaning we assign and the meaning intended. Our personal experiences, our stereotypic responses, and our expectations shape the meaning we attribute to various individuals, things, or events. One embarrassing example we have detected in our own behavior is common among teachers. Teachers have a tendency to interpret a simple request for information as a request for an explanation. Hence we find ourselves giving protracted answers when a simple declarative sentence would have sufficed. As one friend expresses it, "Ask a professor for the correct time, and he'll tell you how the watch is constructed. And then give you the wrong time."

Our perceptions of others' behaviors and attitudes are highly colored by our desires, values, and intentions. Our psychological state therefore can turn a simple comment into a challenge, a slur, or a compliment. We simply fill in the details necessary to create the impression we have decided is accurate and ignore details that would contradict our interpretation.

The role of selective perception in the classroom affects more than social judgments. For students it may deter learning to the extent that they misinterpret the teacher's statements, whether the statements are related to content, classroom procedures, or general conversation. Teachers are similarly prone to misperceive the verbal and nonverbal cues of students. In both cases, the ambiguity of the situation or message characteristics is likely to be responsible, but remains undetected as the problem.

Selective Retention

Everyone has caught a fish that grows by inches with each successive retelling of the tale. The angler's exaggeration is a typical instance of selective retention effects on perception. Just as we structure immediate reality through other selectivities, we write our own version of history through selective retention. The psychological implications are no different here than in the other three; we recall the details of a person or event that are most useful or attractive to us.

The characteristics of the stimulus also affect our ability to retain its details. The more vivid, novel, or intense the stimulus, the more likely it is to be recalled. The first-grade writing experience demonstrates this point and reflects another aspect of selective retention. The details recalled from events that are similar are usually patterned. Reflect on teachers you have had throughout all your years in school. What images flash through your mind? One of the interesting, but unanswered, questions surrounding selective retention effects is whether our patterning of events is due to inherent similarities among stimuli or is a function of our learned need to project order and structure into experience. Which seems most consistent with the hedonic principle we mentioned earlier?

Perception as Communication

The interdependence of the sequences of information processing and perceptual selectivities is an inherent aspect of perception. Each part shapes and is shaped by the others, and the sum of the interdependencies describes for each of us our reality. We stress the perception process in this chapter, because it determines the expectations we form for others. It also defines our individual communication systems. Our perceptions define our version of reality, and this reality is expressed through our communication. We feel the implications of this interdependence are well expressed in Haney's (1973) analogy of the box.

> Visualize each of us as the sole and constant tenant of a box with a top, a bottom, and four sides. There is just one window in this box—one's frame of reference, loosely speaking—through which he views the outside world.
>
> A restricted window. This suggests immediately that one's view is restricted—he cannot see what is happening in back of him, above, to the sides, and so forth. One obviously cannot be ubiquitous and therefore his view is inevitably limited. But there is another restriction that he can overcome to an extent—the size of the window. We all have our "narrownesses"— our areas of naivete. I, for example, was born and reared in a suburb. Suppose you are a country boy and we go out to a farm. We would share the same environment but I would expect that your stimuli and evoked sets would greatly outnumber mine. You would have the preparation, the memory content, to make so much more significance out of the experience than I.
>
> But I have the capacity to learn. Given the time and provided I have the motivation I can acquire some of your sophistication. In short, I can *expand* my window.
>
> Stained-Glass Window. Not only is one's window frame restricted (but expandable largely at his will) but it also does not contain a pane of clear glass. It is rather like a stained-glass church window with various, peculiarly shaped, tinted, and refracting lenses. In one's frame of reference these lenses are his experiences, biases, values, needs, emotions, aspirations, and the like. They may all be distorting media to an extent but are we powerless to overcome these distortions? Hardly, but let us establish one point first.
>
> Does anyone grow up with a clear window? Can anyone be without bias, for example? Quite unlikely, for everyone had to be born at a particular time and in a particular place. Thus he was exposed to particular people and situations all of whom and which taught him *special* lessons regarding values, customs, mores, codes, and so on.
>
> But again man has viability and the capacity to adjust and compensate—he can *clarify* his window. A pencil in a glass of water appears to bend abruptly but if one *understands* something about the nature of refraction he can compensate for the distortion, aim at where the pencil appears not to be, and hit it. So it is more profoundly with a man himself—if he can *understand himself* he can *compensate* for his distorted frame of reference and, in effect, clarify his window. (pp. 69–70)

PRINCIPLES 3.1

1. Expectations are an integral aspect of the communication process.
2. Expectations are learned beliefs, acquired through experience, which individuals use to understand and regulate their environments.
3. Teacher expectations affect students' self-concepts as well as academic performance.
4. Expectations are formed through an individual's highly individualized yet systematic perceptual processes.

FIGURE 3·2 EACH OF US CAN EXPAND AND CLARIFY OUR WINDOWS.

5. Learned patterns of processing information influence the number and type of expectations individuals develop for persons or events.
6. All perceptions, including expectations, are shaped by the operations of an individual's perceptual selectivity processes.

EXPECTATIONS AS BELIEF SYSTEMS

Earlier we defined expectations as beliefs about the relationship between behaviors and their outcomes, which we use to understand and control our environments. The foregoing section on perception has hopefully made you aware of the role of selectivity phenomena in the development and maintenance of expectations. Perceptual data are organized. It is the nature of this organization that determines the characteristics of expectations teachers hold for students, you hold for yourself and others, and so on.

Cognitive Organization: Beliefs, Attitudes, and Values

Much has been written concerning the means people use to organize the rich and varied information they acquire. Since your cognitive world is no more directly observable than any other individual's, we deal with presumed rather than proven matters. Nonetheless, your understanding of communication outcomes will benefit from a brief review of the relationships among perceptual and cognitive elements.

We have already described a view of the information processing system which characterizes human perception and cognition. An information processing approach implies two assumptions that are central to our understanding of communication transactions. The first is that the information processing system is orderly and predictable. The second assumption is equally straightforward. It suggests that we have an inherent need for consistency. Consistency is achieved through imposing structure on the subjective experiences of perception. The structural element of greatest interest with regard to expectations is beliefs.

To understand belief systems we should distinguish beliefs from two other elements of cognitive structure—attitudes and values. Each of these terms is used to describe internal states. Of the three, however, beliefs are probably central to our understanding of human behavior. Beliefs represent the information we have about ourselves and our environment. More specifically, a belief links an object with some attribute. The object of a belief of course may be a person, an institution, an event, or a group, while the associated attribute may be any of a number of traits, properties, characteristics, outcomes, or qualities. The belief, "Teachers are educated people," links the object "teacher" to the attribute "educated."

Values, in contrast, are defined as our relatively stable conceptions of good and bad. Although our values tend to be less amenable to change than beliefs, you cannot establish values without first forming beliefs. Moreover, it is often argued that none of us forms our own values so much as we acquire them through our culture. Perhaps an example will help clarify this distinction. If you were born into an oriental culture, you would believe that humanity was only one among all elements of the universe. In western cultures, however, the belief that humanity is at the center of the universe is a recurrent theme. That distinction in beliefs leads to an entirely different concept of the value of individual life.

Attitudes refer to the affective evaluative dimension of our responses to people, objects, and events. That is, our attitudes reflect our likes and dislikes. You have just read a chapter on self-concept and know that your self-concept is the sum of the information you have learned about yourself from internal and external sources. Your self-concept is thus a set of beliefs about yourself. Your self-esteem, one part of your self-concept, is the evaluative dimension, or the attitude you have about your personal worth.

Teachers and students have attitudes toward one another in instructional settings which definitely influence their perceptions and interactions. These attitudes have a more direct bearing on liking and attraction patterns, however (see Chapter 8), than on expectations. Expectations (beliefs) may affect teacher-student liking patterns, but not to the extent that attraction (attitudes) does. Therefore, to gain insight into the formation of expectations, we must explore the origins of beliefs.

Belief Formation

We can learn much about how teachers acquire their expectations for student performance by examining how we develop beliefs about anything. Whether we are referring to an inanimate object, such as a car or house, or another individual, the process is the same. We can distinguish among at least three types of beliefs that teachers are likely to form concerning their students. Any or all may become an expectation.

We have defined beliefs as ideas or statements which express a relationship between one object and some other object, concept, attribute, or trait. Belief formation, then, is the process of establishing an association between two aspects of the individual's cognitive world. Our most basic or primitive (Rokeach, 1968; Bem, 1970) beliefs are derived from our direct experiences with a particular stimulus. Observation of a student's classroom behavior enables a teacher to form a series of *descriptive beliefs* (Fishbein and Azjen, 1975) about the student's personality, character, social status and, most particularly, academic capabilities and potential. Thus, Jerry's tendency to submit sloppy, hastily prepared work encourages his teacher to believe that he is a lazy or indifferent student. The validity of these observations in the teacher's mind stems from the power of immediate personal experience. After all, what do you trust more than your own sensory information? Descriptive beliefs therefore are likely to lead to strongly held expectations for a student's performance. You may have experienced some of these effects yourself. We call them "halo" effects and "pitchfork" effects.

If you have done well in Spanish I with Professor Carter and can choose to take Spanish II from him or Professor Osalino, which option will you select? We predict that you will join Professor Carter's class and do so with your own set of expectations, including the belief that your good performance in the first class will generalize to the second. This would be a halo effect. On the other hand, what is more dreaded than the prospect of a second course from a teacher whose estimate of your intelligence places you roughly four points above a philodendron? Unfortunately, studies on expectations suggest that pitchfork effects are probably more stable and resistant to change than halo effects. It seems to be more difficult for students to overcome a teacher's negative impression of their performance than it is to lose a positive one. Perhaps negative performances are somehow more memorable than neutral or positive ones. We can explain the persistence of descriptive beliefs by noting that teachers, like everyone else, need to maintain consistency within their belief systems. It is clearly inappropriate, though, for them to "lock students in" at one level of performance.

Interestingly enough, you can find yourself similarly trapped if you follow an older sibling into a teacher's classroom. Seaver's (1971) study revealed that teachers' evaluations of a student's performance, I.Q., and a variety of other measures correlated positively with the older sibling's performance in class. Students who took the same courses from teachers who had not taught their siblings fared substantially better. They did not necessarily receive higher grades, but at least the achievements evaluated were exclusively their own.

A second way in which beliefs are formed involves combining information from past experiences with that gathered from direct observation. *Inferential beliefs* enable us to make a wide variety of judgments about others that would be difficult, if not impossible, to make on the basis of direct observation alone (Fishbein and Azjen, 1975). The expectations a teacher forms by generalizing from previously observed cases are usually stereotypic. Regrettably, inferential beliefs of this sort affect teacher expectations quite frequently, leading to negative learning expectations for minority group students and disruptive students in particular. Because teachers have to deal with so many students in each class, it is inevitable that some shortcuts will be taken in their initial analyses of a classroom group. In Chapters 4 and 5, we explore in depth some of the verbal and nonverbal cues teachers respond to in assessing student performance.

Accents or dialects, for example, often affect teacher perceptions of student performance negatively. Students whose speech sounds different are certainly not always academically deficient. If, however, a teacher has observed over the years that students with unfamiliar dialects are poor spellers, then the teacher is prone to infer that a new student whose speech is accented cannot spell. This particular inferential belief can be changed by the student's spelling performance. When less observable characteristics such as attitude or general learning ability are the attributes associated with certain student behaviors, the possibility of incorrect inferences is increased.

Bruner (1957) suggests that inferential beliefs may be derived through rules of formal logic. Such beliefs usually begin with a descriptive belief or a directly observable event and end with a belief about an attribute that is not directly observable. Consider the teacher who is trying to assess the relationship between students' academic level and their willingness to do optional classroom assignments. Sophomores have completed more assignments than juniors, and juniors have completed more than seniors. On this basis the teacher is likely to believe that seniors are less interested or less attracted to optional assignments, although none of the students has been directly asked about their reactions. Teachers commonly use such indirect measures to assess student interest and form expectations about ability on a group or individual level. Perhaps the least desirable instance of an expectation formed through inferential beliefs occurs when a teacher reasons as follows: Alice obtained a higher score on the verbal portion of the SAT than Clarence. Clarence obtained a higher score than Tony. Alice's achievement in the language and literature program will be superior to Tony's.

The teacher in the foregoing example used the SAT scores to form an inferential belief. The same data could have also been used to generate a final type of belief or a performance expectation. All of us accept information from outside sources about things we have not personally experienced. Each evening we generally accept Walter Cronkite's or John Chancellor's or Harry Reasoner's account of world events without question. If a riot in London is reported, we form the belief that there *was* a riot without benefit of direct observation, past experience with either London or riots, or any prior inferences about the likelihood of riots in London. Beliefs formed through acceptance of information from an outside source are called *informational beliefs* (Fishbein and Azjen, 1975), and these, too, determine the expectations that teachers form. The teacher in our example above could have used the SAT scores to yield the informational belief (and related expectation) that Alice is smarter than both Clarence and Tony.

Other common sources of informational beliefs that influence teachers' informational beliefs about students include personal files, transcripts, GPAs, and comments from fellow teachers or counselors. Any one of these sources may contribute to the development of expectations for a student's academic or social behavior. If Professor Cromwell describes student Charlotte C. as a distinctly mediocre mind during a faculty meeting, teachers who find her enrolled in their classes may or may not treat Charlotte accordingly. The impact of informational beliefs is likely to vary more widely than is the case with descriptive or inferential beliefs. This is because they are not the product of the teacher's own belief system. Acceptance of the information depends therefore on many factors such as source credibility or, in the case of our example, attitudes toward standardized test scores as predictors of academic performance.

Taken together, these three types of beliefs describe the bases upon which teachers form expectations for their students. We have discussed the beliefs in descending order of importance, approximating the position we believe each occupies in the hierarchy of beliefs each teacher develops. That is, beliefs formed through personal experience are stronger than those created through inference or obtained from external sources. Our discussion has been aimed toward demonstrating several implications of expectations in the classroom setting that we feel are critical and often overlooked. The first reiterates a point made early in this chapter: Expectations are a normal part of the process of communication. Without expectations, communication would be almost impossibly complex. Descriptive, inferential, and informational beliefs influence every learning encounter, whether on an individual or group level.

A more subtle, but extremely important, implication emerging from this discussion is that expectations are primarily the *results* of observed performances rather than the causes. Students do not cause teachers to acquire reputations as hard or demanding taskmasters or as "sure suckers for a sob story." Such labels are assigned after, rather than before, the learning encounter. Even when reputations precede a student or a teacher, it is naive to assume that these expectations automatically determine their behavior. Still, we find an alarming tendency within certain educational circles to treat the question of expectations as if it were some dread disease against which we should all seek immediate immunization. A sort of controlled hysteria surrounding the topic leads some writers to make unsupported claims and offer unrealistic solutions (e.g., avoid looking at students' records to prevent inappropriate expectations) to a problem that does not exist, at least in the way that many seem to assume.

Expectations, contrary to popular opinion, are *not always* self-fulfilling prophecies. This frequently abused term was originally coined by Merton (1948) to describe a phenomenon in which a prediction, *initially false*, incites a chain of events that cause the original prediction to become true. Therefore, for a teacher's expectations to become self-fulfilling prophecies, they must be initially inaccurate assessments of a student's capabilities, which are then made realities through the teacher's treatment of the student. Brophy and Good (1974), in an extensive review of research on teacher expectations, argue that more than initial expectations must be considered. The determining factor appears to be whether or not an inappropriate expectation is viewed by the teacher as a permanent, inflexible evaluation of a student's ability. We cannot overstate the importance of this distinction in your understanding of the effect of teacher expectations on student achievement. The picture is neither as bright nor as bleak as it has occasionally been painted. Rather, it is far more detailed and complex than the popularized version of the concept suggests.

The following principles summarize some key points and principles included in our analysis of expectations as belief systems. We suggest that you keep the principles in mind as we examine the ways in which expectations lead to the differential treatment of students.

PRINCIPLES 3.2

1. Expectations are well-organized belief systems regulated by orderly information processing and inherent needs for cognitive consistency.
2. Attitudes and values influence the development of expectations indirectly.
3. Teachers form expectations for student performance through direct observation, inference, and information from outside sources.
4. The strength or stability of an expectation is determined by the way it was formed and the nature of the information.
5. Contrary to popular thought, teacher expectations are not invariably self-fulfilling prophecies.

THE PYGMALION EFFECT

Having established the perceptual and cognitive foundations for the formation of teacher expectations, we now direct our attention to the determinants and effects of these expectations on educational outcomes. Initial interest was sparked by the publication of Rosenthal and Jacobsen's (1968) *Pygmalion in the Classroom.* This book reported the results of the "Oak School" experiment, captured the public's fancy, and generated a controversy that continues today. A brief sketch of the study will show you why one slender volume has stimulated no fewer than 4 books and more than 100 research studies over the last decade.

Rosenthal and Jacobsen were interested in determining whether teacher expectations actually functioned as self-fulfilling prophecies. They selected "Oak School," an elementary school located in an urban, lower-class community. Three teachers from each of the six grades were chosen as subjects for the experimental treatment. The treatment involved giving information concerning students' intelligence test scores to the teachers early in the year. Test scores were not represented accurately to the teachers in two ways, however. First, they were told that the test, which actually measured intellectual ability, was a measure specifically designed to identify which students were likely to "bloom" intellectually during the coming school year. Several students in each of the 18 teachers' classes were randomly selected to be the "bloomers." The teachers were told that these students could be expected to make unusual learning gains.

At the end of the school year, Rosenthal and Jacobsen administered the same test of general intellectual abilities and compared the gain scores of the designated "bloomer" students with those of the other pupils. Students who had been identified as likely to experience large gains did indeed outscore their classmates. Moreover, the Pygmalion effect appeared most pronounced for girls, and the major changes took place at grades one and two. "Bloomers" in grades three through six performed comparably, although the differences in gain scores were not statistically significant. These results demonstrated to the researchers' satisfaction that teachers' expectations, induced by the false knowledge that some of their students would improve dramatically, acted as self-fulfilling prophecies.

Rosenthal and Jacobsen attempted to explain their findings in terms of the probable ways teachers treated the designated "bloomer" students. This explanation is consistent with the theory that differential expectations are communicated through differential teacher behaviors toward different students. Teacher behaviors, however, were not actually measured in the study. Hence the conclusion that the observed difference in learning gains was directly attributable to teacher behavior was attacked with great zeal. In the ensuing years, numerous attempts to replicate the findings of the original study were, almost without exception, unsuccessful. Experimentally induced expectation effects are apparently more difficult to obtain than Rosenthal and Jacobson's study suggests. Thus the educational community remains in dispute, with some constituents firmly convinced of the validity and generality of the Pygmalion effect pitted against an equal number of skeptics who, largely on methodological grounds, reject the original study as a fluke.

Brophy and Good (1974) have reviewed and synthesized the bulk of the research literature on teacher expectations and have concluded that there are indeed instances in which true expectancy effects occur. That is, there is substantial evidence, from naturalistic rather than experimental studies, that teachers form inappropriate expectations for their students. Such expectations manifest themselves through shifts in students' performance levels in the direction of the inaccurate expectations. An even stronger case can be made for a conclusion you are familiar with from your own classroom experience. Studies reviewed by Brophy and Good demonstrate irrevocably that teachers treat individual students differently and in ways that are often self-defeating, although these effects are not generally indicative of a Pygmalion effect. Rather, the Pygmalion effect occurs only when certain very specific conditions are present. Brophy and Good (1974) describe them in this way:

1. Early in the school year, using the school records and/or observations of students during classroom interaction, all teachers form differential expectations regarding the achievement potential and personal characteristics of the students in their classrooms. . . .
2. Teachers begin to treat students differently in accordance with their differential expectations for them. Where teacher expectations are inappropriate and rigid, treatment of the students will be inappropriate.
3. Students treat teachers differently because of their different personalities, and they also respond differentially to the teacher because the teacher treats them differentially. . . .
4. Thus, in general, each student will respond to the teacher with behavior that complements and reinforces the teacher's particular expectations for him. In the case of students toward whom the teacher holds inappropriate and rigid expectations, the students will tend to be conditioned to respond with behavior that more closely approximates and therefore helps reinforce the teacher's expectations.
5. If continued indefinitely, this process will cause students toward whom the teachers hold inappropriate and rigid expectations gradually to approximate those expectations more and more closely. . . . This process will not occur with students toward whom teacher expectations were originally appropriate or were inappropriate but not rigid. . . .
6. If continued over the course of the school year, differential teacher treatment of different students will show differential effects on both process and product measures. Where teacher expectations are appropriate, or where they are flexible so that any inappropriate aspects are quickly corrected, the teacher-student interaction pattern will be largely predictable from knowledge of the student's general personality and specific classroom habits, and his achievement relative to that of his classmates will be highly predictable on the basis of his previous achievement. In other words the classroom behavior and academic achievement of such students will be "about as expected." (pp. 39–40)

Several important issues which the Brophy and Good analysis does not resolve, however, remain to be considered before the implications of the Pygmalion effect can be properly understood. Some of these issues are in our view the truly salient questions, and they will be considered shortly.

DEVELOPMENT OF PYGMALION EFFECTS: TEACHER CHARACTERISTICS

Studies of teacher expectations, whether experimental or naturalistic in nature, suggest that certain teacher characteristics are related to the likelihood that they will form the rigidly inappropriate expectations for a

FIGURE 3·3 TEACHERS FORM EXPEC-
TATIONS FOR THEIR STUDENTS'
ACHIEVEMENTS AND CHARACTERISTICS.

student's performance that are the cause of Pygmalion effects. These characteristics may be considered in terms of a teacher's group orientation and his or her individual orientation.

Orientation Toward Class

It will not surprise you to hear that teachers view their classes as unique entities, possessing personality and achievement characteristics greater than the sum of these traits in individual students. We explore this tendency in some depth in Chapter 9. For the moment, however, the relationship between a teacher's instructional style and the predominance of Pygmalion effects is our specific concern. Available research suggests that the way teachers view their role in the classroom affects their expectations. Specifically, teachers who have, by preference or in resignation, adopted a custodial rather than instructive teaching style seem more prone to induce negative expectation effects among their students. As the term suggests, a custodial orientation indicates a detachment from students with emphasis on the role of the teacher as information dispenser. Such an orientation appears related to the likelihood that a teacher will not only form inappropriate expectations but also react negatively to student behavior that violates these expectations. This is the case even when the behavior reflects improved performance.

Somewhat more optimistic are findings revealing that teachers who hold positive expectations for their entire class promote higher achievement in students than those who have negative expectations. Although there are few data to support the studies, the relevant implication is important. Teachers who communicate positive evaluations to their classes are effective.

Orientation Toward Individual Students

Brophy and Good (1974), among others, have conducted studies which relate elements of teaching style to differential treatment of high and low achievers. These may be roughly rank-ordered in terms of the probabilities associated with the incidence of Pygmalion effects for each type of teaching style. *Overreactive* teachers are those who appear to have a great deal of difficulty in dealing with performance differences in their students. Rather than facilitating learning, these teachers probably impede achievement by aggravating the differences in the performance of high- and low-achievement students. The role of perceptual selectivities in maintaining the overreactive teacher's expectations is readily observable. Even when low-achieving students perform well, they receive less reinforcement and attention. Similarly, these teachers are likely to rationalize by characterizing low achievers as "unteachable" or incapable of learning.

Reactive teachers constitute the bulk of those observed in these naturalistic studies. Essentially, you may think of this teacher as the type who simply allows students to seek their own level of performance. Rather than reflecting negative passivity or a lack of concern for student achievement, these teachers are apparently overwhelmed by what Jackson (1968) described as the frenetic pace at which classroom events evolve. Like most of us, the reactive teacher is frantically treading water just to stay afloat. Generally, these teachers are less likely to form the rigidly inappropriate expectations leading to Pygmalion effects than might be expected. Their classroom behaviors though, often reflect differential patterns of treatment that correspond to the student's achievement level.

Proactive teachers differ from the others in teaching style, primarily in their reactions to differences in the performance levels of their students. One distinct difference emerges from their treatment of low-achieving students. Rather than either emphasizing or passively reinforcing such performance levels, proactive teachers have more planned, controlled interactions with students. Working actively with *all* students, rather than differentiating on the basis of performance, distinguishes the proactive teaching style. This style is least likely to lead to Pygmalion effects and appears to be least hampered by perceptual selectivities or rigid beliefs in dealing with student performance.

These findings suggest several implications in addition to the obvious differences in desirability of the various teaching styles. Lest you assume otherwise, it is important to emphasize that most teachers are unaware of the degree to which their expectations shape their behavior toward students. Overreactive teachers are not the villains they may seem, at least not intentionally. Most teachers do not enter their classrooms thinking, "Today, I shall be a proactive type and really work with my class." These teachers are, as we argued earlier in the chapter, doing what all of us do in every situation, acting on their beliefs.

A second point you should know is that many teacher expectation studies have used novice or student teachers, rather than experienced professional teachers. It is our opinion that this practice makes certain of the inferences based on these data highly questionable. Brophy and Good (1974) seem to support this opinion at least partially by noting that teaching competence affects expectations by reducing the likelihood that teachers will form rigid and inaccurate expectations for students.

The following principles should suggest some questions about Pygmalion effects to you that we have not yet considered. Student characteristics that influence expectations are explored in subsequent sections.

PRINCIPLES 3.3

1. Teacher behavior toward individual students varies as a function of the teacher's expectations for the student's performance.

2. Expectation or Pygmalion effects are less a function of the accuracy of teacher expectations than of the rigidity with which these expectations are held.
3. The incidence of expectation effects is affected by a teacher's beliefs about her classroom role, a classroom group, and her strategies for dealing with students at varying achievement levels.
4. Most teachers are unaware of the scope or impact of their expectations regarding individual students.

SIGNALS OF EXPECTATIONS

Thus far we have focused on how teachers develop expectations for their students' performance. The means by which teachers communicate their expectations to students are equally important. Studies of teacher-student classroom interactions have revealed fairly consistent patterns of teacher treatment of high- and low-achieving students (Brophy and Good, 1974). These patterns are not typical of all teachers or all classrooms. Rather, they should be viewed as the ways teachers can (and sometimes do) create Pygmalion effects. As suggested in Chapter 1, these classroom messages are signaled through two symbol systems, verbal and nonverbal.

Verbal Signals of Expectations

Teachers reveal their expectations verbally in several ways. While on occasion a teacher may declare to a student that he or she is incapable of learning, the message is not usually stated so directly. Rather, the verbal signals are likely to be more subtle. Brophy and Good (1974) suggest that differential treatment emerges through the frequency and quality of verbal contacts between the teacher and the individual student. We consider each of these briefly.

Teachers communicate low expectations to students by calling on low achievers less frequently than on high achievers. Therefore, the low-achieving student is deprived of a critical opportunity to demonstrate or acquire knowledge in the classroom. Even when the student volunteers to answer, he or she is less likely to be chosen than a high-achieving student. Studies reveal that the difference becomes more pronounced as the grade level increases. It seems reasonable to assume that, over time, the student adapts to this treatment by attempting less and less.

More striking instances of the ways teachers communicate their expectations lie in the quality of verbal exchanges. Praise and criticism are the staple teacher responses to pupil performance. Differences in expectations, however, dictate widely varying patterns for high- and low-achievement students. For the low-achieving student, the prospects are, at best, mixed. Some teachers praise any response such a student makes without regard for accuracy or appropriateness. While the teacher's intentions are probably sympathetic, Brophy and Good (1974) aptly note that praising inaccurate responses may only emphasize the student's academic weaknesses. The reactions of the low achiever's peers to his or her unde-served praise are likely to offset any positive effects on future perfor-mance. Moreover, as discussed in Chapter 2, students value accurate feedback from their teachers. Overpraising inadequate responses does little to develop academic self-esteem and may damage your credibility with your students.

In contrast, some teachers frequently are overly punitive toward low-achievement students. Studies reveal two ways in which this ten-dency may be verbalized in classes. One way low expectations are com-municated occurs when teachers praise the correct responses of low-achieving students less frequently or vigorously than those of high-achieving students. Sometimes, correct responses are even ignored. Can the student in this circumstance fail to infer that he or she is not expected to perform adequately?

Criticism also becomes a vehicle of a teacher's expectations for a student's performance. Low-achieving students are substantially more likely to be criticized for incorrect responses than their high-achieving peers. The inappropriateness of this teacher behavior can hardly be over-stated. It is one thing to correct a wrong answer and quite another to criticize a student for attempting to respond. The disproportionate amount of criticism given these students conveys a message that they are failures. As Brophy and Good (1974, p. 331) state, "The situation is clear for lows in certain classes: if they respond, they are more likely to be criticized and less likely to be praised; thus, the safest strategy is to remain silent and hope that the teacher will call on someone else."

Nonverbal Signals of Expectations

Differential treatment of students occurs through nonverbal messages no less frequently than through verbal messages. Researchers have observed three ways in which teachers communicate expectations to their students that warrant our attention. We can describe these in terms of time, spatial relationships, and inclusion.

The treatment pattern for low achievers with regard to time might be described by the single word "less." Generally, these students are given less public class time (e.g., opportunities to answer questions) than their peers, although private contacts with their teachers (e.g., conferences) are about equal for the two groups of students. In a typical class session, however, teachers appear unwilling to wait for low-achieving students to respond to questions. These students are not only given less time to answer but are also quickly passed over if their answers are incorrect. High-achieving students, by contrast, are likely to have more time to answer. Should they answer incorrectly, the high achievers are given more second chances to improve their responses. The teacher's apparent willingness to devote more time to the high-achieving students suggests a difference in performance standards. Students cannot fail to recognize this difference and infer something about their academic worth from the teacher's use of time.

Similarly, spatial relationships reveal teacher preferences for students whose achievement level is high. Brophy and Good (1974) summarize studies which indicate that, when a teacher establishes a seating pattern for a class, low-achievement students are placed further away from the teacher. This physical message of space is ultimately translated into a psychological message of rejection for some students, particularly the low achievers. Their distance from the teacher decreases the likelihood that they will be noticed as individuals. Thus another element is added to a cycle perpetuating mediocre performance. The students with the greatest need for the teacher's attention and efforts are in the least desirable position to obtain them.

Finally, differential treatment of students results from a teacher's expression of nonverbal messages of inclusion. Such messages are conveyed through eye contact, smiles, head nods, and similarly positive signals. Studies suggest a higher frequency of these kinds of messages for students whose achievement level is high. Moreover, these students generally receive feedback (positive or negative) more frequently than low achievers. The latter, of course, are the ones whose need for positive reinforcement is perhaps greatest.

Brophy and Good's (1974) synthesis of studies on the communication of expectations depicts a grim reality of classroom life. Some students are, by virtue of a teacher's expectations, provided an impoverished atmosphere for learning. Fortunately, these observed behaviors are not widespread. This discussion should alert you to some of the ways in which teachers not only reveal, but repeatedly reinforce, their expectations for student performance. The descriptions of the differences in teacher behavior toward certain students should resolve any doubts you may have held about the possibility of Pygmalion effects. They do occur.

DEVELOPMENT OF PYGMALION EFFECTS: STUDENT CHARACTERISTICS

Information on the specific characteristics of students which determine the expectations teachers form for their performance would be the single most valuable contribution toward a unified theory of expectation effects. These data have not, however, been forthcoming. This introduces a question, or rather a series of questions, concerning the extent to which student behavior exerts influence on teacher perceptions, interaction patterns, and performance expectations.

Our discussion of the descriptive, inferential, and informational beliefs that teachers typically form in regard to students suggested quite clearly that teachers do indeed form a variety of beliefs about students, whether on an individual or on an entire class basis. Ask yourself what traits or behaviors you rely on to make judgments about others. We suspect that you might have identified such factors as sex, race, personality, propinquity, socioeconomic status, or even physical appearance. We do know something about the impact of these student attributes on teachers. What we know, however, is that, while these attributes affect teachers in much the same ways as they affect you, they do *not* appear to determine expectations for achievement. That is, any one of these personal characteristics of a student can influence a teacher's attitude toward the student. Too, they may result in differential treatment of the student. These attributes influence the development of attraction and liking between students and teachers and are discussed in Chapter 8, *but they do not determine a teacher's expectations*. We find that this conclusion is too frequently overlooked in discussions of expectation effects. Frankly, it should be reassuring to all of us that what is presently known indicates that teachers can and do distinguish between a student's personal characteristics and his or her academic competence.

What, then, do teachers use to form expectations for achievement? We return to a point made earlier about the nature of the beliefs we use to make predictions. Expectations are usually the results of performance. Teachers rely on student performance cues to form expectations, sometimes on the basis of personal files and always on the basis of their observations of the pupil's in-class behavior. We conclude this section by noting that the majority of teachers observed in naturalistic studies assess student achievement potential accurately and early. Moreover, their expectations tend to be stable, rather than vacillating, from one term to another.

WHAT TO EXPECT ABOUT EXPECTATIONS

We feel at this point like trotting out the old line, "There's some good news and some bad news," to frame our closing thoughts on the Pygmalion question. We depart from our usually conservative reliance on empirical research literature to make a few observations about two issues: the implications of the expectations concept for instruction, and the perspective we recommend for you as a teacher. Following the hedonic principle, we begin in both cases with the good news.

The good news on Pygmalion effects is that they are neither simple nor universal. The popular misconception that many or most teachers exert such drastic effects on student performance is placed in an appropriate perspective emphasizing the interpersonal nature of the teaching event. While this is not particularly helpful in theory development, it is reassuring that teachers appear capable of appreciating and responding to a student's differences independent of their expectations concerning the student's abilities. Further, existing research indicates that, while teacher expectations are unavoidable in the classroom setting, the incidence of self-fulfilling prophecy effects is not at all high. Certainly any instance of rigid and inappropriate expectations is undesirable, but the problem is less prevalent then originally thought.

Now for the bad news. Expectations do affect teacher-student relationships. Data summarized by Brophy and Good (1974) clearly reflect differential treatment patterns in classrooms, most of which discourage students whose achievements are low. Moreover, indications that most teachers are completely unaware of the implications of their behavior toward students reflect poorly on our programs for teacher preparation. To be sure, your primary responsibility in the classroom is to teach a curriculum, but we do not believe this is incompatible with understanding the communication processes involved in effective teaching.

And now, some specific implications for you. Expectations are a reality of classroom life with a detectable effect on performance *in certain settings*. The studies in which we have the greatest confidence are those involving naturalistic observation in elementary classrooms. Hence caution is required in generalizing to secondary or college classroom settings. Elementary teachers, after all, spend hours in the presence of their students daily, with numerous opportunities for influence that the high school or college teacher never has. We reason that this increases the importance of a single teacher's expectations in the elementary classroom setting. Moreover, as discussed in Chapter 2, in the early school years children develop academic self-concepts and are not equipped to weigh the credibility of teachers as more mature students are. In this sense, the impact of your expectations on your students' performance may be reduced if you teach in a high school or college classroom.

Having reassured some of you with the foregoing speculations, we hasten to stipulate that your expectations actually make a difference, regardless of the age of your students or the frequency of your class meetings. Apart from the effects exerted on student performance, your expectations most assuredly influence the way you teach. Your expectations shape your teaching style, your attitudes toward students, and the overall social environment of your classroom. Consequently, it is essential that you monitor the development of your expectations and to a reasonable degree assess their effects on your classroom behavior.

In terms of prescriptions we offer two possibilities. Good and Brophy (1973) argue persuasively that the notion of one standard for all students is arbitrary and inappropriate. We agree and encourage you to exploit every opportunity to individualize instruction, as well as your interpersonal relationships with your students. All students should satisfy the minimal performance standards for a curriculum, but provision should be made for students to work from their level toward realistic rather than arbitrary goals.

Working toward flexibility in your expectations is also desirable. Your ability to influence your students, to assist them in achieving positive educational goals, depends ultimately on your ability and willingness to adapt. Adaptation implies more than playing a reactive role; it involves a commitment to changes that will occur constantly in your students, in the learning environment, and in you. It may not have occurred to you yet, but you are in the best position to make yourself a self-fulfilling prophecy.

PRINCIPLES 3.4

1. Teachers form expectations for student achievement on the basis of their performance and respond differentially to individual students on this basis.
2. Teachers typically communicate their performance expectations for students through the quantity and quality of their verbal interactions with individual students.
3. Nonverbal signals of teacher expectations are expressed through the degree of attention given individual students and the quality of feedback.
4. Personal characteristics of students (physical appearance, sex, etc.) appear to have negligible effects on the expectations a teacher develops for their performance.
5. Expectation effects are most likely to occur when teacher-student contact is frequent over a sustained length of time.
6. The incidence of expectation effects may be mediated by the age and academic self-concept of the students.

REFERENCES

Bem, D. J. *Beliefs, attitudes, and human affairs.* Monterey, Calif.: Brooks/Cole, 1970.

Brophy, J. E., and Good, T. L. *Teacher-student relationships: Causes and consequences.* New York: Holt, Rinehart and Winston, 1974.

Bruner, J. S. Going beyond the information given. In H. E. Gruber et al. (Eds.), *Contemporary approaches to cognition.* Cambridge, Mass.: Harvard University Press, 1957, pp. 41–69.

Fishbein, M., and Ajzen, I. *Belief, attitude, intention and behavior: An introduction to theory and research.* Reading, Mass.: Addison-Wesley, 1975.

Good, T. L., and Brophy, J. E. *Looking in classrooms.* New York: Harper & Row, 1973.

Haney, W. V. *Communication and organizational behavior.* Homewood, Ill.: Irwin, 1973. © Irwin, 1973. Reprinted by permission.

Jackson, P. *Life in classrooms.* New York: Holt, Rinehart and Winston, 1968.

McCroskey, J. C., Larson, K., and Knapp, M. *Introduction to interpersonal communication.* Englewood Cliffs, N.J.: Prentice-Hall, 1971.

McCroskey, J. C., and Wheeless, L. R. *Introduction to human communication.* Boston: Allyn & Bacon, 1976.

Merton, R. The self-fulfilling prophecy. *Antioch Review,* 1948, 8, 193–210.

Rokeach, M. *Beliefs, attitudes and values.* San Francisco: Jossey-Bass, 1968.

Rosenthal, R., and Jacobson, L. *Pygmalion in the classroom: Teacher expectation and pupils' intellectual development.* New York: Holt, Rinehart and Winston, 1968.

Seaver, W. Effects of naturally induced expectancies on the academic performance of pupils in primary grades. Ph.D. dissertation, University of Illinois, 1971.

Chapter 4
The Verbal Symbol System

OBJECTIVES

After reading this chapter you should be able to:

1. explain the futility of teaching principles of language to children.
2. distinguish between intuitive and explicit knowledge of language rules.
3. define linguistic competence.
4. define language code.
5. distinguish between descriptive and prescriptive rules of language.
6. explain how linguists differ from educators in their approach to language.
7. identify and define three verbal coding systems.
8. describe how to distinguish among phonemes of a language.
9. explain why differences in dialect need not provide linguistic barriers to effective communication.
10. provide an example of a syntactically correct sentence which is semantically anomalous.

NOTE: This chapter was written by Robert Hopper, University of Texas at Austin.

11. describe the importance of the nature-nurture controversy in understanding the child's acquisition of syntax.
12. provide examples of words which have different meanings in different sentences.
13. explain the importance of the arbitrary relationships between words and meanings.
14. define pragmatics.
15. list and identify examples of four components of communication situations which speakers take into account.
16. list and identify five functions of communication.
17. define communicative competence.
18. explain the futility of teaching language through correcting children's speech.

> I could tell after listening to that boy say 10 words that he was going to have trouble with fourth-grade work.

This statement, typical of many which can be overheard in teachers' conversations with each other, emphasizes the importance of language in the classroom. Most teachers agree that a student's grasp of language and use of language are a key to academic success at all grade levels. Students who use language poorly are likely to have difficulty learning to read, difficulty expressing themselves orally, and difficulty completing written work. Most teachers believe that students with language difficulties will do poorly in school.

This belief represents an important, yet dangerous, half-truth. Students with language problems *may* do poorly in school; that is the true half. But not all behavior teachers may classify as language problems *really* represents a language difficulty. One purpose of this chapter is to present enough of an overview of the science of linguistics so that you may separate students with language problems (who need special aid) from those whose language is merely different from your own. This is one of the most critical sets of decisions any teacher must make. If you begin to believe that a child's language is likely to prevent academic achievement, then your teaching behavior toward that child may actually hinder his or her success. The concept is called self-fulfilling prophecy: Children often manage to produce precisely the behavior their teachers expect of them. The lesson is that, if you have to make an error in what you expect, err toward expecting excellence.

A second goal of the chapter is to overview the major dimensions of the language code we all use in everyday speech. Following this overview, we discuss how language develops in normal children and how to spot problems in this developmental process. Finally, we discuss ways in which you can help your students develop more useful and precise language habits.

In order to describe verbal coding systems, we must first discuss the form of what you know about language. Most students feel they know little about language. We hope to show that you know a great deal more than you probably guessed.

KNOWLEDGE ABOUT LANGUAGE

What could be more simple than speaking and listening? We do it for a major portion of each waking day. We rarely stop to think about it. When misunderstandings arise, we often puzzle over how they happened: "I told you I would be late getting home tonight. What's the problem?" To most of us, the language in our messages seems quite clear and precise. Others sometimes misunderstand us, and we may explain this by saying, "They weren't listening!", although such an assumption may not be warranted.

Have you ever stopped to consider how many language complexities are involved in a simple act of speaking? Suppose you are telling a story to a friend. You probably speak about 110 words per minute, with gusts up to 150. Each word contains an average of perhaps 5 sounds. You form each of these sounds by moving your tongue, lips, and teeth in rapidly changing patterns to shape the sounds made in your throat as exhaled air passes over the vocal folds in your larynx. Considering that you choose 100 words of 5 sounds each, the choice represents 500 processing decisions of the language code every minute, and not including decisions about content, such as what the story is about or how you adjust the story for different audiences. Speaking, when seen in this light, is at least as complex an act as playing the piano or painting a picture.

Yet, every day we speak, without thinking, as though we were performing the most common of acts. Which in fact we are. Yet it is a common act of incredible complexity, an act of which apparently only humans are capable and which few of us even stop to see as a miracle.

And here's an even stranger point. When you stop to consider the complexity of language, such consideration does little to improve your language performance. If anything, thinking about the difficulty of speech may cause you to hesitate or be unsure of yourself. It's like when you first swing a tennis racket. You might hit the ball very well at first, but after you play a few minutes, you realize how difficult it is and you "choke up." *Focusing too much conscious awareness on language may actually inhibit language use.* We are reminded of an old rhyme by Ms. Edward Craster:

The centipede was happy quite
Until a toad in fun
Asked pray which leg comes after which
And worked his mind to such a pitch
He lay distracted in a ditch
Considering how to run.

The moral is important because most public school instruction uses focused, cognitive exercises to develop skills. In teaching math, we teach principles, and students are aware every moment they study math that it is math they are learning. In history, we study the causes of social movements and try to understand the outcomes of elections. We know we are learning history during a history lesson. Similarly, when studying language, most of you are aware you are studying language. We make no recommendations about this philosophy of education in general, but we argue that its use is questionable in teaching students to use language effectively. *People learn language by using it.* Teaching principles of language may be useful on some occasions but, mainly, students will learn more about language if given chances to talk and listen and then allowed opportunities to talk about matters of concern to them. In fact, too much focused awareness on principles of language and how one sounds can lead to shyness and lack of interaction. Students' fears of making errors can bring a vast silence to the classroom. In this sense, we suspect that talking is different from piano playing or math or history. In piano playing, math, or history, there are sets of principles which guide performance, and which nobody is likely to know until they are taught to them. Most learners must play scales and read music to play the piano, but everyone learns to talk without diagraming sentences. But everybody understands the human language code from early childhood.

Many teachers may challenge the last statement and argue that children do not know how to use the language code until taught to do so. To deal with this issue, we need to discuss what we mean by two expressions: "know" and "language code."

First, let's consider the concept of knowing. If you challenge someone to a game of chess, you take places across a board from each other, and each of you begins to move your pieces in turn. You both demonstrate that you know the rules of chess by moving your pieces appropriately; the bishop moves on the diagonal, and the pawn moves straight ahead but takes other pieces by moving diagonally. You "know" this, but you rarely stop to think about it during a game. You only think about the rules when they are violated, as is the case when someone's pawn tries to take your queen by moving backward. Then you note that pawns cannot move backward, making the move against the rules.

Two levels of knowledge about chess are possible: *intuitive* knowledge, in which you know how to move your pieces and recognize when others are moving their's appropriately; *explicit* knowledge, in which you can recite the rules of chess and talk about them as principles. When we say that most humans know the language code, we mean that everyone possesses intuitive knowledge about language. People show that they know language because they demonstrate awareness of how the language system works when they speak. It's a lot like a fish swimming. There can be no doubt that a fish knows how to swim. The fish knows how to swim better than the most talented and knowledgeable human aquatic physicist. But, even if a fish could communicate, it could not tell us (explicitly) any principles of underwater movement.

Intuitively, each of us knows language, just as a fish knows how to swim. Every speaker shows a knowledge of language by speaking and making himself understood. Every human can tell the difference between a word and a nonword. Every human can assign meanings to sounds. Every human can tell that certain sound combinations are not acceptable in his or her language. Every human can understand language messages. Not everyone, however, can talk about language codes explicitly. But in human communication, as in a fish's swimming, the most important thing is doing it.

Linguist Noam Chomsky has argued this point on an abstract theoretical level. Chomsky notes that each speaker possesses intuitive knowledge of language. This knowledge is something of which speakers may be totally unaware, although it is revealed in their patterns of talking. This underlying knowledge of language is called *linguistic competence* (Chomsky, 1965). Your linguistic competence is what you know intuitively about the verbal coding systems of the English language. We might try to teach you linguistic theory until you are blue in the face, but it is unlikely that your linguistic competence will be affected.

In sum, each of us possesses an intuitive knowledge of the rules of the English language code. We may not know much about linguistics, but we know a great deal about language. We show our knowledge by communicating through language. The implication for teaching is that meaningful opportunities to speak and listen in class may be more important than cognitive learning about language. Earlier we promised to discuss two concepts: knowledge and language code. The *language code is a set of rules pairing sounds with meanings.* The trickiest word in this definition is the word "rules." Our analogies up to this point have been mostly to rules of games. Now we must admit a difficulty with this analogy. There are two kinds of rules: *descriptive* rules and *prescriptive* rules. A prescriptive rule is an order—an injunction. Prescriptive rules are like threats. There is an orderliness laid out and, if it is broken, some penalty is levied. Highway

FIGURE 4·1 EACH PERSON POSSESSES
INTUITIVE KNOWLEDGE OF LANGUAGE RULES.

speed limits are a good example of prescriptive rules. If the speed limit is 35 mph and you go faster than that, you can be cited for speeding and you will have to pay a fine. Most classroom deportment rules are prescriptive rules. Rules about raising your hand before speaking, or about not interrupting others serve as examples. If such rules are broken, the teacher may invoke disciplinary tactics. If you want to know whether a rule is prescriptive, put a "should" in it, and see how it sounds. Thus the following sound fine and can be classed as prescriptive rules:

You *should* do your homework each night.
You *should* respect your teachers.
You *should* not talk too loudly in class.
You *should* keep quiet and stay in your seat during a test.

By contrast, the following sound rather strange:

You *should* use syllables when you talk in class.
You *should* not grow over eight feet tall.
You *should* not flap your arms and fly like a bird.

The last three examples become absurd with "should" in them. Yet there still is a sense in which these statements represent rules. There is a regularity in the fact that people do use syllables when they talk, that people almost never grow eight feet tall, and that they do not fly. These statements serve as examples of descriptive rules. Descriptive rules identify limits in terms of what *is*, not in terms of what should be. The laws of science are descriptive rules. Scientists observe what exists and try to isolate the patterns which are the most regular. The goal of prescriptive rules is order, while the goal of descriptive rules is understanding. *The rules of language, as discussed by linguists, are descriptive rules.* Linguists describe the patterns of actual language use by humans. The question of whether people should talk as they do rarely occurs to linguists.

The difference between a descriptive and a prescriptive rule is not a matter of the structure of the rule. For instance, the rule, "Speed Limit 35," seems clearly prescriptive. It is a rule with a "should" in it, and one which is often disobeyed. Suppose, however, that an anthropologist discovers a culture in which all drivers of automobiles mysteriously always drive at speeds of 35 miles per hour or less. That anthropologist might formulate the descriptive rule, "Speed Limit 35," to describe the driving in that culture. This suggests a second way to distinguish descriptive rules from prescriptive ones. If the rule is frequently violated, it cannot be descriptive. Hence if students frequently misbehave in class, then rules forbidding such misbehavior are prescriptive, not descriptive.

To summarize, prescriptive rules are rules which you can put a "should" in and which are frequently disobeyed. Descriptive rules describe what is. Modern linguists attempt to identify descriptive rules of language. Mastery of the descriptive rules of language constitutes linguistic competence.

This is important to instruction, because parents and teachers often experience difficulty maintaining a descriptive perspective about children's speech. Most parents and teachers believe that students *should* be taught to speak certain ways. We do not condemn this point of view. (Can you see that to condemn this point of view is to use a "should" and therefore is actually to take a similarly prescriptive point of view?) We only ask that you listen to what linguists have to say, descriptively, about the rules of language. Suspend some of your "shoulds" for just a few pages, and let us tell you what linguists say about verbal coding systems. The linguistic perspective cannot solve all language problems in the classroom, but it will help you see more clearly where the problems lie. After learning a little about linguistics, teachers often tell us they are able to hear students speak with a "different ear."

PRINCIPLES 4.1

1. Implicit, intuitive knowledge about language, called linguistic competence, underlies speech behavior.
2. Speakers demonstrate their linguistic knowledge by speaking and understanding the language code.
3. Language is an extremely complex code matching sounds to meanings, but children appear to learn this complex code with little apparent effort, and regardless of the teaching efforts of adults.
4. Linguists emphasize descriptive rules of language and de-emphasize prescriptive rules.

VERBAL CODING SYSTEMS: A LINGUISTIC PERSPECTIVE

To appreciate the complexity of language, compare language coding with simpler codes such as Morse code and secret codes used by spies. These simpler codes usually represent some set of equivalencies, a set of pairings of an item with a meaning. Once you understand the key, the code yields up all its secrets. Language is less simple. There are actually at least three separate levels of coding present all the time we talk. First, there is a level of ordering that involves just the sounds of the language. Second, there is a level of ordering that structures the sounds into sentences, and finally there is a level of ordering which connects sounds and structures to meanings. The study of the sound system of language is called *phonology*, the study of sentence structure is called *syntax*, and the study of meaning is called *semantics*. In the following sections of the chapter, we discuss each of these verbal coding systems in turn and demonstrate that each of these levels of language has a complexity all its own.

The Sound System

The most basic level of order in language is the order which occurs on the level of the sounds themselves. A language does not combine sounds at random. Rather, each language uses a set of sounds that is, to some degree, unique. English uses many sounds, for instance, which simply do not occur in Spanish. Ways of putting sounds together into syllables and words are also likely to be somewhat different in every language. For example, there is a letter in Russian which looks like a capital "W" with a "j" after it ("Wj"). This letter represents a sound sort of like the English letters "schch." This sound is quite rare in English. Say the words "fresh cheese," noting the blend between the last consonants of "fresh" and the first ones of "cheese." That gives a fair approximation of a sound which is actually only one sound in Russian and which appears in many words.

Every sound is not represented by just one letter. For instance, the "sh" sound in English is only one *phoneme*, even though it takes two letters to represent it. A phoneme is the minimal sound unit of any language. Phonemes are the building blocks of language. All languages do not use exactly the same phonemes. Phonemes can be defined only with reference to a *particular* language (Langacker, 1967). In Spanish, for instance, there is no distinction between the phonemes "sh" and "ch," which are two separate phonemes in English. As a result, it is difficult for most Spanish speakers to hear clearly any difference between the words "chew" and "shoe." This provides an interference problem for Spanish speakers learning English. Not only new words and grammar, but a new sound system must be learned as well.

It is important to note that English and Spanish are equally orderly in their sound systems. Neither language can combine sounds in just any old way. An example of how orderly combinations of sounds are in all languages can be found in the phonological rules we use to make plurals in English. Phonology is the study of the sound system. Phonological rules are descriptive rules written by linguists to describe how sounds work in a language. The sound we use to make plurals is basically an "s" sound at the end of a word. But how the sound is pronounced varies according to what kind of sound ends the word:

1. For words ending in the sounds p, t, k, f, or th, plurals are made by adding the "s" phoneme, as in clocks, boats, caps, myths, muffs.
2. For words ending in the sounds b, d, g, v, l, r, y, w, m, n, ng, or th (as in la*the*), plurals are made by pronouncing the "z" sound. (Though it is still often spelled as "s" it is pronounced as "z.") Examples include: trees, doors, pencils, grades, things, sounds, elevators.
3. For words ending in the sounds s, z, sh, ch, or j, plurals are made by adding a sound that is pronounced "iz," which is usually spelled "es." Examples include foxes, fezzes, boxes, buses, causes, beaches, garages. (Fromkin and Rodman, 1974, pp. 81–83)

Thinking about this kind of order in phonological rules leads us to a couple of thoughts. One thought is to wonder whether the groups of sounds represented in lists 1, 2, and 3 above have other things in common besides appearing together in these separate lists. It turns out that they do. For example, the sounds in rule 1 above are called *voiceless,* as compared to the *voiced* sounds in rule 2. The voicing distinction can be clarified by pronouncing the sounds "p" and "b"—not the letters "pee" and "bee," but just the sounds by themselves. You may note that the lips are in about the same place for these two sounds, but when you say "p" you release only a stream of air—a whisper. When you say "b" you make a vocalization. There is a similar difference between "f" and "v," and "t" and "d." We don't wish to become involved in too much jargon but only to note that the groupings in rules 1 to 3 are systematic, not random.

A second line of thought suggested by the plurals example relates to your linguistic knowledge. You may be quite astonished to note that the plural system is so orderly. Yet in a sense you already know this. Even a four-year-old child does. How can I tell you know it? Because you have been using these plural rules appropriately since you were a small child. Try to break some of these rules: Try to say the word "cloth" with an "iz" ending. "Clothiz." Sounds awful, doesn't it? You have known these rules for plural making, intuitively, all along. All we do in this chapter is point out some things you already know. Now you know something more about what you know.

There is more to the sound system than vowel and consonant phonemes and ways to combine them. Things such as tone of voice, pitch, and intonation are also part of the sound system. Linguists call these *suprasegmental phonemes.* We leave this aspect of the sound system undiscussed for the present, since we treat it in Chapter 5 when we consider paralanguage.

One reason it is important for teachers to understand the sound system of a language is that most differences between dialects turn out to be differences in phonology. For instance, we mentioned earlier that speakers of Spanish who learn English as a second language may have difficulty distinguishing the sounds "sh" and "ch." This difference between the sound systems of the two languages may cause some confusion. A speaker might wish to say the sentence:

I went shopping for chairs.

and say instead a sentence sounding like:

I went chopping for shares.

Examples such as this one serve as a major part of the reasoning for educators' efforts to eradicate accents and teach all members of a culture to speak a standard dialect. Their argument is that confusion between the sounds of words such as "chairs" and "shares" could lead to misunderstandings or to breakdowns in communication. Therefore such usages should be eliminated. In actual fact, these sound confusions cause few difficulties in transferring information from one person to another. If someone said to you a sentence sounding like: "I went chopping for shares," you might have to ask for some clarification, but you would probably understand the meaning. That the word "shares" sounds like the word "chairs" in some accents is no more confusing than that the word "two" sounds like the word "too" in most dialects. Every section of the country has some of these sound ambiguities in its dialect. In Texas, the words "pin" and "pen" sound just alike. In New England, the words "guard" and "god" are difficult to distinguish. Also, there are the numerous words with which we construct puns and knock-knock jokes. These all cause some minimal difficulty in language, *but none of them represent serious problems in conveying messages.* Scholars estimate that the English language is about 50 percent redundant anyhow. This means that, if you say a sentence and leave about half the sounds out, a listener will often be able to guess what meanings you were trying to convey. If the listener does not understand right away, answers to a question or two can likely clear up the problem.

There are some difficulties in communication which are connected with dialects and accents (Burling, 1973). The point of this discussion is to note that these difficulties are not primarily linguistic difficulties. The problems emerge not from language, as described by linguistics, but rather from some of our social attitudes toward groups of speakers. For instance, if an educated Anglo-Caucasian Texan finds himself speaking to a dark-complexioned man of short stature with dark hair and eyes who says, "I went chopping for shares," he might infer:

1. This person is a Mexican-American.
2. This person does not speak English very well.
3. This person is likely to be less well educated than I am.

There are a number of other things he might infer about this person: that he is poor, comes from a large family, takes naps in the afternoon, gets drunk a lot, is dishonest, and so on. But the three numbered items listed above are things many Anglo-Caucasian Texans are likely to infer. Similarly, the language of the Anglo-Caucasian speaker might cue some inferences for the Mexican-American speaker:

1. This person is an Anglo-Caucasian.
2. This person is likely to be educated and to have money.
3. This person is probably arrogant and feels superior to me.

The inferences of both speakers about each other are related to language, but they are social inferences that go far beyond language. Speech is just

FIGURE 4·2 COMMUNICATION PROBLEMS ARE OFTEN RELATED TO OUR ATTITUDES TOWARD SPEAKERS OF DIFFERENT DIALECTS.

one means of signaling identity, but it is a very important one. Many Americans are racists to some degree. It is now unfashionable and sometimes illegal to make openly racist remarks, but people still discriminate on the basis of language. The reasons for such discrimination are not linguistic and are not tied to how well language conveys messages. Rather, the reasons are tied to social attitudes toward people of other races (Williams, Hopper, and Natalicio, 1977).

To summarize, every language is ordered in several ways, and one of these ways concerns order at the level of the sound system. Every language is made up of a consistent set of phonemes which appear in ordered sets to make up words and sentences. Different accents and dialects in a language differ from each other mainly at the level of phonology. The discerning and alert teacher should be on the lookout for such differences, so that they will not be diagnosed as ignorance on the part of the child, lazy speech, or a speech problem. Different dialects are mutually intelligible and equally beautiful as far as linguists are concerned. Teachers should respect the varied sounds of students.

Syntax

Just as the English language follows phonological rules, it also follows rules of sentence structure, or *syntax*. Sentence structure can be described by rules that have little necessary connection either with the sound system or with what the sentence means. It is possible to imagine an English sentence which uses coherent English syntax but is silly and meaningless. Examine the following three sentences:

1. The boy hit the ball.
2. The ice cream jumped the liberty.
3. Liberty ice cream the the jumped.

The first sentence is an ordinary English sentence. Sentence 2 uses a similar combination of nouns, verbs, and articles placed in the same order (word order is the major indicator of syntax in English), but the sentence makes no particular sense. A linguist would say that sentence 2 is semantically anomalous, which means it is silly and meaningless. For our purposes, note that sentence 2 has appropriate English syntax (the syntax is quite similar to that of sentence 1) but is meaningless. To show what we mean by asserting that sentence 2 follows rules of syntax, compare sentence 2 with sentence 3. Sentence 3 uses the same words as sentence 2 but combines them in an order which is not appropriate in English syntax. Do you agree that sentence 3 is somehow even more bizarre than sentence 2?

Your ability to see a difference between sentences 2 and 3 indicates your intuitive knowledge (linguistic competence) of English syntax. As noted above, English syntax is revealed mostly through word order. Articles and adjectives generally appear before nouns, the subject noun phrase generally appears before the predicate phrase which contains the verb, and so on. The dependence of English syntax upon word order is shown by our scrambling the words in sentence 3 and therefore destroying its syntax. Scrambling words does not destroy the syntax of sentences in all languages. Some languages, such as German, Russian, and Latin, show syntax primarily through inflectional endings placed on nouns, verbs, and modifiers. These inflectional endings identify each word in terms of tense, number, gender, and case and therefore clarify which modifiers, nouns, and verbs belong together. English uses inflectional endings too, to indicate plural and tenses. The "s" endings for plurals are examples of such inflectional endings. But most syntactic information in English is carried by word order. Thus you can make sentences in English by doing little more than keeping nouns and verbs in familiar sequences, as Lewis Carroll demonstrates in his poem, "Jabberwocky":

> 'Twas brillig and the slithy toves
> Did gyre and gimble in the wabe;
> And mimsy were the borogoves,
> And the mome raths outgabe.

Carroll also shows in this poem that you can make nonwords that sound (phonologically) like English words.

To summarize, linguists are able to describe sentence structure by using rather abstract sets of rules. The implication is that there is something in your head which is roughly analogous to these rules, and that this knowledge helps you process sentences. There is no suggestion that the rules exist in the form we've discussed here. That would be like suggesting that fish know differential calculus because their swimming can best be described mathematically. Still, the complexity of theories of syntax presents difficulties when you think about small children learning to talk. No one suggests that fish *learn* how to swim. Rather, they swim by instinct. They also swim as soon as they are born. Children, however, do not speak until rather late in infancy, and their speech changes through learning experiences for several years. Could it be that children learn something as difficult as the rules of syntax we've been discussing? If not, what is the relationship between rules of syntax and what children learn?

It is important for teachers to consider these issues about syntax, because they plunge us into the middle of the age-old controversy over how much about language is learned and how much it is innate. Some theorists claim that language is obviously learned because children learn the language of the speakers around them. If your parents are British, but you were born and raised in a small Chinese village, there is a high probability that you will speak both languages. Another evidence for learning is that children often imitate adult speech. This makes it seem that they are practicing how to talk.

On the other hand, there is some evidence that language is innate. Only humans talk. No nonhumans can reliably be taught to use language. Some apes have become pretty handy with nonverbal sign languages, but even in these experiments the capacity shown has been far short of what humans do routinely. Also, while it is true that children sometimes imitate grown-ups and other children, there is little real evidence that this imitation is that helpful in learning syntax. Some children rarely imitate, and there is no evidence that their development is hampered in any way.

There is truth in both these positions. Children obviously have mental capacities and motor skills that make language use possible. Of these skills, the capacity to organize the syntax of sentences is perhaps the most startling. Children show no capacity for syntax until almost two years of age, and by the age of four most are spouting rather difficult syntactic constructions. It's difficult to imagine how all this could have been learned from scratch.

Most syntax is learned miraculously fast, but certain syntactic rules are learned slowly. The rules that are learned late in childhood are special exceptions to more general rules. These would not be of much importance, except that violations of syntax rules seem to attract adult attention—to stick out like the proverbial sore thumb. For example, note the following two sentences:

4. Dad asked Sally to do the dishes.
5. Dad promised Sally to do the dishes.

Sentence 4 is the usual case. Dad does the asking, and Sally does the dishes. If the verb is "ask," "order," "command," "pester" or most others, it remains that Sally is scheduled as dishwasher. In sentence 5, however, Dad does both the promising and the dishes. A typical six-year-old is likely to assume that the structure remains the same even for promise and therefore to misunderstand sentence 5. Thus a child whose syntax learning is virtually complete might still believe that Sally will do the dishes in sentence 5 (Chomsky, 1969).

Usually such examples of syntax incompleteness simply seem quaint. Adults recognize such usages as typical of children and simply ignore them or laugh a little. Occasionally an argument may come about over an issue such as whether Wilbur really did promise that he would clean his room or whether he agreed that someone else would do it. Teachers and parents may wish to take care of pronoun use at such times to avoid ambiguities: "Wilbur, promise me that *you* will clean your room today."

There are some differences in syntax which are due not to immaturity but to dialect. These differences, like those we just discussed, are generally quite small and do not create many misunderstandings. Like the examples above, however, these instances of dialect differences in syntax seem to call attention to themselves in conversation. For instance, examine the following sentences:

6. I don't have any crayons.
7. I have no crayons.
8. I don't have no crayons.

Sentences 6 and 7 are acceptable in syntax to all speakers of English. Sentence 8 is not, because of a usage callled a *double negative*. Let us examine, however, the differences among these three sentences. Sentences 6 and 7 differ only in what linguists call the *right shift rule*. This allows the negative particle to move to the right of the verb without causing problems. The speaker has the option of saying it either way. Sentence 8 is unacceptable to many English speakers (and most teachers) but remains the normal usage in some dialects of English. The point stressed here is that the difference between sentence 8 and the other two sentences is slight. Sentence 8 uses the negative particle in *both* places. Some teachers claim that this is illogical—that two negatives make a positive. This argument ignores the fact that many languages, including French, Spanish, and Old English employ double negatives (Burling, 1973).

It would be a rare speaker indeed who actually failed to understand the syntax of a double negative. The real problem of double negatives and several other dialect usages is that teachers and others may fail to accept them. Why do teachers not accept double negatives? The answer is that this is a low-prestige construction historically used by black people and other disadvantaged minority groups. It's not really a matter of the language itself, but rather a matter of language use—in this case, a matter of the class of people who have been associated with this usage.

To summarize, differences in the syntax of different speakers rarely interfere with understanding what a speaker says, but they somehow seem to call attention to themselves. Sometimes listeners take such differences to show speaker immaturity. At other times, similar differences are used to stereotype children as being members of minority groups or unsuccessful students.

Historically, the response of teachers has been to correct such usages as double negatives whenever they occur. This strategy, for reasons not totally clear, has never worked very well in trying to change speech behavior. For some reason, correcting the syntax of children or adolescents only rarely is effective in altering the features corrected. Perhaps syntax just has to be learned in the give-and-take of everyday conversation. Perhaps when teachers correct syntax features which parents and friends use, value conflicts are set up for the student, causing him or her to reject the educational experience.

Whatever the reasons, correcting syntax differences, whether the differences are due to immaturity or to dialect, rarely brings about the desired change in the student's speech. A preferable strategy is to have the teacher use forms she or he favors and to engage students in conversation in settings in which they contribute. This is not a very complete solution, but syntax remains a mysterious business. Features of syntax seem to be learned either with lightning speed or agonizing slowness.

Semantics

The final subset of verbal coding systems is semantics, or meaning. Semantics is perhaps the least understood aspect of language. Apparently speakers follow semantic rules just as they follow syntactic and phonological ones. Languages are codes—sets of symbols which stand for things. In a way, they are similar to simpler codes such as Morse code. Morse code, as you probably know, is a way of combining dots and dashes (or longer and shorter sounds) to stand for letters of the alphabet. Morse code is a simple code because it uses a one-to-one correspondence between a symbol and what it stands for. For instance, a single dot always stands for the letter "E." Language is less simple, though we don't often stop to think about it. Many words have a large number of meanings and don't mean the same thing each time you say them. Consider, for instance, the word "time." Let's use this word in several sentences:

> The referee called *time* out.
> I don't have *time* to talk to you.
> Would you *time* how long it takes me to run to the mailbox?
> By the *time* I get to Poughkeepsie, she'll be rising.
> A long *time* ago, we were born.
> You're just in *time* for supper.

At first glance, you may think these words all mean about the same thing, but closer examination shows that each shade of meaning is slightly different. This is actually more difficult than a word such as "crane" which has at least two widely different meanings—a bird and a construction machine. In actual fact, there are hundreds of words used in common everyday speech that have several meanings. It has been estimated that the 100 most frequently used words in English have an average of 85 dictionary meanings each. Look up some common words such as, "out" or "charge," in an unabridged dictionary. You'll be amazed at how many meanings are listed. You will be even more amazed that you know (intuitively) most of these meanings, in the sense that you would have understood the word's meaning if it had been used in a conversation.

It may seem curious to you that so many words have multiple meanings. It seems so inefficient, and potentially dangerous, to use a system which allows so many possibilities for slippage or misunderstandings. Wouldn't it be more efficient to have a language in which every word had one clear meaning? Yet no human language operates with one set of meanings. Ambiguity and homonyms (words that sound the same but have different meanings) are common in all known languages. It seems that, mysteriously, the human mind is better able to process languages which use a somewhat smaller number of words, the most common of which are connected with many meanings (Hopper and Naremore, 1978).

A further complexity of language is that symbols of language are arbitrarily paired with meanings. This means that there is no particular connection between words and sentences and the meanings they convey. There is no particular connection between the word "happy" and the emotion(s) to which it refers. The word "horse" looks very similar to the word "house," but there is little similarity between the two items referred to by the words. The word "house," used in English, is not at all like the word "maison," which has a very similar meaning in French. The connections between sounds and meanings are largely arbitrary. There are a few exceptions: the words "buzz," "puke," and "bang" sound somewhat like the concepts they represent. But generally, language coding is arbitrary pairing. This can be contrasted with coding in nonverbal communication, which is discussed in Chapter 5. A smile is not arbitrarily paired with the happiness it often represents. Rather, the smile can actually be considered part of the happiness, and the smile goes along with the happiness, belongs with it. Further, all other things being equal, a big smile probably means more happiness than a small smile from the same person. But the word "HOUSE" doesn't necessarily mean a bigger object than the word "house."

Unfortunately, our lack of understanding about semantics also makes possible a number of forms of exploitation. Politicians who fail to answer questions, scholars who hide behind confusing jargon, and makers of television ads who state impressive but empty claims often use semantic traps on the unwary.

Perhaps the best example of a semantic trap is *bifurcation*. Bifurcation occurs when language categories trap us into either-or thinking. Words seem often to describe polar opposites of concepts. This is especially true of adjectives:

deep—shallow
happy—sad
angry—pleased
good—bad
beautiful—ugly
faithful—unfaithful

Reality is not made up of such clear opposites, but rather there exist in the world thousands of shades of gray and other colors. But communicators can grow to believe that reality has the clear-cut categories that seem to be represented in the meanings of words; we have let words play a trick on us. If you say, "You are either for me or against me" or "If you go out with him you're no love of mine" or "You look just beautiful tonight," then you are falling into this trap to some extent.

In Chaucer's *Canturbury Tales*, we are treated to the story of a young man saved from death by a witch. The witch claims the right to marry the young man, which she does. When the man expresses horror, the witch allows him two choices: either she can stay ugly and be a faithful wife or she will turn beautiful but play him false. The man agonizes over this dilemma but finally refuses to make a choice between the alternatives. At the moment he refuses to choose, the witch becomes a lovely beauty who promises eternal devotion. This story may seem exotic, but actually the inference pattern it represents is quite common. There are two bifurcated meanings which are paired into one simplified continuum. The usual result is stereotyping: A beautiful woman is a "dingbat"; a woman who has sex casually will make a bad wife; a black person who speaks with a racial dialect is a bad job prospect; if minority groups move into a neighborhood, property values will plummet. All these examples represent the same kind of double-dimension evaluative choices faced by the young man in Chaucer's story. And it is surprising how often we come face-to-face with these issues in the classroom. For instance, a family of Latvians moves into your school district. Not surprisingly, since everyone knows Latvians have too many children, it turns out to be a large family, and one of these students is admitted to nearly every class level. Teachers are worried about the new students, fearful that they will be shiftless and lazy, that they will be unprepared to work at their grade level, and that they might cause discipline problems. Many teachers would see a set of choices as unpleasant as those in Chaucer's tale. You could try to be friendly to these students, and they probably would respond by causing trouble, or you could use strong disciplinary tactics leading the children to sullen silence. This second choice would avoid trouble, but would hinder the children's achievement. The point we wish to emphasize is that there may be many other choices besides these two.

The overall point of this section on semantics is the often-repeated phrase that meanings are in people more than in words and sentences. Further, meanings are not always logical. To some extent, meanings are what a consensus of persons believes them to be. Take note of your categories.

PRINCIPLES 4.2

1. The major subsystems of the verbal coding system are phonology, syntax, and semantics.
2. The sound system of a language is ordered. Only certain sounds appear, and these appear in a particular order.

3. The major differences between dialects of English are in the sound system, and these need not affect individuals' understandings of each others' speech.
4. English syntax is largely handled through word order.
5. Syntax seems to be the most clearly innate part of language. Children master it quickly at a very early age.
6. Many words in the English language can have more than one meaning.
7. Pairings between words and meanings are arbitrary.

PRAGMATICS: LANGUAGE USE

Up to this point we have been discussing the forms of language: the nuts and bolts and parts of verbal messages and how parts of sentences fit together. Forms of language have traditionally been treated as important by teachers, especially by teachers of English and the language arts. A predominant mode of language instruction is to concentrate on teaching forms. This focus may be appropriate on some occasions, but there is also importance in learning how language is used. In normal conversation, the discussion of language forms is rare. If someone asks you a question, you answer the question; you *use* language rather than comment on it. If you discuss language form, it usually brings about an abrupt change in the topic:

"Can I go to the store?"
"You mean *may* I go to the store?"

In this brief dialogue, the focus on form basically evades the topic of conversation. Most talk is not like this; rather, communicators focus attention on patterns of use.

In the following section we turn our attention to language use, or pragmatics. We argue that how language is used for communication is as important as forms of language.

Communicators use language to accomplish everyday goals and purposes. We express our ideas, make our feelings known, try to get our way with other people, and exchange information. The most cynical expression of the importance of how language is used was expressed by Lewis Carroll:

"When I use a word," Humpty Dumpty said, in rather a scornful tone, "it means just what I choose it to mean—neither more nor less."
"The question is," said Alice, "whether you *can* make words mean so many different things."
"The question is," said Humpty Dumpty, "which is to be master—that's all."

You do not need to agree with Humpty Dumpty's statement to understand that language becomes the messages for which it is used. Language is not just coding system parts put together, it is also the purposes for which the pieces are put together. For the rest of this chapter, we demonstrate that language use shows as much variety, and probably more instructional opportunity, than language form. In fact, it even seems that communication is best taught by emphasizing function over form. This means that people's language forms become more diverse and appropriate as speaker-listeners come to grips with the communication demands and opportunities of various situations.

For example, the way language forms are used varies with the setting. Students speak differently at school than when socializing with their peers. They speak differently in the schoolroom than out of the schoolroom. They speak differently to adults than to children. It is important that students be able to adapt their language to these various settings. Therefore one of the key language skills they need to learn is how to vary their language behavior to meet the demands of particular communication situations. Traditionally, schools have taught that there is one appropriate way to talk. People who did not speak this way were thought to lack education, intelligence, or both. Now it is clear that there are many ways to talk that are appropriate in some settings. Some students who become adept at school talk, but never learn appropriate forms for other occasions, may have difficulty communicating effectively with mechanics, store clerks, or neighbors.

In sum, language is used to communicate. Teachers probably have more to teach students about connecting language forms to speech situations than is generally realized.

There are four main parts of any communication situation which any speaker must take into account in order to communicate effectively (Wood, 1976).

Persons If you hear a spicy, off-color joke, you generally wait for an appropriate audience before retelling it. You do not ordinarily tell the joke to the clerk at the grocery checkout. If you are a teacher who is furious about something, you do not describe your mood to the principal in the same way that you would to a co-teacher. Everyone makes hundreds of adjustments in speech behavior according to their audience each day without ever thinking about it. Students, however, often can use help in developing such skills. There may be better and worse ways to make adjustments to situations. For example, students can be taught to soften their language when talking to an authority figure to enhance the probable impact of the message.

Tasks In looking at any conversation, it is useful to ask what speakers are trying to accomplish. For example, if a parent says to a child, "Will you please take out the garbage," the parent is not ordinarily asking an idle speculative question. Rather, he or she is issuing a command. If you keep the parent's probable goals of this interaction in mind, as well as those of the child, there are few problems in understanding what is happening. Keeping track of the task can be helpful to teachers who find themselves correcting details of children's speech throughout the school day. For instance, suppose a teacher asks an arithmetic question, and the child answers, "Two and two be four." A teacher who responds by correcting a detail in the child's use of a verb chooses to ignore that the purpose of both teacher and student in this case is to study addition. When the teacher interrupts the math lesson to comment on the child's language, he or she ignores the fact that the child has supplied the correct reasoning in terms of the math lesson. Our general advice is that teachers should generally confine corrections about details of language use to those portions of the school day when language use is the specific topic for study. During the rest of the day, or in subjects such as math, science, or history, give students a chance to make language mistakes and learn by doing. Of course, this doesn't mean that teachers must tolerate obscenity or other clearly unacceptable language behavior at any time.

Topics   Any teacher knows that the topic under discussion makes a great deal of difference to children's language behavior. Some children rarely talk during history lessons but have a great deal to say about science, or vice versa. All people of all ages prefer some topics to others, and most people don't like to talk about language mistakes at any time. A possible lesson from this is that language lessons can take the form of discussions of topics that children are interested in. For example, suppose that the goal of a unit in a fifth grade class is to have students speak up in a group setting to support their views. If the teacher presents the goal to students in this form, the assignment might be greeted by long periods of silence. But if the teacher introduces topics of interest to the children, such as petty thefts which have recently occurred and what to do about them, the children are likely to use this as an occasion to perform the behaviors the lesson calls upon them to practice.

Children learn to communicate by communication practice. The same seems to be true of older students, and even adults. When teachers make an effort to find out what topics are prominent in the students' out-of-class discussions and to integrate such topics into the curriculum, such effort is likely to result in enormous benefits. Effective teachers often do this, and we emphasize that it must be done anew with each new group of students. One group, for instance, may be very interested in cars, while the next group is more interested in football or foreign policy. Use your intuition. Don't just use the old commonplace subjects, such as student government or school spirit, unless interest has been expressed in these topics.

Settings   The time-place dimensions of any interaction situation have a great impact on language behavior. Students are extremely sensitive to changes in scene. They are often apprehensive about changes from home environments to school classrooms. If they are taught that classrooms are places in which they are primarily rewarded for keeping quiet, then it may become rather difficult to convince them to practice speaking skills there. In the lower grades, teachers have the task of making the classroom an inviting context for children to speak in. One way to do this is to emphasize that, in class, there are times to talk and times to remain silent. For instance, the time to talk is during group discussions, when called on, at lunch, or at show and tell. In secondary settings, students might be cued by the teacher to adapt their speaking and listening patterns. For instance, a history class might use each Wednesday as a time for informal discussions of current events. These discussions might be based upon materials or ideas (newspaper clippings, etc.) brought in by the students. Each Wednesday, to signal the change in format, the teacher might arrange the class chairs in a circle or make some other alteration in the setting.

All the above suggestions are related to one principle: It is important for students to learn the difference between times for speaking and times for remaining silent. Such learning requires that they experience a rich selection of occasions for silence and for talking.

To summarize the preceding discussion, all speakers learn to take into account the participants, task, topic, and physical setting of communication situations, and most speakers adjust messages according to constraints introduced by these factors. One aspect of communication that is important in considering pragmatics is the *function* for which a speaker uses language behavior. Functions are uses which language can perform. Speakers use language to transmit information, to persuade others, to express feelings, to perform social rituals, and to exercise the imagination (Allen and Brown, 1976). Following are five functions.

Informing   A textbook is primarily an informative message. Authors and readers share the assumption that the writer has something to tell the reader which the reader does not already know. The informing function is the "I've got something to tell you" function. Teachers, for example, perform this function when they lecture, describe assignments, or answer questions. For students, the purest form of informing is the custom of "show and tell" used in many elementary classrooms.

FIGURE 4·3 THE BEST LANGUAGE LESSON
IS A DISCUSSION ON A TOPIC OF INTER-
EST TO STUDENTS.

Controlling Such behaviors as arguing, convincing, nagging, correcting, and the like, can be identified as primarily serving the function of controlling another's behavior. To some degree, all communication has a control aspect, just as all communication is to some extent informative. Observations of school classrooms suggest that controlling behavior is practiced in many forms by teachers and students alike (Wrather, 1976). People try to control each other in any setting, but some methods of persuasion may seem preferable to others. One method which has time-honored status is giving reasons for the point you argue. Some reasons are more cogent than others. Of course, teachers know a great deal about this, and the construction of messages filled with reasons is the focus of most instruction.

Expressing Feelings If one communicator tells another about the emotions he or she is experiencing, a kind of communicative sharing takes place which is different from a purely informing or controlling function. It has often been acknowledged in recent years that American adults experience difficulty in expressing feelings to others. We do not argue that expression of feelings is all-important, nor that such expression is always wise. We only argue that students should be allowed to express feelings in the classroom setting. Such expression contributes to the development of trust in student-teacher relationships and enhances the development of a positive social environment for learning.

Ritualizing There is much language behavior which functions mainly as a kind of repetitive organization of life. Religious rituals and ceremonies such as pledging allegiance to the flag are obvious examples. But much everyday interaction serves primarily a ritualizing function. For instance, when two acquaintances meet on the sidewalk, they exchange highly stereotyped greetings, such as, "Hi, how are you?" The words are almost as predictable as those of a song or poem. The major indicator of ritual is the predictability of what happens. To the degree that ritual behaviors have traditionally been taught, they have been stressed in the form of good manners or proper ways to behave.

Imagining Imagining is a bit different from the first four communication functions we have discussed. Messages which serve the imagining function may sound much like other messages, except that there is the notion attached to them that they are somehow unreal. Imagining messages include pretending, storytelling, acting, and most other forms of play. Dramatic activity, for example, has long held a place in school curricula. Actually, classroom work in almost any kind of function we've listed has some imaginary component, since classroom events have a quality of simulation.

Now that we have discussed five kinds of functional relationships students learn about and use as they communicate, we can add a few general points about the functional perspective. First, you probably have noted that many utterances can serve more than one function simultaneously. A high school student who gives a persuasive speech may seem to be performing only the persuading function. But new information is often a prime persuader. Further, a persuasive speech is often most effective when the audience can clearly perceive that the speaker has strong feelings on the subject. A speaker also follows certain rituals, such as standing on a podium facing the audience. Finally, the whole exercise is imagining, which makes it a simulation.

You may ask, "If many messages perform several functions simultaneously, what is the purpose of having a system of functions?" The purpose is that each of the functions represents a descriptive rule about communication. For instance, the informing function represents the fact that communication involves an exchange of informational signs. All communication involves information. Similarly, it has been argued that all communication is persuasive to some degree in that it seeks to control behaviors of others. Most communication also involves the feelings of communicators to some degree. All communication also involves ritual in that communicators follow rules. Rule-governed structures underlie communication, especially the language coding system. Finally, all communication involves distinctions between reality and imagination.

One final point about these functions of communication may be helpful. These functions have been discussed here largely from the standpoint of a message sender, but the perspective of a listener is equally relevant. Just as you impart information to others, you seek information through efficient listening and questioning. Just as you control others, so you are controlled. Just as you express feelings, you respond to feelings of others.

DEVELOPING COMMUNICATIVE COMPETENCE

Throughout this chapter and this book, we focus upon the aspects of communication which can aid teachers in understanding classroom interaction. In closing this chapter, it seems worthwhile to consider briefly the actual teaching of communication skills themselves. This is important both for readers who become teachers in some area of communication, such as reading, writing, speaking, or listening, and for those who consider communication skills critical to success in any area of study or employment (Allen and Brown, 1976).

Earlier in this chapter we discussed the concept of linguistic competence: the intuitive knowledge about language rules which we all have that underlies our speaking behavior. This perspective helps us understand language behavior, but linguistic competence is only part of what we know that underlies our speech behavior. In addition to knowing about rules of language (linguistic competence) we must also know rules of pragmatics, including when to speak and when not to, what kinds of words to use and not to use, how to address strangers, and many other social skills. So, a child or an adult has a competence in or an intuitive knowledge of both language and pragmatics, constituting *communicative competence* which makes speaking and listening possible and meaningful.

The concept of communicative competence is broader in two ways than the concept of linguistic competence. First, as discussed above, communicative competence includes both knowledge about language and knowledge of social patterns of usage. Second, communicative competence is more than a repertoire of rules. It also includes strategies for selecting which rules a communicator may apply in particular settings.

The relationship between linguistic competence and communicative competence is a lot like the difference between knowing the rules of a game such as chess and being a good player of the game. You can learn the rules of chess in a few minutes. If you don't have experience playing the game, however, then any experienced chess player will beat you easily. You may find the game baffling at this level. With practice, and perhaps some instruction, you learn tactics which help you to succeed. In complex games you can continue to improve in your playing skill throughout your whole lifetime. Linguistic competence is like the rules of chess. Communicative competence includes knowing what you have to do in order to play effectively.

This analogy has some implications for the teaching of communication. Researchers (e.g., Brown, 1973) have illustrated that a child five years of age has already learned most of the rules of his or her native language. But the five-year-old child is just beginning to gain experience in pragmatics. Learning about effective usage goes on for a whole lifetime. Instruction about the details of language per se is likely to be not only boring but inefficient, rather the focus should be on providing opportunities for speaking and listening effectively.

One counterargument to this position is that students can have trouble in later life if their language does not sound like that of the middle class. Instruction in details of language, however, has proved ineffective for many students. Rather than trying to change language usage habits, efforts should be directed toward improving communicative range.

To say that a five-year-old knows grammar is not of course to claim that he or she can diagram sentences. Nor is it to claim that children make no mistakes in speech. Everyone makes speech mistakes. In addition to slips of the tongue, memory lapses, and other real errors, children often say "they was" or "two shoe" or "I goed home." But none of these utterances are absolutely ungrammatical. Such sentences or phrases follow

FIGURE 4·4 CHILDREN AND ADULTS
KNOW A GREAT DEAL ABOUT BOTH
LANGUAGE AND PRAGMATICS.

some language rules, although the patterns might be unacceptable in certain settings.

Correction of students' speech by adults is a particularly important problem. Think of what happens to you when a student says, "I ain't got two hat." If you are like us, you probably feel some urge to correct such usage. The habit of correcting speech is ingrained in most educated adults. It is particularly strong in college degree holders who were successful in English classes. Perhaps there is occasionally some value in the correction of speech by teachers, but there is no good evidence that anyone's speech ever improved significantly as a result of such correction. All of us had our speech corrected as children, and most of us learned to avoid the patterns that were corrected. But was our behavior changed because of the correction? Probably not. Many people who were corrected a lot did not change, and some who were not corrected speak as correctly as others who were.

If teachers should concentrate on students' messages and pay less attention to language forms, then you may ask why we have written a chapter about details of language for this book. There are a number of reasons. First, you need to know something about the linguistic perspective to understand the importance of instruction in pragmatics. Second, teachers may spot genuine language problems on occasion because they know some details of language theory. If a student's sentences are actually unintelligible, that student should be referred to a speech or language clinician.

So, think pragmatics and work on your own attitudes. Most of you are probably somewhat bigoted about language. New varieties of language are becoming acceptable in a wider variety of settings. You may be sure that you will hear many varieties of spoken language in your classroom.

PRINCIPLES 4.3

1. Pragmatics is an important aspect of verbal coding systems.
2. Four parts of any communication situation which speakers take into account are persons, tasks, topics, and settings.
3. Speakers and listeners adjust messages and interpretations according to the functions of communication.
4. Five important functions of communication are informing, controlling, expressing feelings, ritualizing, and imagining.
5. It is useful to think of communication abilities as one holistic process of communicative competence, or knowledge about language and its use.

REFERENCES

Allen, R. R., and Brown, K. L. (Eds.) *Developing communication competence in children.* Skokie, Ill.: National Textbook, 1976.

Brown, R. *A first language*. Cambridge, Mass.: Harvard University Press, 1973.

Burling, R. *English in black and white*. New York: Holt, Rinehart and Winston, 1973.

Chomsky, N. *The acquisition of syntax from 5 to 10*. Cambridge, Mass.: MIT Press, 1969.

Chomsky, N. *Aspects of the theory of syntax*. Cambridge, Mass.: MIT Press, 1965.

Fromkin, V., and Rodman, R. *An introduction to language*. New York: Holt, Rinehart and Winston, 1974.

Hopper, R., and Naremore, R. C. *Children's speech*. New York: Harper & Row, 1978.

Langacker, R. *Language and its structure*. New York: Harcourt Brace Jovanovich, 1967.

Williams, F., Hopper, R., and Natalicio, D. *The sounds of children*. Englewood Cliffs, N.J.: Prentice-Hall, 1977.

Wood, B. *Children and communication*. Englewood Cliffs, N.J., Prentice-Hall, 1976.

Wrather, N. Describing communication functions in a first grade classroom. Master's thesis, University of Texas at Austin, 1976.

Chapter 5
The Nonverbal Symbol System

OBJECTIVES

After reading this chapter, you should be able to:

1. define nonverbal behavior.
2. explain why it is important for teachers to understand nonverbal behavior.
3. discuss the nature and origin of meaning in nonverbal behavior.
4. identify two levels of meaning in nonverbal behavior.
5. discuss and provide examples of nonverbal stereotyping.
6. explain the implications of nonverbal stereotypes for classroom communication.
7. describe sign, action, and object language.
8. define and provide examples of kinesic cues commonly observed in classrooms.
9. define and explain the significance of proxemic cues in teacher-student relationships.
10. discuss the concept of classroom territorial behavior.
11. provide a rationale for greater tactile communication between teachers and students.

12. define and explain the significance of paralinguistic information in classroom communication.
13. discuss the impact of physical appearance cues in shaping teacher perceptions of pupil performance.
14. identify the ways in which time affects communication processes in the classroom.
15. discuss the implications of time as a determinant of student learning and attitudes.
16. compare and contrast verbal and nonverbal symbol systems.
17. describe the interdependence of verbal and nonverbal symbol systems.
18. identify and provide examples of nonverbal cues in self-presentation.
19. identify and discuss the ways teachers and students use nonverbal cues to convey rules and expectations.
20. identify and discuss the ways teachers and students use nonverbal cues to serve metacommunicative functions in classroom transactions.
21. identify and discuss the ways teachers and students use nonverbal cues for feedback and reinforcement.
22. explain the relationship between teacher nonverbal activity and teaching effectiveness.
23. discuss the implications of the teacher effectiveness–nonverbal behavior relationship for instruction.

"You don't have to say it to say it."

At first reading, this sentence may strike you as gibberish, but each of you has experienced the communication principle underlying the statement. That is, every face-to-face interaction contains messages that are exchanged without the use of words. Think about it for a minute. When are words unaccompanied by gestures, facial expressions, general movements, and changes in vocal emphasis? All these nonword behaviors contribute greatly to the total message communicated. They may supplement, modify, or even contradict spoken words. Moreover, these effects may occur without the conscious awareness of either participant in the communication transaction. Such subtle yet important messages comprise the domain of *nonverbal behavior*—all behavior other than the spoken or written word to which people attribute meaning.

Most of us have at least an intuitive grasp of the area of nonverbal behavior and some appreciation of its importance. We all have learned, for example, that certain nonverbal symbols have very explicit meanings.

The hitchhiker's thumb expresses his message quite effectively, without words. What the hitchhiker may not realize is that his thumb is not the sole or perhaps even the most important nonverbal message he conveys. His very presence at the roadside, gazing expectantly at each onrushing vehicle, probably expresses his intent before the thumb is extended. His success may depend upon other factors, such as physical appearance and dress, posture or bodily orientation, and even facial expression. Similarly, you as a teacher may be aware in a general way that your nonverbal behavior influences your students and that theirs in turn affects your own behavior. You may not be very sensitive, however, to the variety of nonverbal messages you convey or observe in a classroom and, more importantly, the profound impact these messages have on your effectiveness as a teacher. Our purpose in this chapter is to expand your awareness of nonverbal behavior in the classroom and, hopefully, improve your ability to understand the multitude of nonverbal messages you receive from your students.

Don't be misled. This chapter will *not* enable you to read another complex, multifaceted human being "like a book," much less 20 or more of them at the same time. We obviously believe, however, that there are certain benefits to be gained from the analysis of nonverbal behavior. Two considerations seem particularly relevant to teachers.

Nonverbal Behavior in Student-Teacher Transactions

Most of us tend to focus our attention on what is said during interactions, assuming that accurate communication is largely a matter of matching words with thoughts and stating these words in a grammatically acceptable way. A frequent result of this preoccupation with words is inaccurate communication based on incomplete information. All of us begin life as totally nonverbal creatures and are subsequently taught to use language. Students, young ones in particular, are usually less verbally proficient than teachers. The teacher's specialized training and daily professional activities, however, emphasize communication via the spoken or written word. Thus it is hardly surprising that most teachers attribute great power to words and, as a result, may rely on words to the exclusion of nonverbal information. This difference in the level of verbal dexterity between students and teachers makes awareness of nonverbal behavior essential for accurate student-teacher communication.

Similarly, knowledge of nonverbal cues enables a teacher to analyze his or her own behavior with regard to critical learning outcomes. You as a student could probably provide your instructor with some astonishingly accurate assessments of his or her attitudes toward the subject matter of the course, yourself and your classmates, and even this textbook.

FIGURE 5·1 MOST OF US FOCUS ON WHAT IS SAID DURING INTERACTIONS.

"Psyching out" the instructor is a time-honored classroom activity that depends greatly on nonverbal cues observed in the teacher. Like the classic tale of the psychology professor driven to lecturing from a corner to maintain positive reinforcement from his students, "psyching out" may be too easily dismissed as inconsequential or merely inevitable by teachers. The fact remains, however, that teachers make countless statements nonverbally that their training and experience would never permit them to make. In this way, it is entirely possible for a teacher to devalue a subject, a student, or even his or her own credibility without uttering a single negative word. Nowhere is this point better illustrated than in the case of the teacher who professes a genuine commitment to student participation in classroom decision making but spends most class time carefully explaining *her* plan for an upcoming unit. Students quickly recognize the realities of such a situation and respond accordingly. Sometime later, the same teacher may be heard decrying student apathy and disinterest in classroom activities. It is unfortunately equally likely that the students have dismissed the teacher as a phony and have discounted her course on that basis.

Conversely, teacher nonverbal behavior may have positive effects on pupil achievement, as Rosenthal and Jacobsen's (1968) *Pygmalion in the Classroom* suggests. As you may recall from our discussion of this study in Chapter 3, a group of elementary pupils was given standardized I.Q. tests prior to entering school. Without regard to actual scores on the "intellectual blooming test," some students were labeled high scorers, suggesting that they would show unusual intellectual development during the coming school year. Teachers of these students were given this information. I.Q. tests administered at the end of the school year reflected a dramatic rise in the scores of the randomly labeled "intellectual bloomers."

Although Rosenthal and Jacobsen (1968) account for this in terms of teacher expectation, thereby provoking a controversy, their interpretation of the way teachers responded to their "blooming" pupils provides a vivid illustration of the potential role of teacher nonverbal behavior.

> To summarize our speculations, we may say that by what she said, by how and when she said it, by her facial expressions, postures, and perhaps by her touch, the teacher may have communicated to the children of the experimental group that she expected improved intellectual performance. Such communications together with possible changes in teaching techniques may have helped the child learn by changing his self-concept, his expectations of his own behavior, and his motivation, as well as his cognitive style and skills. (p. 180)

In the remainder of this chapter we identify the specific nonverbal systems operating in classrooms and discuss their functions in the instructional process.

A MULTIPLICITY OF MEANINGS

We began this chapter by defining nonverbal behavior as all behavior other than the spoken or written word to which people attribute meaning. In the broadest sense, this definition is accurate. For obvious practical reasons, however, some limitations of this definition are desirable and necessary if the role of nonverbal behavior in the classroom is to be understood. Perhaps a good starting point is a consideration of meaning in nonverbal communication.

Attempting to define the nonverbal domain led Sapir (1963, p. 556) to describe it as "an elaborate code that is written nowhere, known by none, and understood by all." Given the elusive nature of the nonverbal idiom in ongoing communication events, Sapir's description is most apt. The kind of understanding or meaning to which he refers is an intuitive and incommunicable insight born of ordinary experience in human communication. In other words, we are all practiced nonverbal communicators. While our skills in interpreting nonverbal messages may vary, all of us continuously receive and translate nonverbal information. Meaning, then, does not exist in the nonverbal act itself but in the *interpretation* given the act. With the exception of the sign language used by the deaf and a narrow range of nonverbal cues which have a specific culturally defined meaning (the hitchhiker's thumb, the peace sign, the up-yours gesture), called emblems, nonverbal behaviors lack definitive referents.

Although a common culture and similar personal experiences enable us sometimes to agree on the interpretation of nonverbal acts, they do not ensure that our interpretation will always be correct, or even close to correct. To facilitate accurate interpretations of nonverbal cues, it is useful to distinguish at least two levels of meaning with regard to nonverbal acts. These distinctions, developed by Ekman and Friesen (1969), reflect essentially different types of information conveyed through nonverbal activity. On one level, meaning may be described as *idiosyncratic*. A nonverbal behavior has idiosyncratic meaning when it appears consistently in one situation but is peculiar to a single individual. All of us probably have certain behaviors in our nonverbal repertoire that fall into this category. For a fellow graduate teaching assistant of ours, skin splotching was a generalized response to teaching. Immediately preceding and during her classes, this young woman's face and neck became mottled with blazing patches of varying size which subsided shortly after her classes ended. For those who worked with her, it was never necessary to ask when her classes met. As in the old cliché, her face told all.

Nonverbal acts have *shared* meanings when the circumstances surrounding their appearance are common across an identifiable group of individuals. Commonly recognized visible symptoms of stage fright such

as trembling hands or knees, excessive perspiration, and vocal dysfluencies in a beginning public speaking class exemplify the shared meanings
value of specific nonverbal cues. Experienced teachers can also readily
describe the shared meaning of the technique students have perfected to
make daydreaming appear to be attentive listening. Unlike idiosyncratic
meanings, *shared meaning usually occurs when a particular group of
observers is in agreement about the information conveyed by an act.* The
more common the behavior, in terms of frequency of occurrence and sets
of individuals exhibiting it, the greater the shared meaning associated
with that behavior.

It should be noted that the terms "idiosyncratic" and "shared," as
used here, do not refer to the nonverbal acts themselves but rather to the
meanings associated with the acts. To assume that the mere appearance of
a certain cue invariably signifies a particular message is to engage in
nonverbal stereotyping. Despite the claims of some popular books on the
subject, such as Fast's (1970) *Body Language* and Whiteside's (1974) *Face
Language,* folded arms do not always indicate stubbornness, nor does
observing the way a woman holds her cigarette give you accurate information about her sex life. Stereotyping of this type leads to miscues in
interpersonal communication which ultimately may be more damaging
than cues that are missed altogether. Hall (1966) relates a story of
classroom interaction which makes this point admirably. A newly certified
teacher from the east was encountering some difficulties in classroom
management in her small southwestern city school. Most of her students
were Anglo-American with a few Mexican-Americans and blacks. While
administering midyear examinations, the teacher detected several students cheating and, to investigate the issue, questioned each suspect
individually. Of the students interviewed, a quiet Mexican girl named
Maria was the least convincing in denying her guilt. Although Maria's
grades had always been quite satisfactory, the teacher interpreted Maria's
avoidance of direct eye contact, expressionless face, and short answers as
sullen indifference and hostility. It was not until the case was referred to
the assistant principal, a lifelong resident of the area, that the teacher
realized her error. Maria's nonverbal cues were less indicative of attempted deception than of her cultural background, emphasizing de-
ference to authority, and a generous amount of apprehension. The
teacher's stereotypic interpretation in this case caused a highly traumatic
experience for an innocent student.

Of overriding importance to meaning, whether idiosyncratic or
shared, is the regularity or consistency of a specific nonverbal cue's appearance over time. All of us engage in random, meaningless behaviors
occasionally, which signify nothing or which may be extremely atypical of
our usual behavior. The students whose nonverbal behaviors you observe
are no exceptions. As a teacher you interact with your students in a

context that is unique in that the classroom setting elicits behaviors from them that may never emerge outside the classroom. For this reason, our tendency to generalize the meanings of nonverbal cues from other, nonacademic settings to the classroom requires restraint. Your task as a discerning teacher, therefore, includes discriminating between erratic, random nonverbal behaviors and the patterns of behavior which emerge over time as meaningful indicators of student response. To this end, we now turn our attention to nonverbal coding systems.

PRINCIPLES 5.1

1. A significant proportion of the meaning in student-teacher transactions is conveyed by nonverbal information.
2. Nonverbal behavior includes all information beyond the spoken or written word to which meaning is attributed.
3. Nonverbal behavior is a learned, culturally determined, contextual, inevitable element of interpersonal communication transactions.
4. Accurate communication is dependent in part on an individual's skill in understanding his or her own and others' nonverbal behaviors.
5. Nonverbal stereotyping results from the misconception that nonverbal behaviors have inherently specific meanings. Meaning is actually determined by the total context rather than by the characteristics of the behavior itself.

NONVERBAL CODING SYSTEMS

Although there is wide agreement concerning the importance of nonverbal information in human communication, there is a conspicuous absence of agreement on the boundaries of the nonverbal domain. Early theorists Ruesch and Kees (1956) identified three areas: sign language, action language, and object language. *Sign language* includes all communication in which words, numbers, and punctuation are replaced by gestures. The hand language of the deaf, the clenched, upraised fist of the militant, and a colorful array of "street" gestures reflect sign language. *Action language* refers to all movements made without a specific intent to communicate. A student might be observed squirming about in her seat, not because she is trying to communicate a message to the teacher but merely because she is uncomfortable. The teacher, however, might infer that she is inattentive, that she needs to be excused, or some other explanation. *Object language,* the broadest of the three categories, embraces all intentional and unintentional displays of material things: from clothing to architectural structures, from art objects to personal artifacts, from the size and color of a book to the typeface use; all are considered object language.

Other catalogings (Barker and Collins, 1970) include such categories as dreams and extrasensory perception, smelling, animal and insect communication, and skin sensitivity. In compiling the following nonverbal codes we have chosen to emphasize those most applicable to classroom encounters. In our view these codes constitute the primary elements of nonverbal classroom communication.

Kinesics

Kinesic behavior, alternatively referred to as body motion, includes a wide range of nonverbal behaviors. All gestures, movements of the limbs, torso, and head, postures, facial expressions, and eye movements (blinking; frequency, duration, and direction of gaze; pupil dilation) are types of kinesic behavior. Familiar classroom examples are the frantic waving of a hand in the air to attract the teacher's attention, the steady gaze the teacher might use to quell classroom disturbances, or the shuffling of feet and closing of notebooks that frequently precedes the ending of a class.

Given the sheer number of possible kinesic cues from a single individual, it is obvious that such cues vary in terms of specificity, communicative intent, and information conveyed. To give you some perspective on this vast area, we refer to Ekman and Friesen's (1969) five-part classification scheme for analyzing body motion. *Emblems* are nonverbal actions which have a single, direct verbal translation that is culturally defined. In this sense, emblems correspond to sign language as discussed earlier. Students and teachers tend to use emblems intentionally when verbal channels are blocked or are for some reason inappropriate. Less specific than emblems are *illustrators*, defined as nonverbal activity used to amplify a spoken message. When you point to give directions, use gestures to indicate size, shape, or motion, or physically accent a word or phrase (e.g., snap your fingers as you say, "Just like *that!*"), your kinesic behavior details your verbal message by illustrating it visually.

Nonverbal behaviors used to maintain or control interaction between two or more individuals are labeled *regulators*. Most of us use regulators unconsciously to indicate to others that we are listening or that they should speed up or slow down, change the subject, or stop talking entirely. Head nods and eye movements constitute most of the regulators, although some hand gestures are used to regulate conversation. Although we appear to use regulators without conscious awareness, we are extremely sensitive to these cues when they are sent by others. Probably the most common regulator in classroom interaction is the head nod, used by teachers and students alike to signify, "Keep going, I'm following your thought."

In sharp contrast to emblems, illustrators, and regulators are *adaptors*, body motions which are highly idiosyncratic and serve no clear purpose in an interaction. Psychologists speculate that adaptors are actually remnants of once-complete behavior patterns designed to satisfy our emotional or physical needs in childhood. Thus it is reasoned that the adult swinging his leg during a tense verbal exchange is exhibiting aggression that is denied complete expression by his adult status or the dictates of the particular situation. It has been suggested that the specific adaptor may aid the individual by reducing his internal pressures. Although each of us has adaptors in our nonverbal repertoire, we use them unconsciously.

Emblems, illustrators, regulators, and adaptors are kinesic behaviors which originate primarily from the body, as opposed to the face. Ekman and Friesen's final category, *affect displays*, is concerned with communication via that most expressive area of our bodies. Affect displays are facial expressions which reveal emotional states and usually appear in conjunction with verbal statements of liking or disliking, pleasure or disgust, happiness or sorrow, and so on. Affect displays function somewhat like illustrators in that they may augment or reinforce a verbal message. They may, however, contradict or be totally unrelated to what is said. Most instances of affect displays are spontaneous and unintentional.

Proxemics

Most of us are accustomed to thinking of space in geometric, physical terms: Objects occupy space, jumbo jets fly through space, and we write our name in the allotted space. Symbolic and expressive uses of space are equally important, if not more so, in understanding human communication. In this regard, Altman (1971, p. 291), a psychologist, has written, "... individuals... do not deal with one another in an environmental vacuum. Their exchanges occur within a physical environment and involve *active use* of that environment to cope with and structure their social relationships." Hall (1959), an anthropologist, coined the term *proxemics* to describe the study of the relationship of humans to the spatial dimension of their environment. From an instructional perspective, our major interest in proxemics is in how teachers and students structure their microspace, how they relate physically to other people with whom they interact, and the meaning they attribute to these physical relationships.

Considerations of particular interest to classroom teachers include the concepts of personal space and territoriality. Both concepts are a part of daily experience for all of us and appear to be essential to our best performance and sense of well-being. Our individual, personalized concepts of space are in part derived from cultural norms which dictate "proper" distances for interactions. According to Hall, our culture respects four basic distance levels. The first of these, *intimate distance*, is characterized by a high probability of physical involvement. In terms of physical space, intimate distance ranges from 3 to 18 inches. Interactions at this distance are reserved for family members and close friends. Dis-

FIGURE 5·2 EACH PERSON HAS AN INVISIBLE BUBBLE OF PERSONAL SPACE.

tances of 18 to 48 inches between interactants connote *personal distance,* the range at which we interact with intimate or close associates with whom we maintain less sensory involvement. Private conversations are frequently carried on at this range. *Social distance,* involving distances of from 4 to 12 feet is normally used for interactions with business associates and friends. Finally, *public distance* encompasses the formal or informal gatherings of groups who space themselves from 12 to 25 feet from a communicator.

Based partially on social norms and partially on personal characteristics (size, personality traits, ethnic background), each of us acquires a notion of our own personal space requirements. We use this "pulsating halo" or "invisible bubble" to help us organize our perceptions and regulate our interaction with our environment. The bubble surrounding an individual varies in size based on the personal and situational characteristics. We all accept the realities of crowded elevators and long lines at grocery stores gracefully, if somewhat grudgingly. If, however, a student stood that close to you in an empty classroom, what would your reaction be?

Individuals often include elements of their environment in their personal space bubbles. Students, even if not assigned a regular place, tend to select a particular seat and continue to sit there throughout the school year. The term "territoriality" is used to describe this behavior. Social psychologists maintain that the territorial impulse, also observed in animals, is useful to humans in establishing a sense of personal identity. When deprived of the opportunity to establish and maintain territory, individuals frequently become hostile, frustrated, and irritable. Many of you have had the experience of walking into a classroom only to find "your" seat already occupied or of finding yourself seated in a crowded lecture hall next to an "armrest hog." Your feelings of being invaded, or the lack of them, should give you some insight into your own territory-claiming needs.

Haptics

Kinesics and proxemics blend to form *haptics,* or tactile behavior, the special class of events that take place when two people come into physical contact with one another. The physical experience of touch in our culture is one which is closely supervised. Many schools, for example, prohibit corporal punishment, and the informal norms regulating physical contact between a teacher and student of the opposite sex are often rigidly enforced. This seems to be in direct opposition to a wealth of data suggesting that touching is essential for healthy development, particularly in infancy (Knapp, 1972; Montagu, 1971). Many educational administrators believe, however, that learning should proceed on a mind-to-mind basis with as little physical contact as possible between pupil and teacher. At least two arguments might counter this belief. On one level, most teaching requires a certain degree of physical involvement beyond mere presence in a classroom. Teachers move about the room, rearrange desks or books, or supervise students' work on a project. Assume that a motor skill is being taught, such as printing numerals or letters. Restricting touch between student and teacher places an unnecessary and unrealistic restriction on such learning. If the teacher is unable to guide the motions of the pupil's hand, physically, the amount of time and effort required for learning will be greatly increased.

Regardless of whether a task involves concept or motor learning, however, a second argument for physical contact is worth mentioning. Touching, from infancy on, is one of the most powerful reinforcers in human experience. Cheek patting, chin chucking, and head patting are among the most positive signals of affection and regard. These acts convey immediate, direct approval far more convincingly than words. Similarly, tweaking the nose or ears, rapping the knuckles, or swatting the bottom signify disapproval swiftly and succinctly. Learning theorists argue that such clear and direct reinforcement enhances learning. In most instructional settings, however, touching is recognized as activity reserved for extreme situations only. It is appropriate to cuddle an injured or weeping child or to restrain a student physically from hitting another, but for the day-to-day business of learning? Probably not.

Haptic communication patterns are culturally determined. That is, each culture has informal norms indicating who may touch whom under what circumstances. While almost all cultures forbid the touching of erogenous areas of the body by nonintimates, variations in touching other parts of the body are remarkable. Latin and Middle Eastern cultures generally encourage physical contact, both within and outside instructional settings. American culture, however, is based on British traditions, particularly in terms of educational practices. Haptic experiences between student and teacher are primarily for the purpose of punishment through canings, spankings, or slappings. It is somewhat ironic that most school systems permit physical contact between students and teachers only when it inflicts pain or expresses hostility. The positive reinforcement value of touch is largely ignored after the early elementary school years.

Paralanguage

Spoken language does not consist solely of the words uttered. In some cases the true meaning of a message lies in the way it is said, rather than in what is said. Paralanguage deals with vocal phenomena which make each individual's voice as unique as his or her fingerprints. The slow drawl, the nervous stammer, and "uhs" and "ums" all are within the domain of paralinguistics. Probably because we are so accustomed to hearing voices, we are often at a loss to describe adequately why certain voices appeal to us or why others make us want to stick our fingers into our ears up to our elbows. This inability, however, does not prevent us from using vocal information in making important interpersonal decisions including judgments about personality, intelligence, or attractiveness. Voices, it seems, contribute greatly to our total perceptions of another person. As a teacher you may find that your students' impressions of your credibility, warmth, and competence are influenced by your vocal cues. You in turn should be aware that your judgments of their abilities may be affected by the sound of their words rather than by their words alone.

The mechanics of speech production are rather complex and cumbersome to explain. Factors which contribute to paralinguistics, however, are comparatively simple and straightforward. We believe it may be helpful to you in understanding the vocal behavior of others, as well as your own, to be familiar with the components of paralanguage. If you keep in mind how much classroom time is spent in speaking or listening to others speak, the following list may seem less tedious.

Trager's (1958) early classification of paralanguage includes four major components. The first three are aspects of vocalized sound, which may or may not be a consistent part of an individual's voice; the fourth is common to all voices. *Vocal characterizers* include laughing, sobbing, moaning, whispering, sniffing, clearing the throat, swallowing, and gulping. *Vocal qualifiers* refer to intensity (too loud, too soft), pitch height (too high, too low), and extent (drawl, clipping). *Vocal segregates* are actual linguistic sounds present in language which do not appear in sequences we call words, such as "shh," "uh," "um," "uh-huh," and silent pauses. *Vocal qualities* modify every voice and include pitch (spread, narrowed), range (vocal lip control), articulation (forced, relaxed), rhythm (smooth, jerky), resonance (resonant, thin), and tempo (increased, decreased). The mutual effects of these acoustic phenomena result in the composite, unique sound that is your vocal signature.

Your voice of course is probably your most basic teaching tool. Apart from the forming of words, your voice fulfills other functions in your daily exchanges with students; it orders, coaxes, praises, whines, or drones. Moreover, it does all these things *regardless* of the words you are saying. Paralinguistic cues are present whenever words are spoken. From this vocal information your students can infer a great deal about your attitude toward yourself, the subject matter you teach, and themselves as individuals. For example, consider the question of reinforcement. In our earlier discussion of haptics, the absence of touching as a means of expressing approval or disapproval in classrooms was noted. Most theorists agree that touching has been replaced by vocal cues which convey similar, less immediate meanings. Frank (1957) describes the substitution in this way.

This infantile tactuality... is gradually transformed as the child learns to accept mother's voice as a surrogate, her reassuring tones of voice giving him an equivalent for his close physical contacts, her angry scolding voice serving as a punishment and making him cry as if hit. (p. 218)

In terms of inferring teacher attitudes, paralinguistic information is second only to facial expression as a source of information. In a series of studies, Mehrabian (1971), asked people to judge the feelings of an individual. People relied on words for only 7 percent, on facial expression for 55 percent, and on vocal cues for 38 percent of the information about the individual's feelings. A familiar example that demonstrates this principle well is sarcasm. It is not the words themselves that carry the meaning, but the way they are said. Thus the positive meaning usually associated with the expression, "Oh terrific!" can be changed to a negative meaning (frustration or disappointment) if the words are uttered sarcastically. Almost all the meaning in sarcastic messages is conveyed through paralinguistic cues.

Vocal cues also provide information about your immediate feelings toward yourself or another individual. Generally, the more positive your feelings the greater the pitch variation, rate, and volume of your voice. If you are anxious or overtired, your paralinguistic cues will probably reflect your feelings. You as a student are aware of the differences in tone of voice your teachers use and the meanings that accompany these differences. Vocal cues can indicate which students are liked or disliked, as well as those who have performed well and those whose efforts are only adequate.

Finally, paralinguistic information contributes greatly to the social environment of the classroom. Vocal cues can create an environment that is warm and supportive or one that is harsh and threatening to students. The implications for successful learning should be apparent to you. Vocal cues are not the only sources of influence in shaping the mood of a classroom. But what do teachers do more than anything else? They talk. An unpleasant appearance or a constant frown may not be noticed by all students. As your own experiences indicate, many students hardly ever *look* at their teachers. All students, however, must listen. Even if they are not consciously trying to hear the teacher's voice, such a vocal stimulus is difficult to escape. It is for this reason that paralinguistic cues are important.

Physical Appearance and Artifacts

Depending on the state of your self-image, you will be either (1) delighted or (2) distressed when we tell you that physical appearance is clearly one of the most influential nonverbal cues in the classroom, or indeed, any other communication setting. As might be predicted, research (Kleinke, 1975; Knapp, 1972; McCroskey, Larson, and Knapp, 1971) indicates that individuals judged as physically attractive tend to have higher initial credibility, fare better in courtship and marriage decisions, and may be able to parlay their physical attributes to earn higher grades and status occupations. This is due in part to the way the person perception process operates. At first encounter with a stranger, be he or she a student or a teacher, we all respond to what are termed *object characteristics*. Size, general appearance, skin color, hair, clothing, scent, or demeanor all produce powerful first impressions. Thus, before the first words are exchanged, both you and the stranger have made several judgments about each other. Given time and continued contact, perceptions usually shift from object characteristics to less obvious qualities. We refer to *personal characteristics*—those amorphous qualities of personality, style, attitude, and values that are not readily apparent at first glance. It is as yet unknown whether the impact of physical appearance is ever totally obscured in interpersonal communication. Your personal experiences, like ours, probably suggest that personal characteristics ultimately predominate, particularly in educational settings. This in no way, however, resolves the dilemma for you as a teacher.

Because our culture adheres to democratic ideals, if not always to democratic practices, we are reluctant to admit personal prejudices. This tendency is heightened when physical attractiveness is considered, because our culture teaches that "beauty is only skin deep." Thus we all more or less play a game with ourselves and with others by pretending that we are indifferent to the way someone looks or dresses. You will inevitably find, however, certain students initially more attractive than others. Your attraction to them may be based on highly idiosyncratic grounds or on deeply ingrained cultural standards of physical beauty. Regardless of its foundation, the impression is firmly imprinted, and your subsequent reactions to these students will be colored by it.

The reverse is equally true. Some students may by virtue of appearance cues irritate or even repel you. Others, perhaps most, may elicit no strong reaction in either direction. If you are thinking that over time these differences will erode, consider the findings of the following study by Singer (1964). This research was designed to examine the use of physical attractiveness by females to obtain higher grades from college professors. After finding that male and female students did not differ with regard to a psychological tendency toward Machiavellianism (willingness to use any means to gain desired ends), Singer became interested in discovering whether female students expressed this tendency by exploiting their physical attractiveness. To this end, he gathered 192 photographs of first-year women students and had the pictures rated on an attractiveness scale by 40 faculty members. When the professors' ratings were compared with GPAs and birth order, a positive relationship between being a firstborn, attractive female and GPA was obtained.

Further analysis revealed that Singer's manipulative intent hypothesis was supported. Firstborn females were found to be more socially conscious of their appearance than later-borns. When asked to estimate ideal body measurements and their own measurements, these women were not only more accurate in stating their own measurements and those of the ideal female form, but also were more likely to distort their measurements in the direction of the ideal. Similarly, firstborns engaged in more positive "exhibition" behaviors in the classroom, increasing the likelihood that instructors would remember them, hence give them the benefit of the doubt in grading. Observations of in-class behaviors and self-reports from these women disclosed their tendency to sit in the front of the room, remain to talk to the instructor after class more often, and make more frequent appointments to see their instructors during office hours.

Our concern in this discussion has not been with the fact that you as a teacher classify your students on the basis of their personal appearance cues. As noted earlier, this is an inevitable part of the person perception process. What is *not* inevitable, and well within your control as a teacher, is the tendency to let these cues dictate or influence the performance expectations you hold for a student. You have already seen the profound effect of teacher expectations on student achievement. In this regard we might all do well to remember that a good student is not always good-looking.

The role of dress and other personal artifacts such as jewelry, glasses, or cosmetics in determining interpersonal responses is not entirely clear. That these factors contribute to the total image an individual projects is obvious. Less obvious is the degree to which we selectively attend to details of apparel rather than, or in concert with, other appearance cues. We may indulge in some speculations about the functions and effects of clothing in classroom settings.

On a very basic level, clothing and other artifacts may be used by an individual to satisfy needs for attention, group membership, and esteem. For many students group identification is expressed by dress in terms of fraternity or sorority clothing styles. For others the standard uniform of jeans performs the same function. Consider your immediate classroom situation. From the rear view, would anyone have much difficulty in discriminating between teacher and student on the basis of dress alone? Probably not. We might infer then that, for the wearer, clothing choice represents an attempt to control the reaction of others. For an observer, it provides a means by which individuals may be socially classified.

Time

The final coding system we examine is, like space, a backdrop for all interpersonal communication events. Our perceptions of time are similarly conditioned by cultural norms. Many of these cultural norms permeate the way teachers and students view class time. For example, there is an emphasis on punctual arrival for classes that reflects a preoccupation in American society. A lack of punctuality nonverbally signals a lack of concern or respect for the appointment. Teachers, as any consistently tardy student will tell you, do not reward such behavior.

Harrison (1974) has described the monochronistic use of time that has sifted from our culture into the classroom. The term "monochronistic" refers to the allotment of time so that only one thing is done at any moment. Hence you spend three hours a week in a communication class, five hours in chemistry, and so on. Even within the larger structure of class hours, teachers tend to subdivide time to permit concentration on a single topic, project, or assignment. In this way, it is believed, the learning process may proceed in an orderly progression.

Apart from these cultural norms, classroom interactions are affected by at least two other uses of time worth mentioning. The first of these refers to the way teachers shape student perceptions toward a subject matter area by the time allotted to a topic. In a sense, teachers function much like the mass media in agenda setting. That is, Walter Cronkite usually does not tell you explicitly what to think or believe about world and national affairs, but through his selection, ordering, and emphasis of news items, makes it abundantly clear what to think *about*. In like fashion, we spend weeks teaching students how to manipulate human behavior through verbal and visual symbols and devote one or two class periods to discussing the ethics of persuasion. Can the nonverbal message, whether intentional or unintentional, be escaped?

Time, as a dimension of nonverbal classroom communication, has implications for students' attitudes toward instruction. Would it surprise you very much to read that many students view interactions with their teachers as positive reinforcement? Madsen and Madsen (1970), after extensive observation of experimental contingency-managed school systems, report that one of the rewards elementary students enjoy most is "time-with-teacher." While we should be cautious in generalizing this finding to students at all levels, we can state with some assurance that students respond favorably to instructors they perceive as open, receptive, and approachable.

THE SILENT PARTNER: NONVERBAL CUES IN VERBAL COMMUNICATION

If this chapter is your initial exposure to nonverbal communication, there is a chance that you may misunderstand our motive. The presentation of verbal communication and nonverbal communication as separate symbol systems may seem to emphasize a dichotomy that does not exist. Actually, verbal and nonverbal communication should be viewed as intertwined parts of the same process. Now that you are somewhat familiar with the basic elements of each, we explore the ways in which nonverbal and verbal systems interact.

Generally speaking, there are more differences between verbal and nonverbal coding systems than similarities. Verbal coding systems are represented by written and spoken language, a complex, multilevel structure composed of discrete elements and governed by rules of syntax. We know that language is a learned behavior. The nonverbal code, on the other hand, is not a single unitary code at all. Rather, it consists of fragments of many codes (tactile, kinesic, etc.) composed of continuous elements with no readily apparent rules of syntax or grammar. We are not entirely certain whether all nonverbal behaviors are learned. There is increasing evidence that some primary facial expressions are innate.

Of the two coding systems, there is little doubt that the verbal code occupies a superordinate position. We rely on language to make coherent the often chaotic experience of living. It is equally true that nonverbal cues accompanying the verbal code are emitted, consciously or unconsciously, for the purpose of conveying information to a receiver. Both codes are necessary for optimal communication accuracy. Knapp (1972) has identified six ways in which the nonverbal code interacts with the verbal code. A brief view of these functions will highlight the interdependence of the two systems and give you some insight into their mutual impact in the classroom.

Repeating

A variety of gestures is used to reinforce or reiterate a verbal message through visual illustration. Pointing is probably the most frequently occurring instance of nonverbal repetition in the classroom. When a student asks where he or she is to sit, your answer is likely to be accompanied by a gesture indicating the appropriate location.

Substituting

Nonverbal cues can function as a sort of verbal shorthand, replacing the verbal message with combinations of gestures and facial expressions that convey the same information. Observe the nonverbal behavior of students as they walk from their seats to the front of the room to turn in completed examinations. Their facial expressions, walk, and especially the way they hand in their papers conveys their reactions far more eloquently than puny words. One professor staunchly maintains that he can predict performance accurately about 70 percent of the time on this basis alone. In public places, substitute nonverbal displays can be used to correct an individual's behavior in a face-saving way. Even the most chronic gossip can be silenced by a well-placed nudge in the ribs or rap on the ankle.

Complementing

Nonverbal cues often reveal the basic attitudes or intentions of one individual toward another person or toward the topic of conversation. The information conveyed is not so much a repetition of what is said as it is an extension or elaboration contributing additional information. When a teacher admonishes her students, "Keep your eyes on your own paper," the accompanying facial expression and vocal cues communicate whether the statement should be interpreted as a mild rebuke or a final warning. Knapp (1972) suggests that complementary cues are used to signal changes in the nature of a relationship between two people. If you can remember any of your first dates, you can probably recall the agonies of your fixed smile, forced laughter, and studied postures which gradually dissolved as you became better acquainted with each other. These changes in relaxation cues would lead an outside observer to predict that the verbal content had fewer vocal dysfluencies, more interruptions, and a more spontaneous quality.

Contradicting

When nonverbal cues do not agree with verbal message content, the disagreement may reflect confusion, uncertainty, anxiety, or outright deception. We are all familiar with numerous examples of this type of conflict. The amorous man carefully scrutinizes his lady friend's nonverbal cues to determine whether "no" really means "yes," or at least "maybe." An angry wife might say to her husband, "Nothing's wrong," but her fierce facial expression, refusal to look him in the eye, and the fact that she slammed the door on his big toe inform him otherwise. These and similar classroom examples are frequently characterized as *double-bind* messages, in that they convey contrary evaluations to a receiver. It falls to the receiver to decide which of the conflicting messages carries the true meaning.

Interpretation of double-bind messages presents special problems. One common assumption states that, because they are more difficult to control, nonverbal cues can be trusted more than words. While some research findings (Mehrabian, 1972) support this assumption, the problem is not so simple. Consider a typical classroom deception situation. You have failed to complete an assignment that is due today, and you have to provide an explanation to your instructor. Your assignment is not ready because you went to a party last night, but you feel your teacher will not consider this a very compelling excuse. What are you going to do? Re-

FIGURE 5·3 NONVERBAL CLUES MAY CONTRADICT THE VERBAL MESSAGE.

gardless of the specific excuse you offer, your nonverbal behavior will probably include the following: direct eye contact, concerned facial expression, and sincere tone of voice. Most of us are fairly skillful nonverbal liars—at least as far as the face is concerned. If your teacher is wise in the ways of nonverbal cues, she may note that you are twining one foot around the other, or that your fingers are beating a nervous tattoo on your notebook, and infer a discrepancy between your verbal and nonverbal behavior. Two factors, then, limit the reliability of nonverbal messages in double-bind situations. Certain nonverbal cues are more reliable than others because they are harder to control consciously. Also, some of us are simply better at conveying contradictory information than others.

Your previous communication experiences generally, and those with a single individual whose verbal and nonverbal messages you are trying to decipher, seem likely to influence which system you rely on. Just as some individuals seem to be more proficient in masking nonverbal information than others, there are individuals who depend heavily on nonverbal cues to express their messages. Interestingly enough, some research (Mortensen, 1972) suggests that these individuals are also most accurate in interpreting nonverbal cues. In any case, when your knowledge of an individual's communication style is insufficient, you interpret a double-bind message according to which code has proved most reliable in the past. If this is the verbal code, you will doubtless be accused of taking everything too literally. If you place greater emphasis on the nonverbal code, you are doomed to spend an inordinate amount of time asking yourself, "What did he mean by *that*?" How's that for a double-bind?

Accenting

When we wish to emphasize a single point or dramatically underscore the significance of an entire segment of dialogue, we often use nonverbal behaviors to achieve the desired effect. Teachers frequently use head movements, hand gestures, and touch to accentuate key phrases during a lecture or individual conference. One pipe-smoking professor we know well relied on his favorite briarwood for more than the pleasures of tobacco. His pipe-wielding behaviors varied according to the relative importance of the material being discussed. During routine statements, the pipe remained in the corner of his mouth or cushioned within his half-open palm. When summarizing the major points of a discussion, however, the pipe stem became a visual exclamation point, impaling each idea to be impressed on the student's mind.

Relating and Regulating

Maintaining contact with all participants in a communication event and ordering the flow of communication among participants are frequent and important uses of nonverbal cues during verbal interactions. Teachers, for example, use eye contact to indicate to students that they are aware of their presence and monitoring their responses. In class discussions, students usually wait for an acknowledging head nod from their instructor before beginning to speak. While speaking, the student's eyes return to the instructor, whose eye behavior, shifts in posture, or head nods let her know whether to continue speaking or yield the floor to someone else. The presence or absence of relational cues can give you valuable information about listener response to your remarks. Ignoring feedback of this type can create serious disruptions in communication accuracy.

PRINCIPLES 5.2

1. Nonverbal coding systems are usually defined in terms of broad categories of directly observable behaviors.
2. Kinesics encompasses the broadest range of nonverbal behaviors and includes a majority of body motions observed in classroom or other communication settings. The kinesic code is a multichannel, multimessage system contributing to all the communication functions defined by nonverbal behavior.
3. Proxemic codes deal with the symbolic and expressive uses of space. Proxemic behavior reveals the interpersonal attitudes, status, and personality characteristics of teachers and students.
4. Haptics or tactile behaviors are severely restricted in most instructional settings, because of cultural rules concerning intimacy. The tremendous reinforcement value of touching is often only negatively displayed through disciplinary acts.
5. Paralinguistic codes are critical in teacher-student interactions. Vocal cues contribute greatly to the impression formation, reinforcement, and expression of attitudes and feelings functions of classroom communication.
6. Physical appearance cues have a direct bearing on the impressions students and teachers form of each other. Physical attractiveness enhances the attribution of positive personal and academic qualities.
7. Time codes are particularly influential in establishing patterns of classroom behavior. Students observe a teacher's use of time to infer his or her attitudes toward themselves, course material, and the instructional process in general.
8. Verbal and nonverbal coding systems are inextricably interdependent. Of the two, language plays the dominant role in most student-teacher exchanges, although nonverbal information functions by elaborating or modifying every verbal message.

FUNCTIONS OF NONVERBAL CUES IN THE INSTRUCTIONAL PROCESS

The foregoing discussion of the interdependence of verbal and nonverbal coding systems has obvious implications for an analysis of nonverbal behaviors in the classroom. The supportive role of nonverbal cues accompanying verbal information is reflected in the process of instruction no less than in any other communicative process. There are, however, several classroom functions that are uniquely nonverbal in nature that warrant separate treatment.

Self-Presentation

Much of what it means to be a student, or a teacher for that matter, takes place on a nonverbal level. Appropriate behaviors for a student or teacher are learned largely through experience within classrooms rather than by more systematic instructional methods. Although you are currently enrolled in a course designed to teach you something about being a teacher, your impression of what it means to teach and go to school is already rather complete. If asked, you could probably provide a lengthy list of behaviors that teachers and students should perform. Most of this information was acquired nonverbally, and you in turn may ultimately pass it along to your students through your nonverbal behavior.

Goffman (1959) has described self-presentation as largely a matter of role enactment. This simply means that you probably have an image of yourself in the classroom setting which determines how you will behave. If, for example, you believe that the role of the teacher is information giver, you probably also believe that students are essentially information receivers, passive unless prodded into some sort of activity by the teacher. Although this description sounds rather grim, reflect on your classroom experiences and ask yourself how many match our example. Your perceptions of appropriate role behaviors are probably so thoroughly ingrained that you cannot quite recall how you came to "know" them. Nonetheless, it may be useful to explore some of the ways in which self-presentation norms appear in the classroom.

Silence is basic to the role of the student in most instructional settings. Students who do not comply in this aspect of self-presentation are promptly labeled disruptive or considered behavior problems. While silence has never been identified as learning, the ability to be quiet, from the elementary years onward, is the first distinguishing characteristic of a successful student. Those who wish to present themselves as ideal students in the classroom master other relevant behavioral cues, such as looking as if they are listening, nodding their heads to indicate understanding, and the strategic aspects of hand raising.

Teacher behaviors are equally well-defined in terms of nonverbal role enactment. In contrast to students, teachers are almost never expected to be quiet, passive, or compliant. Rather, their role demands that they move, speak, and control the behavior of their students. Controlling behaviors appear to be a rather significant aspect of the teacher's in-class role. The rap of the knuckles on the lectern to gain attention, the steady gaze that connotes disapproval, and the wagging finger are but a few representative examples of such behavior. One observational study (Grant and Hennings, 1971) revealed that about 63 percent of teachers' nonverbal activity was control-oriented.

Identification of Rules and Expectations

Teachers sometimes provide students with precise behavioral objectives for their courses, but it is interesting to note that these objectives rarely describe actual, day-to-day classroom performance. You may be told that you are expected to participate in class discussions, but the issues of when and how much are rarely made explicit. Yet, over a period of time you learn to distinguish between a teacher's rhetorical questions and those which require a verbal response. Whether the nonverbal R.S.V.P. comes from paralinguistic information, facial expression, or a gesture is not important. The point is that you have a basis for discriminating between the two types of questions and know the expected response, if not the correct answer. This example should give you an idea of how classroom rules and performance expectations are conveyed and learned nonverbally.

While specific classroom rules may vary widely in number and scope, they are almost invariably concerned with the regulation of interaction between student and teacher or student and student. Of particular interest here is the concept of channel control, which refers to the determination of who speaks to whom in the classroom. Channel control is a privilege teachers tend to guard rather jealously. One small-group communication instructor we know required each class member to lead a class discussion at least once a semester while he sat at the back of the room as an observer. You can probably predict the outcome more quickly than we can write it. Without fail, the instructor was unable to relinquish control, regardless of how the discussion was proceeding. By the end of these practice sessions, the luckless leader of the day was occupying the observer's position in terms of the direction and frequency of interaction.

Perhaps the most important nonverbal cue in channel control is eye contact (Argyle, 1969). By engaging another's eyes, we signal a willingness to interact, and that we are attending to what they are saying. You as a student know the power of the instructor's gaze. In most classrooms it signals your access to the communication channel, and singly, or when paired with other nonverbal cues, withholds the opportunity for talking. Expectations are similarly indicated by eye behavior. When you think you have answered a question completely and your instructor continues to hold your eyes, what is your response? Well, you may not be able to deliver, but you most assuredly know that the teacher is nonverbally implying that you should answer further.

Metacommunication

Ruesch and Kees (1956), following extensive observations of nonverbal behavior in therapeutic settings, determined that certain nonverbal cues act as qualifiers of verbal statements. The qualifying function is metacommunicative in that it indicates how the words ought to be understood. Galloway (1972) describes metacommunicative behavior on the part of a student in the following way:

> . . . a student at his desk may say that he is working and simultaneously act out the appearance of being busy, believing that this kind of behavior is more convincing. Even if he is actually working... much of his energy may be spent in trying to look studious and dedicated. (p. 3)

Metacommunicative messages in the classroom may be conveyed intentionally or unintentionally. More often than not, it is the unintentional message that turns missed cues into miscues. Consider, for example, the teacher who unconsciously smiles while she tells her students that she will under no circumstances accept term papers after the stated due date. When some students' papers are not submitted on time, she is surprised and irritated. The students whose papers are rejected react angrily, protesting that she failed to make it clear that the due date was inflexible. They responded to the metacommunicative message—the smile that led them to believe it was all right to turn in the paper late.

For metacommunicative information we appear to rely chiefly on facial expressions and paralinguistic cues. The tone of voice accompanying a verbal message is particularly important in this regard. By subtle shadings in tone, a devastating criticism may be softened to a mild reprimand or a seemingly innocuous comment turned into a stinging insult.

Feedback and Reinforcement

Given the realities of the classroom setting, highly individualized reinforcement systems are often infeasible or even undesirable. In much the same way, although for different reasons, it is frequently impossible for teachers to receive verbal feedback from their students. Thus nonverbal cues carry a significant amount of evaluative freightage during student-teacher interactions.

A wealth of research has demonstrated the importance of feedback for communication accuracy. Our own experiences confirm these findings. In the instructional setting, feedback is especially important because education at any level usually involves the learning of new skills or information. Without feedback, learning becomes more a matter of chance than of design. You are probably accustomed to thinking of feedback in terms of an evaluation, usually in the form of a letter grade, that you receive from your instructor. Evaluative feedback may also be expressed

nonverbally, through the instructor's facial expressions, bodily orientation, and other cues.

As a teacher you may find yourself somewhat less concerned with
evaluative feedback from students and more interested in assessing feedback for comprehension cues. While it might be possible to stop and ask
your students if they have grasped each concept you discuss in class, the
long-range effects of such a practice would be rather negative. Thus you
are likely to rely on nonverbal cues, such as head nods, smiles, or note-
taking behaviors, to gauge understanding. Such cues, unfortunately, may
be exhibited as a function of self-presentation norms rather than as indicators of attention or learning. Moreover, available research suggests that
even experienced teachers are unable to assess comprehension accurately
on the basis of visible student behaviors. Until the nonverbal behaviors
specific to learning are identified, the most reliable cues are likely to be
those that connote boredom, inattention, or restlessness.

Reinforcement of course is a form of feedback. On the nonverbal
level, reinforcement has a powerful effect on a student's perception of
himself, of school, and of his instructor. The specific cues—smiles,
frowns, eye contact, touch—are not really relevant. Each teacher's style is
somewhat unique. We are most particularly concerned here with the
dynamics of the student-teacher relationship. Regardless of whether a
teacher has 10 students or 50, his or her encounter with each is essentially
a two-person relationship. The realities of that relationship are likely to be
defined, from the student's perspective at least, by the nonverbal behaviors of the teacher. Through nonverbal influence, the teacher gives
each student an estimate of his or her self-worth, not just as a student but
as a total human being. A professional observer (Galloway, 1971) describes the impact of nonverbal reinforcers this way:

> I was there to observe specific students for an entire school day. I noticed
> that these students looked at teachers but teachers did not necessarily look
> back. This was true, even though the students had different teachers for
> every class period. From class to class these students trudged to their seats,
> but their presence was never acknowledged. . . . In spite of absence of con-
> tact with some students, teachers managed to view other students dif-
> ferently. When teachers talked, they looked at some students to suggest that
> everything was going well. In these instances, mutual glances were ex-
> changed between teacher and students in a positive manner. . . . But there
> were all kinds of visual discriminations going on and the differences in eye
> contact were amazing. Eyes that looked up or down transmitted, "I reject
> you." Eyes that avoided contact suggested, "you are not included." Eyes that
> stared at students revealed, "I dislike you." As I sat there watching all of this,
> I mused that these teachers didn't know what was happening. . . . I was sure
> that their reaction would be one of disbelief. So that I won't be misun-
> derstood, let's make it clear: these teachers were not unlike teachers any-
> where. They were doing their job as they saw it. (p. 229)

FIGURE 5·4 CUES THAT CONNOTE BOREDOM, INATTENTION, OR RESTLESSNESS ARE NOT DIFFICULT TO DETECT.

Through nonverbal cues, a teacher can make a student an active participant in the learning transaction or a nonperson.

NONVERBAL COMMUNICATION AND TEACHING EFFECTIVENESS

Research on the nonverbal dimension of classroom interaction is still in the descriptive stage. Precise relationships between the various nonverbal codes are not yet understood, and their differential impact on learning outcomes is at best a matter of speculation. Thus we are some distance from a precise rhetoric of body movement and expression for classroom teachers. In lieu of a precise routine of the "right" nonverbal moves to make in the classroom, we think it more appropriate to present an instrument used to record teacher nonverbal behavior. The instrument was developed on the basis of extensive observation of the nonverbal behaviors of elementary and secondary schools. The behaviors identified in the instrument therefore reflect some of the important nonverbal teaching practices.

Love-Roderick Nonverbal Categories
and Sample Teacher Behaviors
1. Accepts Student Behavior
   Smiles, affirmatively shakes head, pats on the back, winks, places hand on shoulder or head.
2. Praises Student Behavior
   Places index finger and thumb together, claps, raises eyebrows and smiles, nods head affirmatively and smiles.
3. Displays Student Ideas
   Writes comments on board, puts students' work on bulletin board, holds up papers, provides for nonverbal student demonstration.
4. Shows Interest in Student Behavior
   Establishes and maintains eye contact.
5. Moves to Facilitate Student-to-Student Interaction
   Physically moves into the position of group member, physically moves away from the group.
6. Gives Directions to Students
   Points with the hand, looks at specified area, employs pre-determined signal (such as raising hands for students to stand up), reinforces numerical aspects by showing that number of fingers, extends arms forward and beckons with the hands, points to student for answers.
7. Shows Authority Toward Students
   Frowns, stares, raises eyebrows, taps foot, rolls book on desk, negatively shakes head, walks or looks away from the deviant, snaps fingers.
8. Focuses Students' Attention on Important Points
   Uses pointer, walks toward the person or object, taps on something,

thrusts head forward, thrusts arm forward, employs a nonverbal movement with a verbal statement to give it emphasis.
9. Demonstrates and/or Illustrates
   Performs a physical skill, manipulates materials and media, illustrates a verbal statement with a nonverbal action.
10. Ignores Student Behavior
    Lacks nonverbal response when one is ordinarily expected. (pp. 295–296)

Studies using the Love-Roderick (1971) scale and similar instruments (Civikly, 1973; French, 1971; Koch, 1971; Willett, 1975; Willet and Smythe (1977) revealed two fairly consistent findings. First, teachers who were classified "effective" were *more active* than teachers designated "ineffective." Movements and nonverbal cues appeared more frequently for these teachers in almost all categories. This should not surprise you. Any stimulus, whether it is a student or a teacher, is considerably more compelling when it is varied, vivid, or novel. When was the last time you heard someone exclaim, "Wow! What a dynamite teacher. All through the lecture he stood behind the lectern and read his notes, lifting his eyes only when he turned a page." Teachers whose nonverbal activity level is low are usually perceived as less interesting and informative in the classroom.

It should be noted, however, that activity itself is probably not enough to enhance teaching effectiveness. The Love-Roderick scale does not include a category for "personal moves," those peculiar habits we all use unconsciously. For Johnny Carson, personal moves include playing with his tie, straightening his cuffs, and smoothing back his hair. Your own might be rubbing the side of your nose, or twisting a strand of hair around your finger when you are thinking. Consider the teacher who asked you to read this chapter. You can probably mimic a number of personal moves that are especially typical of your teacher. We mention personal moves here to make an important point. Although they may constitute as much as 33 percent of the total number of nonverbal moves a teacher makes, personal moves do not enhance learning or teaching effectiveness. Rather, they function as adaptors for the teacher and as relatively useless, distracting cues for the student. Teaching effectiveness therefore is at least partly due to *purposeful* nonverbal activity.

A second, perhaps more important, finding from studies of teacher effectiveness and nonverbal cues is that teachers can be trained to improve their nonverbal behavior. Love and Roderick, as well as others, have found that workshops and seminars on nonverbal classroom behavior enhance teachers' performance. The improved performance is not due to learning "six new and dynamic gestures to try on your students." Uniformity of teacher behaviors is hardly a desirable goal. Instead, prospective or practicing teachers are exposed to the dimensions of nonverbal activity much as you have been in this chapter. They are given practice sessions in which classroom situations are simulated and different approaches may be tried. Most importantly, they view videotaped recordings of their own teaching activity. In this way, the teachers learn to develop their nonverbal teaching potential.

You may, in the course of your preparation for teaching, have had a similar opportunity. Examining your own nonverbal teaching cues maximizes your ability to help your students learn. Whether through videotapes or the report of an observer, such information is invaluable. There is no single "right" nonverbal teaching style, but there are many we might label "wrong." If your goal is effective teaching, your task includes the components of every learning situation: awareness, evaluation, and change. Reading this chapter should help you achieve that critical first step. The next two, we hope, will inevitably follow.

A CONCLUDING NOTE

This chapter focused on the symbol system we have practiced longest and probably understood least: nonverbal behavior. Our definition of nonverbal behavior as all behavior beyond spoken or written words to which people attribute meaning emphasized the scope and impact of this symbol system on face-to-face interactions. Nonverbal behavior is pervasive and completely inevitable in human experience. Much of the meaning conveyed in messages, classroom or otherwise, comes from the nonverbal symbol system.

Our major purpose in this chapter has been to sensitize you to the dynamics of nonverbal cues in the instructional setting. It is our contention that teaching effectiveness can be realized only through an understanding of the elements of the learning equation. The contribution of nonverbal behavior to student *and* teacher perceptions of the classroom is indeed substantial. By now you should be aware that your ability to convey nonverbal information accurately to your students and interpret nonverbal information from them has important implications for the intellectual and emotional outcomes of instruction.

Meaning of course has been a central issue. The tendency when discussing nonverbal cues to imply a single meaning for every movement is inevitable. The process of communication would be more manageable if this were true, but it is simply not the case. On the contrary, it is essential that you realize that *nonverbal meaning arises from the context in which the nonverbal behavior occurs*. This context includes (at least) you, another individual, a physical setting, and a social environment. Moreover, the context probably includes another symbol system, spoken language. It is only when context is considered that the meaning of nonverbal cues may be inferred. Given that you probably teach about 20 to 200 students per semester, it is rather unlikely that you will be able to learn to read 1, much less all, of them "like a book." Can students read teachers? The probability is considerably higher that, given time, they can. Remember that your students have only 4 or 5 teachers per semester and that, regardless of class size, each student views his or her interactions with a teacher as an interpersonal rather than a one-to-many relationship. It is for this reason that we have taken a somewhat teacher-centered, functional approach to nonverbal classroom behaviors.

The functional approach in this chapter has highlighted the impact of nonverbal cues on classroom interactions. We have not attempted to provide you with a structural analysis of nonverbal codes. We believe that it is more essential for you to become aware of the major types of nonverbal systems operating in the classroom and their potential influence on learning outcomes. The degree to which kinesics, haptics, proxemics, paralinguistics, or any of the other nonverbal codes interacts in your case is unpredictable. You may be sure, however, that others attach meaning to the way you move, sound, dress, or look. Most perceptions of you, your subject area, and your classroom that your students develop are based on nonverbal information. The image you present as a teacher, class rules, feedback, and the teaching style you project are largely a function of nonverbal behavior. Since all these behaviors are learned, it is possible for you to analyze your interactions with your students and alter your behaviors to achieve the best results.

PRINCIPLES 5.3

1. Self-presentation functions of nonverbal cues are realized through role enactment. Nonverbal profiles of teachers and students reveal markedly similar behavior patterns across classrooms.
2. Identification of rules and expectations function is conveyed largely through kinesic and paralinguistic behaviors of the teacher. Control and regulation of interaction are primary examples.
3. Metacommunicative nonverbal messages reveal communicator intent, affect the quality of the classroom social environment, and are usually conveyed by facial and vocal information.
4. Feedback and reinforcement functions may be achieved through all the nonverbal coding systems. The power of these cues in shaping the academic and social self-concepts of students can hardly be overstated.
5. Nonverbal activity of effective teachers differs from that of average teachers, primarily in terms of more positive action-oriented behaviors and fewer personal motions.
6. Increasing evidence suggests that nonverbal skill development programs improve teachers' effectiveness in promoting student learning.

REFERENCES

Altman, I. Ecological aspects of interpersonal functioning. In A. H. Esser (Ed.), *Behavior and environment.* New York: Plenum, 1971.

Argyle, M. *Social interaction.* New York: Atherton, 1969.

Barker, L., and Collins, N. Nonverbal and kinesic research. In P. Emmert and W. Brooks (Eds.), *Methods of research in communication.* Boston: Houghton Mifflin, 1970, 343–372.

Civikly, J. A description and experimental analysis of teacher nonverbal communication in the college classroom. Ph.D. dissertation, Florida State University, 1973.

Ekman, P., and Friesen, W. The repertoire of nonverbal behavior: Categories, origins, usage and coding. *Semiotica,* 1969, 1, 49–98.

Fast, J. *Body language.* New York: Evans, 1970.

Frank, L. Tactile communication. *Genetic Psychology Monographs,* 1957, 56, 209–255.

French, R. Analyzing and improving nonverbal communication: A model for in-service education. *Theory into Practice,* 1971, 10, 305–309.

Galloway, C. Nonverbal: The language of sensitivity. *Theory into Practice,* 1971, 10, 227–230. © Theory into Practice, 1971. Reprinted by permission.

Galloway, C. Analysis of theories and research in nonverbal communication. Special project for the National Center for Educational Communication, Washington, D.C., 1972. ERIC No. ED 059 988.

Goffman, E. *The presentation of self in everyday life.* Garden City, N.Y.: Doubleday, 1959.

Grant, B., and Hennings, D. *The teacher moves: An analysis of nonverbal activities.* New York: Teachers College Press, Columbia University, 1971.

Hall, E. *The silent language.* Garden City, N.Y.: Doubleday, 1959.

Hall, E. *The hidden dimension.* Garden City, N.Y.: Doubleday, 1966.

Harrison, R. *Beyond words: An introduction to nonverbal communication.* Englewood Cliffs, N.J.: Prentice-Hall, 1974.

Kleinke, C. *First impressions: The psychology of encountering others.* Englewood Cliffs, N.J.: Prentice-Hall, 1975.

Knapp, M. *Nonverbal communication in human interaction.* New York: Holt, Rinehart and Winston, 1972.

Koch, R. Nonverbal observables. *Theory into Practice,* 1971, 10, 288–294.

Love, A., and Roderick, J. Teacher nonverbal communication: The development and field testing of an awareness unit. *Theory into Practice,* 1971, 10, 295–299. © Theory into Practice, 1971. Reprinted by permission.

McCroskey, J., Larson, K., and Knapp, M. *An introduction to interpersonal communication.* Englewood Cliffs, N.J.: Prentice-Hall, 1971.

Madsen, C., and Madsen, C. *Teaching: Discipline: Behavioral principles toward a positive approach.* Boston: Allyn & Bacon, 1970.

Mehrabian, A. *Silent messages.* Belmont, Calif.: Wadsworth, 1971.

Mehrabian, A. *Nonverbal communication.* Chicago: Aldine-Atherton, 1972.

Montagu, A. *Touching: The human significance of skin.* New York: Columbia University Press, 1971.

Mortensen, C. *Communication: The study of human interaction.* New York: McGraw-Hill, 1972.

Rosenthal, R., and Jacobsen, L. *Pygmalion in the classroom.* New York: Holt, Rinehart and Winston, 1968.

Ruesch, J., and Kees, W. *Nonverbal communication: Notes on the visual perception of human relations.* Berkeley: University of California Press, 1956.

Sapir, E. The unconscious patterning of behavior in society. In *Selected writings of Edward Sapir in language, culture, and personality.* Berkeley: University of California Press, 1963.

Singer, J. The use of manipulative strategies: Machiavellianism and attractiveness. *Sociometry,* 1964, **27,** 128-151.

Trager, G. Paralanguage: A first approximation. *Studies in Linguistics,* 1958, **13,** 1-12.

Whiteside, R. *Face language.* New York: Frederick Fell, 1974.

Willett, T. A descriptive analysis of nonverbal behaviors of classroom teachers. Unpublished report, University of Missouri, 1975.

Willett, T., and Smythe, M.-J. A descriptive analysis of the nonverbal behavior of college teachers. Paper presented at the Speech Communication Association, Washington, D.C., 1977.

Chapter 6
The Physical Environments of Classrooms

OBJECTIVES

After reading this chapter you should be able to:

1. explain why classroom seats are often uncomfortable.
2. identify the effects of color on productivity and mood.
3. describe how color can be used to create stimulating environments in schools and classrooms.
4. identify the effects of windowless rooms on student behavior.
5. describe the effects of overcrowding.
6. identify how people are likely to respond when the temperature is too high.
7. discuss the effects of room attractiveness on mood and learning.
8. identify the action zone in classrooms and explain its importance.
9. explain why students who sit in the action zone participate more than students sitting elsewhere.
10. describe the consequences of row-column seating arrangements.
11. draw five different classroom seating patterns and identify the type of activity most appropriate for each.

A few years ago Robert Coles (1969) asked elementary school children what they would do to make their school better. One little girl, Margie, gave this reply:

> I'll tell you one thing, I'd tear *this* building down. There's nothing to do but that. Then, if I could build a new school, I'd make it pleasant-like. I'd get rid of all the desks, every one of them. I'd have us sit around a table, and maybe we could have cookies. I'd have the teacher be better. She could laugh a lot, and there wouldn't be a clock up there, making noise every minute that goes by. We could open and close the windows and they wouldn't be stuck like now. We could have a big rug here in the room, so if you fell down you wouldn't get hurt, like I did. And they could have some places, some big sofas maybe, where if you didn't feel too good, you could lie down, or you could just sit in them sometimes, and you'd be more comfortable. (p. 48)

Margie was obviously concerned about the physical environment of her school. Is physical environment important? We think so, for as you will see in this chapter, it can affect learning, as well as the moods you and your students experience and the ways in which you respond to one another. Furthermore, the structure of one important element of the schoolroom, seating arrangement, has a great impact on the interaction which occurs in your classes.

EFFECTS OF PHYSICAL ENVIRONMENT

The major problem in dealing with the physical environment is that most of us are unconscious of it. Having already spent so much time in schools, the setting seems very natural to you. Even though you may have vague feelings of unpleasantness or fatigue in a certain classroom, cafeteria, or library, you are probably unable to pinpoint the cause of such discomfort. One of our purposes in this chapter therefore is to increase your awareness of *how* the environment affects your behavior and that of your students.

You might be saying to yourself about now, "So what? I can't single-handedly tear out walls, hang Sheetrock over cracking plaster, replace furniture, and repaint my classroom even if I wanted to." We realize that. At the same time, no good can come from unquestioning acceptance of the status quo. No matter how bad the classroom is in which you find yourself, you can improve it. At the least, decorations can be added and furniture rearranged, and these two simple acts can produce dramatic results. In addition, we believe that becoming informed about the effects of environment can have some far-reaching results. Many school boards construct buildings and decorate and furnish entire schools without benefit of the reliable information teachers could provide about the consequences of such decisions. Perhaps after being exposed to this chapter you will be more willing to express your views regarding the type of environment in which you would like to work.

Even the most perfect of environments does not ensure good interpersonal relationships, effective communication, and learning, but bad physical settings can work effectively against the attainment of all three.

To begin, let's take a close look at classrooms to examine furniture, color, lighting, density, temperature, and attractiveness and consider how these aspects of the physical environment affect how we feel, and subsequently how we act and interpret the actions of others.

Furniture

I'd like comfortable chairs, like ones that had cushions so your back doesn't hurt and your bottom either. (Coles, 1969, p. 50).

Can you remember the seats in your high school? They probably didn't look very inviting, but disregard that consideration for the moment and remember how they felt. If you were to select a chair in which you had to sit for six or more hours a day, would you choose the hard, wooden bottom and back of the typical school seat? Not likely.

Can a chair make a difference in how a person feels? A number of Copenhagen café owners believed so. They were concerned about customers who stayed too long in their seats without making additional purchases. According to Sommer (1969), these businessmen sought the aid of Henning Larsen, a Copenhagen furniture designer. Larsen's task was to design a chair which would cause unpleasant pressure on a person's spine when occupied after a short time. The purpose of course was to make the customers uncomfortable and cause them to move on, making room for new customers.

We have no evidence that Mr. Larsen has ever designed chairs for American classrooms, but many students might conclude that the seats in their classrooms produce pain not unlike that of the Larsen chair.

The fact that classroom seats aren't pleasant to sit in isn't surprising, at least in Sommer's (1969) opinion. He claims that furniture manufacturers make little effort to evaluate the furniture they produce for comfortableness, other than to consider in general ways the sizes of the bodies the pieces are designed to hold. Classroom seats are designed for functional efficiency: They must last for many years and be easy for the janitor to sweep around. At least, these often seem to be the features of importance to school board members who make the selection.

Color

Color, like furniture, affects how we feel. Architects working in industrial settings have found that color selections can have powerful consequences for worker behavior. Coordinated colors have increased production, raised morale, and lowered absenteeism (Papadatos, 1972). Research has also shown a relationship between school achievement and color. In one such investigation, children in three separate schools were studied (Ketcham, in Rosenfeld and Civikly, 1976). One school which needed painting was not painted. A second school was painted in the traditional fashion with buff-colored walls and white ceilings. In the third school, the advice of architects for coordinating colors was followed. Rooms which faced the north were of a pale-rose color, while those facing the south were done in shades of cool blue and green. To create contrast and focus attention, the walls at the front of the room were painted darker colors than the side walls. Achievement in the areas of social habits, health and safety habits, language arts, arithmetic, social studies, science, and music was greatest for the third school. Children in the school painted with the traditional color scheme ranked second, while those in the unpainted school were last in gains.

The findings from Ketcham's study are supported by others. The State Department of Education in Connecticut found that several changes took place when schools were repainted in different colors: Student pride in the school increased, and behavior problems, specifically vandalism, decreased (Rosenfeld and Civikly, 1976).

Despite the research evidence from industrial and educational settings, many schoolrooms, particularly in our cities, are painted monotonous shades, such as pale green. How should they be painted to break the monotony and create a stimulating environment? Architect Steven Papadatos, who has made a detailed study of the effects of color, offers these suggestions:

1. A light tone that will reflect sunlight should cover the wall in a classroom opposite the windows. The wall with windows should be painted a cool medium tone.
2. Walls at the front and back of the room should be a nondistracting natural tone.
3. In classrooms exposed to the north, light colors should be employed to compensate for the sun's rays.
4. To decrease the tunnel effect created by long, straight halls, paint doors and the space above doors in bright dark tones, leaving the walls in a contrasting lighter tone.
5. For areas with great amounts of wall space such as cafeterias and lobbies, designs should be applied to the walls in contrasting and complementing colors. Focal points of interest can be created in hallways by the use of bright colors and designs around water fountains and exit doors.

Colors may have the effects found in the research reviewed here, because people tend to associate moods with specific colors and act in accordance with the mood created. Wexner (1954), for example, asked people to associate moods with eight different colors. For some moods, a single color was consistently chosen by many individuals (e.g., red was exciting-stimulating, while blue was tender-soothing), indicating a high degree of agreement.

What mood(s) do you associate with the color(s) used in the classrooms you now attend? If you were selecting colors and combinations of colors to make your classrooms maximally pleasant and attractive, would you choose the colors now used?

Lighting

> And it's too dark in school, way too dark. And once you're inside, you never see the outside until the big bell rings and you can leave. (Coles, 1969, p. 52).

The long, rectangular shape of the schoolroom which most of us take for granted originated out of a need to illuminate the entire room with natural light—the front of the room being determined so that light could come over the left shoulders of the pupils (Sommer, 1969). Before inexpensive electricity was available, natural sunlight was commonly the only source of lighting in schoolrooms.

Have you ever attended a school without windows? If not, how do you think you would respond? Would it feel strange not to see sunlight? Would you experience claustrophobia? Would you tire more quickly?

If the notion of classrooms without windows seems unnatural, it's reasonable for you to expect unpleasant effects from spending time in such rooms. But what can research tell us about how students and teachers *actually react* to windowless schools?

According to Tognoli (1973), one of the most extensive investigations of windowless schools was conducted by the Architectural Research Laboratory of the University of Michigan. The authors of the research report do not claim firm conclusions. They did find, however, that pupils in the study showed little response to the removal of windows, with the exception of favorable comments on new bulletin boards and bright colors added to the rooms. While dissatisfaction might have been expected from teachers long accustomed to having windows, such reactions were absent. In fact, teachers were generally satisfied with the windowless rooms because they believed student attention increased as a result of fewer outside distractions.

In a study by Sommer (1969), students in discussion sections of a college course were assigned to either a windowless room or a room with one long wall of windows. Sommer wished to determine if the rooms had effects on student participation. He found no differences in participation between the classes meeting in the two rooms; neither were there differences in grades. Some additional effects of interest, however, did emerge. One instructor assigned to the windowless room took his students from the building and assembled them on the lawn outside. In the other class meeting in the windowless room, the students requested several times that the class be moved outside. Hence in both course sections meeting in the windowless room, "escape" reactions from both instructors and students were evident.

Why is the issue of windowless schools of concern? One reason is related to the scarcity of energy which is expected to become more of a problem in the future. The absence of windows permits rooms to be heated and cooled with much greater efficiency, and the electricity required to provide artificial lighting in place of sunlight is much less than that required for temperature control. At least one authority predicts that by necessity we will have to spend increasingly more time in environments devoid of natural light (Birren, 1972).

Humans need light. Its importance has been underscored by Wurtman (in Birren, 1972) who claims that, next to food, light is the most critical environmental variable controlling our bodies' functions. Light dilates the blood vessels and increases circulation, increases the amount of hemoglobin in the blood, stimulates the adrenal gland, and controls a number of critical biological rhythms.

How will we compensate for the absence of natural sunlight? Probably through the extensive use of ultraviolet radiation. For several years students in the Soviet Union have received ultraviolet light in their classrooms to provide the beneficial effects of sunlight not furnished by the fluorescent light used for illumination. Birren (1972) reports that under such conditions children have been observed to grow faster than usual, demonstrate greater learning, and have fewer sinus-related infections.

In the future it is quite likely that you may teach in a school without windows, perhaps even one which is totally underground. Such an environment may take some initial "getting used to," but there is little evidence to suggest that such changes will be harmful or that you will be unable to cope with them.

Density

The physical environment of schools and classrooms consists not only of the furniture, decoration (e.g., color), and lighting, but also of the number of people present (Proshansky, Ittelson, and Rivlin, 1970). Currently we are not experiencing on a nationwide basis the overcrowding that occurred in schools in the 1950s and 1960s as the children of the post-World War II baby boom went from kindergarten through high school. It is a fact, however, that significant population shifts are taking place in our country. Many northern states are losing people who are migrating to the popular southern Sunbelt. If this trend continues, it seems likely there will be an increased need for more classroom space in the southern region. Even if the population does not grow in northern states, however, there will be a need to replace deteriorated school structures in this area. Yet, with increasing costs of school construction, local districts are less able to finance new buildings. In addition, with the public's growing disenchantment with education and the high price tag it carries, voters may be increasingly reluctant to support new school bond issues. As a result, no matter where you live, you may be teaching in a room which contains more pupils than it was designed to hold.

If crowding in classrooms occurs, what will be the consequences? Will students learn less and less efficiently? Will feelings of claustrophobia be common? Will teachers and students find it simply more difficult to get along with one another? As with the effects of windowless schools, there is surprisingly little research on the effects of overcrowding on humans in any setting, not just that of the school. This is the case despite the fact that the world's population continues to grow at an alarming rate and each of us has less space to call one's own.

While there have been relatively few controlled studies of the effects of overcrowding on humans, numerous studies have been made with animals. The results are dramatic. When mice are put in a fixed space and given food and water, they reproduce rapidly. When their number reaches a certain size, however, severe disruptions in their social behavior occur. Mating and young-rearing behavior becomes erratic, with the result that infant mortality is high and the population declines.

Freedman (1971) hypothesized that, if overcrowding produces stress in humans, as it apparently does in animals such as mice, such stress should have negative effects on the ability of humans to perform complex activities. To test this hypothesis, Freedman placed subjects (many of whom were high school students) in either a crowded or an uncrowded room, usually for four hours at a time. His research is of interest to us because several of the tasks he asked subjects to do were similar to learning activities students perform in classrooms. For example, he had them complete memorization tasks as well as problem-solving ones (e.g., thinking of novel ways to use bricks, constructing words from a group of letters). The high-density condition Freedman set up *was* crowded—so crowded that there wasn't space for even one more person to sit in the room. Despite this, no differences in ability to perform the tasks were found between the crowded and the uncrowded rooms. In this study, at least, recall and problem solving were unaffected by room density.

In a related study, Griffith and Veitch (1971) found that individuals who participated in an experimental study in a crowded room reported more feelings of fatigue than people in a room with a low density. Further, persons in the crowded room rated the room as less attractive, pleasant, and comfortable. This negative reaction seemed to carry over to their rating of the experiment. They found the experience less pleasant and less interesting than individuals who completed the task in the low-density setting.

Finally, Sommer and Becker (1971) studied students' and teachers' reactions to a college classroom over a three-year period. During that time 32 classes, ranging in size from 5 to 22 students, met in the room. They found there were nearly twice the number of complaints about ventilation, room size, and overall satisfaction in the large classes as compared with the small ones.

Is overcrowding harmful? The research we have reviewed here suggests that, for relatively short periods of time, overcrowding doesn't affect learning. Overcrowding does have a negative influence, however, on how people feel about themselves, the environment, and their purpose for being there. The long-term effects of these reactions on learning, as well as on interpersonal relationships in the classroom, are unknown.

Temperature

We noted in the discussion of windowless schools that a scarcity of energy may cause significant changes in the physical environments of schools. What would be the consequences of eliminating or greatly reducing the use of air-conditioning to control the thermal environment? In schools which presently do not have air-conditioning, how are people likely to respond when it "gets too hot?"

Research findings support the experience each of us has had that when the temperature is too high we become irritable and interpersonal relationships suffer. In Griffith's (1970) study, people indicated how much they liked strangers under two temperature conditions. Under the "hot" condition (90.6 degrees Fahrenheit), strangers were liked less than under the "normal" condition (67.5 degrees Fahrenheit).

In a later study, Griffith and Veitch (1971) found that under the hot condition individuals responded with a variety of negative reactions. They reported feeling more aggressive, less elated, less social, more sad, and less vigorous than at the normal temperature. Furthermore, individuals rated the room and the experiment as less pleasant when the room was hot.

In research conducted in the naturalistic setting of actual schools, Gingold (in Tognoli, 1973) examined the effects of old and new school buildings on 200 elementary and junior high pupils. In the "new" environments, characterized by improved temperature control (in addition to other environmental changes), students showed improvement in attention and in attitudes toward their classrooms.

What can we conclude about the consequences of classroom temperature? Not as much as we would like to be able to, unfortunately, because the research is incomplete in two ways. First, we don't know how heat affects learning. Second, we don't know what effects cold has on how people learn or how they feel with respect to mood and perceptions of others. We can expect, though, that classrooms which are too hot produce a number of negative reactions from all persons assembled there.

Attractiveness

When you look at a room you can isolate your reaction to each of the aspects of the environment we have previously discussed. Additionally, you have an overall perception of the way in which the colors and furnishings combine to make it attractive or unattractive. Does the attractiveness of a schoolroom affect how students and teachers feel? A famous study by Maslow and Mintz (1956) provides some insight regarding an answer to this question.

In the Maslow and Mintz investigation, subjects were given a task to perform and assigned to one of three rooms. The first room was "ugly" and had been prepared to resemble a janitor's closet in disarray. The second was "average" (a professor's office). The third was "beautiful" in that it was clean and orderly with attractive furniture, drapes, and a carpet. Not surprisingly, individuals tried in various ways to avoid spending time in the ugly room. The ugly room was also reported to produce headache, fatigue, hostility, and other negative feelings. In contrast, the beautiful room produced feelings of pleasure and energy for those performing the task in that setting. This study, then, provides evidence that the attractiveness of a room influences how we feel. Of equal or greater concern to teachers is the effect of room attractiveness on cognitive learning. A recent study by Franzolino (1977) sheds some light on the relationship.

Franzolino assigned three small groups of college students to different rooms. As in the Maslow and Mintz study, the rooms were intended to be ugly, average, or beautiful. In the ugly room the walls were painted a pale "institutional" green, the plaster was cracked, the windows were covered with yellowed venetian blinds, and the wooden tables and chairs were scarred with initials and other graffiti. The average room had beige-colored wallpaper, the chairs were of a modern design with vinyl seats, the tables had formica tops in good condition, and the floor was covered with linoleum. The beautiful room had dark wood paneling, attractively framed oil paintings, soft-cushion seats, new wooden tables in undamaged condition, and a carpet. All three rooms were approximately the same size. Temperature, lighting, and the time of day at which the study was conducted were held constant.

Students listened to tape-recorded instructions on how to play the game "Risk." Each student then individually completed a multiple-choice paper and pencil test to assess his or her understanding of the game. Then, pooling their knowledge, they again completed the test, this time working together as a small group. The individual and the group scores on the test did not differ between the beautiful and average rooms, but both sets of scores were higher for these two rooms than those obtained by students in the ugly room.

From these two investigations, and others which we have not discussed here but which provide similar findings, we can conclude that the attractiveness of classrooms is important: Individuals feel better and learn more in attractive surroundings than in ugly ones. The implication of course is that you should attempt to make your classroom as attractive as possible. While you may have little control over color, temperature, overcrowding, furniture, and lighting, you do have the potential to influence the attractiveness of the environment. And doing so does not have to be costly. We have seen austere "institutional" rooms dramatically transformed into pleasant settings simply through the addition of a few travel agency posters, plants, brightly colored crepe paper, and student artwork. Margie, the little girl whose comments introduced this chapter, had some very specific ideas about how she would change her classroom. You may be quite surprised to find how much more attractive your room could be if students are given the opportunity to apply their imaginations to its decoration.

In this section we have seen that specific aspects of the school and classroom environment can affect how people learn and how they feel about themselves and others. The following principles are intended to summarize the conclusions which can be drawn from our review. In the next section we examine the direct effect another aspect of the environment, seating arrangement, has on interaction in the classroom.

PRINCIPLES 6.1

1. We are largely unaware of our environment and the ways in which it affects us.
2. The use of coordinated color selections in schools can have positive effects on student achievement and attitudes.
3. Research findings have failed to demonstrate that windowless classrooms produce harmful consequences.
4. Overcrowding for brief periods has negative effects on mood and satisfaction with the environment and tasks, but not on learning.
5. Excessive heat has negative effects on mood and on liking for the environment and tasks.
6. Unattractive surroundings have negative effects on mood as well as on learning.

CLASSROOM ARRANGEMENT

Stroll down a school hallway and peer into classrooms. You are most likely to see the teacher standing or sitting at the front of the room, with students in chairs arranged in an orderly pattern of rows and columns. We noted earlier that one design authority, Robert Sommer, suggests that the row-column arrangement evolved because of the necessity to use natural light for illumination. But why does this pattern still prevail today? Probably not because teachers experiment with a variety of patterns and find the row-column to be the best, but rather because of tradition. You grew up with the row-column arrangement. You know it. You feel comfortable with it, and you and your students are probably reluctant to leave the security of the known for the uncertainty any new structuring will bring. Because classrooms can be arranged in ways limited only by your imagination, however, we believe it is important that you understand how the structure of a classroom affects the communication which takes place there. After reading the following section you may decide to use the row-column pattern in your classroom. That's your decision. You should, however, be aware of the consequences of ordering your environment in this way, and of alternatives to the row-column pattern and the advantages they possess.

Adams and Biddle (1970) used hidden cameras and microphones to make videotape recordings of 32 lessons in 16 classrooms. Half the lessons were in social studies and the other half in arithmetic or mathematics. Classes at the first-, sixth-, and eleventh-grade levels were observed. Teachers were equally divided as to sex, while half were under 30 years of age and the other half were over 40. While Adams and Biddle were interested primarily in *what* teachers and students said to one another, we are most concerned with their findings regarding *who* spoke in the classroom. Obviously, teachers talked—a lot. But which students participated? The videotapes revealed that almost all pupils who made comments sat in the front-center section of the room—an area the investigators called the "action zone." As can be seen in Figure 6.1, this area consisted of the three positions lying in a central zone down the center of the room and the two seats at the front on either side of this vertical line. Students in these seats not only made the most comments, they were also the most frequent targets of comments made by the teacher. This pattern, with slight variations, was observed in all the classrooms studied, regardless of the subject matter, grade level, or sex or age of the teacher.

There are at least two explanations why students in the action zone seats participate more than students sitting elsewhere. The first suggests that greater visual contact occurs between the teacher and students in the front-center location. Breed and Colaiuta (1974) found that students in the action zone looked at the teacher more than students in other seats.

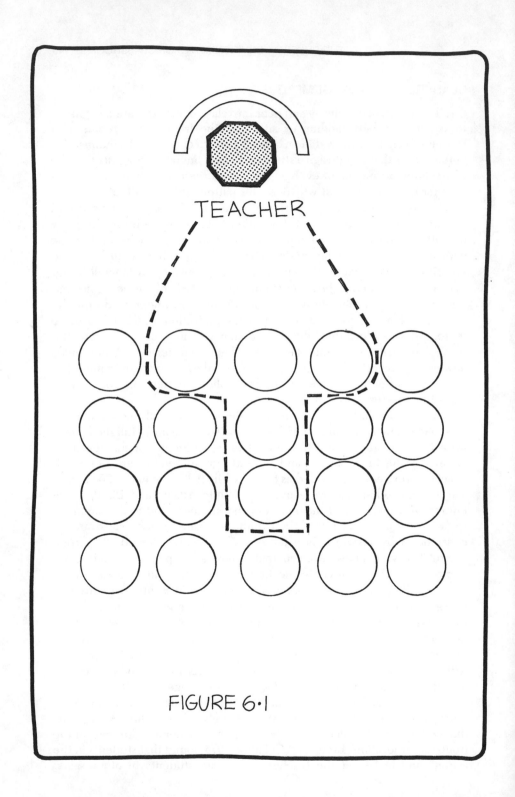

TEACHER

FIGURE 6·1

Because teachers tend to occupy the center-front of the classroom, it seems quite reasonable that they are best able to see the eyes of students in the action zone, and vice versa. Franzolino (1975) has suggested that such eye contact serves two functions which influence student attentiveness and participation:

1. *Eye contact regulates interaction.* Speakers tend to look away when beginning long statements, looking back at their listeners when finished. In this way speaker-listener roles are transferred. Because pupils in the action seats are able to view the teacher's eye movements, they may be better able than students in the back and side positions to determine when it is appropriate to comment.

2. *Eye contact serves as a stimulus to participate.* A teacher might make eye contact with a student not merely to indicate that he may say something if he wishes, but also to indicate that the teacher *expects* him to comment. A prolonged gaze might also be used to warn students to be more attentive. Students sitting outside the action zone would be expected to be less affected by the stimulatory effect of the teacher's gaze.

The second explanation for the existence of the action zone is that students choosing these seats desire more interaction with their teachers than students who sit elsewhere. Walberg (1969) found that students who chose to sit in the front of the room were likely to fit the stereotype of the model student: They liked school, believed it was important to be bright and get good grades, and wanted to be considered hard workers by teachers. In contrast, students who chose the back of the room didn't like school, were unconcerned about high grades, and tended to be more introverted, expressing a preference for work that allowed them to be by themselves.

According to Mehrabian (1971), there is a universal tendency for people to approach things they like and draw away from things they dislike. Walberg's study suggests that students who sit in the action zone like classroom activities. Those choosing to position themselves at increasingly greater distances from the teacher may be expressing a negative attitude.

In addition to attitude toward school and specific subjects or teachers, the extent to which a student simply enjoys talking in class may influence his or her seat choice. Koneya (1973), for example, observed college students in one setting and identified them as "high," "moderate," or "low" verbalizers. He found that in the traditional row-column classroom setting, high verbalizers chose action zone seats more frequently than moderates or lows.

To summarize, we have reviewed research which suggests that students seated in front-center seats participate more because of the increased visual interaction they experience with their teacher. On the other hand, there is evidence that students selecting these seats participate more because they have positive attitudes toward classroom activities and like to talk more than pupils who sit at the back and sides. Which explanation do you favor? Koneya's research suggests that both may be correct—seat location as well as the personal characteristics of students seem to influence participation. This conclusion is based on his finding that moderates who sat in the action zone participated more than moderates who sat outside the central area. The same was found for high verbalizers. Low verbalizers, however, tended to maintain their silence no matter where they sat.

Having taken you through this rather lengthy examination of student participation patterns in row-column seating arrangements, let's consider the consequences of using such a seating structure:

1. *Students who sit outside the action zone do not participate much.* Should you be concerned about participation, and if so, why? As noted in Chapter 1, the basic reason for putting students and teachers together is the assumption that interaction will facilitate learning. Adams and Biddle (1970) believe that teachers should try to maximize participation for two reasons: (1) Student responses provide the teacher with information about how well they are learning; and (2) by participating, students may become more involved and develop a greater interest in learning.

2. *Interaction between and among students is severely restricted.* Students at the front of the room can't see (and may also have difficulty in hearing) students at the rear, and vice versa. At any moment, only one pupil or the teacher can be talking. The rest of the students must be passive listeners. Comments exchanged between seat neighbors must usually be discouraged. Discussion is restricted to a single topic at a time. To maintain order, the teacher must take on the role of the autocrat, deciding who may speak, in what order, and for how long.

3. *Teachers will be distant from many students much of the time.* Adams and Biddle's (1970) videotapes revealed that teachers tended to utilize only three areas of the room: the "center stage" (center-front), the "inland strip" (up the middle), and the "ring road" (around the perimeter).

   When the teacher moves about the room, such movements tend to take one of three patterns: the "footlight parade," the "inland excursion," and the "grand tour." Adams and Biddle describe each of these travel patterns. In the following description note particularly the amount of time teachers spend in each of the three sections:

1. The footlight parade covers an area across the front of the room but mainly at the center-front. Teachers on an average spend sixty-eight percent of their total time there.
2. The inland excursion consists of a track leading from the center-front of the room, up the middle of the room and back. Teachers visit with specific children in the inland for some eight percent of the time.
3. The grand tour is a general perambulation around the room. For fifteen percent of the time that they are in the classroom, teachers perambulate. Characteristically, the grand tour involves sight seeing only—no visits are made. The primary purposes it seems are to indicate interest, show a supervisory "flag," or to provide exercise for the teacher. (p. 65)

It appears, then, that with continued use of the row-column arrangement, teachers tend to stake out certain areas of the room (notably, the front-center) just as students claim seats to which they return day after day. In addition, just as students tend to defend "their" seats from would-be invaders, teachers tend to keep pupils from the space they have claimed in the classroom. Adams and Biddle report that in 27 of the 32 class sessions they studied, students *never* entered the teacher's zone during the lessons.

For the 68 percent of the lesson time the teacher remains at the front of the room, students at the rear and sides are certainly not within easy conversational distance of the teacher. In fact, to be heard in a room with poor acoustics, a young child may literally have to shout. At a distance of 25 to 35 feet, it is also difficult (if not impossible) for the teacher to create the impression that he or she is dealing with each pupil on a personal and individual basis.

Are there no activities for which the row-column seating pattern is suitable? Unquestionably, there are, and we will identify some shortly. What teachers need to do, however, is to use row-column seating *only* when it is appropriate and not to use it when other patterns are more suited to the activity planned.

Alternative Seating Arrangements

Richardson (1970) has suggested five different patterns of seat arrangement designed to facilitate five different classroom activities. First, let's consider the row-column pattern. Whenever you wish to minimize interaction between students, such as while they are taking a test or doing independent seatwork, the row-column arrangement is appropriate. When the activity requires work in small groups, however, interaction can best be facilitated by pushing the desks together so that students can sit face-to-face and talk with one another. This pattern also permits maximum space to exist between groups to minimize distractions (see Figure 6.2).

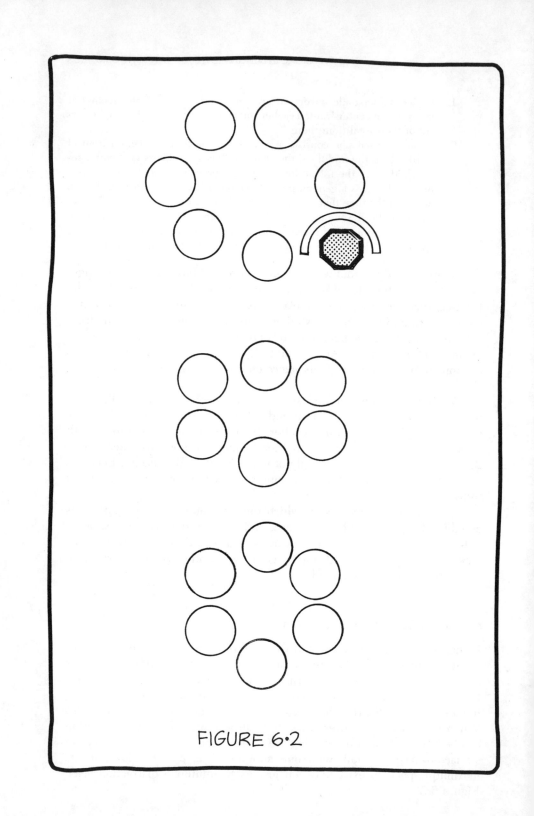

FIGURE 6·2

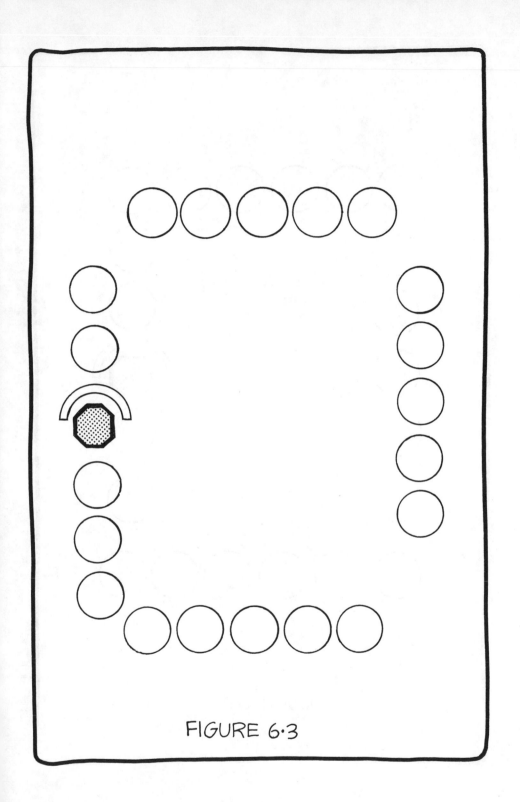

FIGURE 6·3

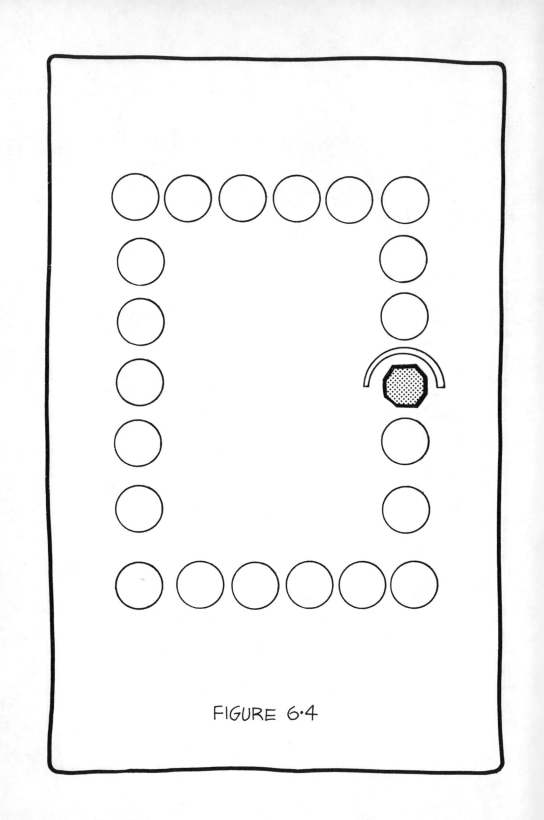

FIGURE 6·4

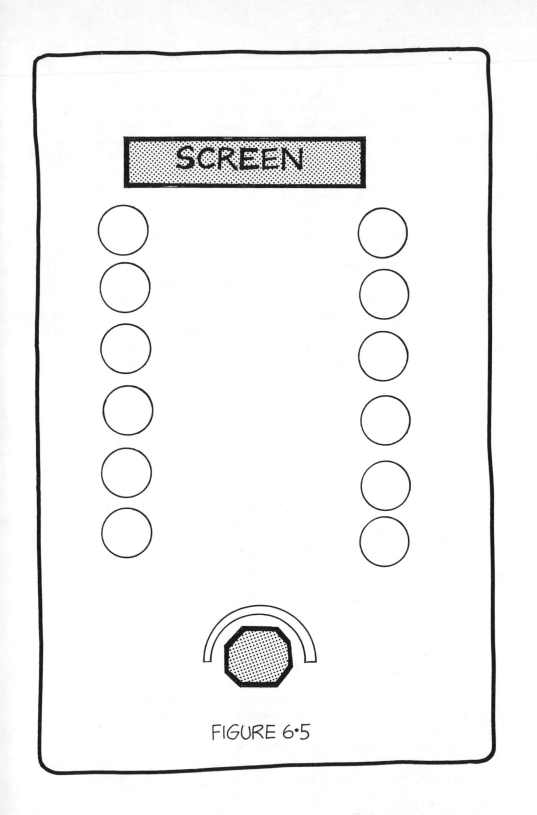

SCREEN

FIGURE 6·5

Suppose that after the small groups have completed their tasks you wish to have each group make a report to the rest of the class. What arrangement would you choose? For this activity the members of the group making the report could arrange their desks in the shape of a long table at the front of the room. The remainder of the desks could be pushed against the wall and the students who were audience members could arrange their chairs in a large horseshoe or semicircle (see Figure 6.3).

Discussion involving all members of the class is a goal you may frequently seek, so let's consider large-group discussion as the fourth activity. To maximize student involvement and minimize your role as controller of the discussion, use the hollow rectangle arrangement shown in Figure 6.4 and select a seat for yourself in the formation.

Finally, consider activities in which you are using a film, slide, or overhead projector to show images on a screen at the front of the room. If the chairs are divided into two lines along the sides of the room, leaving a wide aisle in the center, students can alternate between looking at the screen and at you as the activity demands (see Figure 6.5).

As Richardson explains, each seating arrangement is designed to facilitate a different pattern of interaction. In the first, the teacher wishes to keep interaction at a minimum. In the second, there is no central leader directing the interaction of all the students, although the teacher is free to move about the room, providing advice when students seek it. In the third arrangement, the teacher delegates the leadership role to the small group of students making the presentation. The teacher underscores his or her role as an audience member by sitting with the other students. In the fourth pattern the teacher may assume leadership of the discussion with either little or great involvement as the situation demands. Leadership can also be delegated to a student, while the teacher assumes the role of a group member. In the fifth pattern, the teacher uses media to provide information, still allowing students an opportunity to interact with him or her and each other in a more effective fashion than can be achieved with row-column seating.

A CONCLUDING NOTE

We have tried in this chapter to increase your awareness of the physical environment of the classroom. As you have seen, this environment can have a significant influence on learning, moods, and interpersonal communication. You should realize, however, that the ultimate effect of the environment depends on how people adapt to it.

A student we know recently interviewed professors and students to discover their reactions to a new university classroom building. The building was a school designer's dream: Lighting and acoustics were excellent, a variety of multimedia devices was built into each room, and all rooms were carpeted and attractively painted and furnished. Those who taught there had maximum flexibility in the use of space, as all chairs, and in some rooms even walls, were portable. Despite these model conditions, the interviews revealed that few professors had changed their teaching methods. The majority continued to lecture without using the slide, movie, or overhead projectors available. Few rearranged the portable seats to better facilitate discussion. Instead, row-column seating was the norm, and classroom activities in the new building could have as readily been conducted in the oldest structures on campus. The point here is that it does little good to change the environment if teachers are unwilling to change their teaching methods.

Just as teachers are creatures of habit in the ways they respond to the classroom environment, so too are students. Confirm this observation for yourself. At the beginning of the term go to each of your new classes early and scatter the chairs about the room. It has been our experience that arriving students invariably rearrange the chairs in a row-column arrangement. We have observed this response even in very small classes where it was highly unlikely that the professor would conduct the class by the lecture method.

Many students expect to sit in rows and columns, and, for the most part, be passive. Hence they may be very resistant to changes in the seating arrangement and require time to adjust. You shouldn't expect, for example, that, as soon as you put the chairs in a horseshoe pattern, the whole class will suddenly participate in the discussion. After several days of using the pattern, however, some marked changes in participation should be evident.

As Friedrich, Galvin, and Book (1976) have observed,

> it is the interrelationship of people with the environment that creates learning and communication situations. The physical setting creates an atmosphere which is more or less conducive to certain types of communication but it is the human factor that activates or ignores the potential. (p. 34)

PRINCIPLES 6.2

1. In a row-column seating arrangement, pupils in the front-center section participate the most.
2. The high participation of students sitting in the action zone may be a function of seat location as well as the personal characteristics of the students.
3. When a row-column seating arrangement is used, students who sit outside the action zone have low participation rates, interaction between and among students is limited, and the teacher is distant from many students much of the time.
4. Rather than constantly using the row-column arrangement, teachers should try to match the seating pattern to the classroom activity.

REFERENCES

Adams, R. S., and Biddle, B. J. *Realities of teaching: Explorations with video tape*. New York: Holt, Rinehart and Winston, 1970.

Birren, F. The significance of light. *American Institute of Architects Journal*, 1972, **58**, 16–19.

Breed, G. and Colaiuta, V. Looking, blinking and sitting: Nonverbal dynamics in the classroom. *Journal of Communication*, 1974, **24**, 75–81.

Coles, R. Those places they call schools. *Harvard Education Review*, 1969, **39**, 46–57.

Franzolino, P. The relationship among classroom seating preference, student personality characteristics, and course achievement. Master's thesis, University of Texas at Austin, 1975.

Franzolino, P. Effect of aesthetic environment on individual and group task performance. Unpublished manuscript, Department of Speech Communication, University of Texas at Austin, 1977.

Freedman, J. L. The crowd—Maybe not so madding after all. *Psychology Today*, 1971, **5**, 58–61.

Friedrich, G. W., Galvin, K. M., and Book, C. L. *Growing together: Classroom communication*. Columbus, Ohio: Merrill, 1976.

Griffith, W. Environmental effects on interpersonal affective behavior: Ambient effective temperature and attraction. *Journal of Personality and Social Psychology*, 1970, **15**, 240–244.

Griffith, W., and Veitch, R. Hot and crowded: Influences of population density and temperature on interpersonal affective behavior. *Journal of Personality and Social Psychology*, 1971, **17**, 92–98.

Koneya, M. The relationship between verbal interaction and seat location of members of large groups. Ph.D. dissertation, University of Denver, 1973.

Mehrabian, A. *Silent messages*. Belmont, Calif.: Wadsworth, 1971.

Maslow, A. H., and Mintz, N. L. Effects of esthetic surroundings: I. Initial effects of three esthetic conditions upon perceiving "energy" and "well being" in faces. *Journal of Psychology*, 1956, **41**, 247–254.

Papadatos, S. A. Color in the classroom. *School Management*, 1972, **16**, 26.

Proshansky, H. M., Ittelson, W. H., and Rivlin, L. G. The influence of the physical environment on behavior: Some basic assumptions. In H. M. Proshansky, W. H. Ittelson, and L. G. Rivlin (Eds.), *Environmental psychology*. New York: Holt, Rinehart and Winston, 1970, pp. 27–37.

Richardson, E. The physical setting and its influence on learning. In H. M. Proshansky, W. H. Ittelson, and L. G. Rivlin (Eds.), *Environmental psychology*. New York: Holt, Rinehart and Winston, 1970, pp. 386–397.

Rosenfeld, L. B., and Civikly, J. M. *With words unspoken: The nonverbal experience*. New York: Holt, Rinehart and Winston, 1976.

Sommer, R. *Personal space: The behavioral basis of design*. Englewood Cliffs, N.J.: Prentice-Hall, 1969.

Sommer, R., and Becker, F. D. Room density and user satisfaction. *Environment and Behavior*, 1971, **3**, 412–417.

Tognoli, J. The effect of windowless rooms and unembellished surroundings on attitudes and retention. *Environment and Behavior*, 1973, **5**, .191–201.

Walberg, J. W. Physical and psychological distance in the classroom. *School Review,* 1969, **77**, 64–70.

Wexner, L. B. The degree to which colors (hues) are associated with mood tones. *Journal of Applied Psychology,* 1954, **38**, 432–435.

Chapter 7
Influencing Student Attitudes: the Process of Persuasion in the Classroom

OBJECTIVES

After reading this chapter, you should be able to:

1. explain why it is important that students have positive attitudes toward learning, the schooling process, and the subject matter you teach.
2. define the concept of attitude.
3. explain how you can identify students' attitudes.
4. provide examples of what students are likely to say or do when they like the subject matter you teach.
5. describe the possible outcomes of any persuasive attempt.
6. describe what conditions must exist before you can conclude that your persuasive efforts were successful.
7. identify two reasons why students differ in their responses to your persuasive efforts.
8. identify and explain three principles from learning theory which can be applied to the persuasion process.
9. provide examples of tokens which are appropriate for the classroom context.

10. identify advantages and disadvantages of using tokens to reward.
11. provide examples of verbal and nonverbal teacher praise.
12. identify advantages and disadvantages of using praise to reward.
13. explain the relationship between credibility and persuader effec-
    tiveness.
14. identify and describe three dimensions of credibility.
15. define initial and derived credibility.

In the previous chapters we considered the verbal and nonverbal
coding systems and the process of communication as it takes place in
classrooms. In short, we examined *how* teachers and students communicate. In later chapters we continue our study of factors which affect the
communication process. At this point, however, we shift the focus to
consider one important reason *why* teachers communicate.

Why do teachers communicate? Obviously they do so in large part to
bring about a desired change in learners, be it concerned with the *knowledge* required to solve linear equations, the *skill* required to adjust a
carburetor, or the *attitude* necessary to appreciate art. Regardless of the
nature of the learning objective, or the age or ability of students, all
teachers should also communicate to achieve this goal: to have students
acquire favorable attitudes toward learning, the schooling process, and
particular subject matter. This goal is of critical importance for two reasons.

Gagné and Briggs (1974) suggest that it is impossible to overemphasize the impact of students' attitudes on how readily they learn. You
can quickly confirm the truth of this observation for yourself. If you had
acquired a negative attitude toward learning and the schooling process,
you undoubtedly would not be reading these words. Perhaps, however,
you did dislike a particular subject or course. Our experience suggests
that virtually everyone has not only disliked, but has really *hated* some
course or subject encountered along the way. If so, recall how that dislike
affected your willingness to come to class, pay attention in class, cooper-
ate with the teacher, do homework, and even try to learn. It's a safe bet
that when students dislike a subject they avoid doing all the above. The
result? Learning about the subject becomes more likely *not* to occur.

The second reason teachers should be concerned with the attitudes
of students deals with the future. It is Mager's (1968) view that teachers
should be interested in more than just short-term changes in their students. You know from your own experiences that you were able to complete most (if not all) of those required courses you simply couldn't avoid.
You gritted your teeth and stayed with it—no matter how painful. But
what about after the courses were completed? Did you seek opportunities

FIGURE 7·1 STRIVE TO SEND STUDENTS AWAY WITH POSITIVE FEELINGS ABOUT LEARNING.

to use the knowledge you had acquired? Did you take more advanced courses in the field? Our guess is that you stayed as far away as possible from anything resembling the dreaded area. Now, when a student leaves a course feeling so negatively about the subject matter, can the teacher be satisfied, no matter how well the student has mastered the learning objectives?

Mager says "no!" Students should acquire knowledge, skills, and attitudes for some use in the future, be they to satisfy life, career, or new learning needs. When a student leaves a course disliking the subject matter, he or she is likely to avoid the area in the future and quickly forget what has been learned. Furthermore, negative attitudes developed toward a particular course may become generalized to the whole schooling experience. Probably very few children arrive at the schoolhouse steps for the first time with intensely negative attitudes toward learning and education. There is an abundance of evidence, however, that after spending time in school many develop exactly such feelings. The acquisition of a hatred of learning and school at whatever grade level can virtually ensure that the child or adolescent will be highly resistant to any attempts by teachers to assist him or her in learning in all subsequent grades.

We might conclude, then, that all teachers should strive to send students away with positive rather than negative feelings about learning and schooling, as well as about specific subjects. In this condition students are willing to use what they have learned and eager to learn more, not only about a particular subject but about all subjects.

Attaining the goal of developing positive attitudes in students requires teachers to be effective persuaders. We have already given some attention to the process of persuasion in Chapter 2, when we considered how teachers can influence students' self-concepts. In this chapter we examine in greater detail the nature of persuasion and persuasive strategies teachers can employ.

THE NATURE OF INFLUENCE

Karlins and Abelson (1970, p. 2) have observed that the act of persuasion is as old as humanity: "Eve accomplished it in Eden; so did Mark Antony and so does Madison Avenue." Furthermore, the art of persuasion has been studied and written about for thousands of years. According to Simons (1976, p. 4), "One of the first books in recorded history could be considered a treatise on the subject; it was a handbook on how to flatter the Pharoah." While study of the process of influence is thus very old, the systematic scientific study of it is relatively new. Given its importance in our lives and our fascination with it, it is not surprising that more social scientists are actively engaged in its study today than at any other time. Beiseker and Parson (1972) noted that, from 1954 to 1972, more than 1500 reports of research investigations on some aspect of the process of persuasion appeared in professional journals alone. Since the date of their observation, the massive stream of such research studies has continued to pour forth.

Despite this extensive research effort, we still do not know all about how humans influence one another, and particularly how teachers persuade students. Yet, these studies have yielded principles which can serve as helpful guidelines for designing persuasive efforts. Of course, you have been persuading others all your life. No matter how successful you have been in influencing mom and dad, brothers and sisters, and friends, however, you can expect to find that persuasion in the classroom presents some unique challenges. The more you know about the process, the more likely you are to be effective.

Where do we go from here? Well, achieving success in persuasion, as in most other endeavors, requires careful planning. It is first necessary to define precisely your objectives as a persuader. In the following section this objectives-setting process is considered in detail.

IDENTIFYING YOUR PERSUASIVE OBJECTIVES

Your persuasive goal is to have students develop positive attitudes toward learning, the schooling process, and the subject(s) you teach. How will you know when you have succeeded? Well, it makes sense that you will first have to be able to recognize positive and negative attitudes when you see them.

This presents a problem. Despite the fact that each of us has thousands of attitudes, no one has ever seen one. Attitudes are internal states. They represent your evaluations of people, things, ideas, and events with regard to whether you like or dislike them. Although unseen, these generalized feelings of liking and disliking are important because they influence the choices you make—the person you vote for, the color of your car, your college major, and so forth (Gagné and Briggs, 1974).

Because attitudes influence choices, we infer a person's attitudes by observing what he or she chooses to do and say. For example, suppose you see a classmate, Frank, refuse a cigarette. On the basis of just this one observation, you wouldn't be ready to conclude that Frank has a negative attitude toward cigarettes. But imagine that you observe these additional incidents: Frank asks another person to put out a smoldering cigarette from which smoke is drifting into Frank's face; Frank wears a button proclaiming "Stamp Out Smoking"; Frank displays a sign on the dashboard of his car reading "Thank You for Not Smoking." What would you conclude? Frank doesn't like cigarettes! You infer this negative attitude from what you have heard Frank *say* and seen him *do*. And you could also infer that this generalized feeling of dislike toward cigarettes accounts for the whole set of different actions you have seen Frank perform.

Once you have identified Frank's attitude, you can become more accurate in predicting a variety of responses he will make in the future involving the attitude object—cigarettes. For instance, on the basis of what you already know, would you expect Frank to sign a petition supporting a ban on smoking in public places? Yes. What about the chances of his making a donation to the cancer society? Pretty good, right?

To quickly summarize, our likes and dislikes constitute our attitudes. We infer people's attitudes from our observations of how they choose to act. Once we have identified a person's attitudes, we can often improve our accuracy in predicting how that individual will choose to act in the future. If, for instance, we determine that a student has a negative attitude toward school, we would expect him to avoid school as much as possible, such as by playing hooky, feigning sickness, or dropping out.

Now that we have considered in a general way the nature of attitudes, let's return to the problem of identifying the specific attitudes students hold. How do you know what attitudes students have? Remember that attitudes must be inferred from what people say and do. Since you're a student, why not take a look at yourself? What are five things you are likely to say and/or do when you *like* a college course?

1. _____
2. _____
3. _____
4. _____
5. _____

We can't examine what you wrote, but it wouldn't be surprising if you found some of your statements in the left-hand column in Table 7.1. The right-hand column is likely to include some things you might say or do when you dislike a class.

This list isn't exhaustive, and it isn't intended to be. Rather, its purpose is to provide you with a few illustrations of responses students make which reveal their attitudes. Can you make additions to the list? Blanks are included at the bottom of both columns for you to do so.

To identify other signs of positive and negative attitudes, you might take a close look at your fellow students in your courses for the current term. As we cautioned earlier, however, you can't infer a person's attitudes on the basis of only a few observations. With observation of a classmate over several course meetings, however, you can make a judgment about his or her attitude toward the course. Likewise, if you consciously look for signs of positive and negative attitudes in the responses of

Table 7.1   ATTITUDE INDICATORS

SIGNS OF POSITIVE ATTITUDES	SIGNS OF NEGATIVE ATTITUDES
Arrives at class on time, or early	Arrives late to class
Rarely misses class meetings	Cuts class at every opportunity
Gives close attention to lecture, discussion, or seatwork	Sleeps, reads comic books or other material unrelated to class, talks to neighbors, looks out window, watches clock
Smiles at teacher when appropriate	Frowns most of the time
Asks questions and makes comments	Refuses to answer questions, is silent, grumbles, makes noises (e.g., barnyard animals)
Appears to be comfortable in seat	Fidgets and squirms in seat, leaves seat, leaves classroom
Looks at teacher	Refuses to look at teacher
Stays after class to talk with teacher or other students	Immediately flees class when period ends
Tells others: "I really like this course"	Tells others: "I really hate this course"
Does unrequired outside reading and attends unrequired course-related activities	Avoids unrequired reading and activities like the plague
Completes assignments	Doesn't complete assignments
Turns in assignments on time	Turns in assignments after due date
Seeks contact with teacher outside of class	Avoids contact with teacher outside of class at all costs
Others?	Others?
_____	_____
_____	_____
_____	_____
_____	_____

your students when you are teaching, you will be able to place each student on the following scale:

STUDENT ATTITUDE TOWARD WHAT I TEACH

(7) _____ Extremely positive
(6) _____ Very positive
(5) _____ Positive
(4) _____ Neutral
(3) _____ Negative
(2) _____ Very negative
(1) _____ Extremely negative

Students whose attitudes you identify as being at point 7 on the scale are those whose responses can be interpreted on all (or almost all) occasions as signs of liking for the subject matter. Attitudes at point 1, in contrast, always (or almost always) indicate disliking. Under most circumstances you can expect most students to be somewhere between these two extremes.

While you should be concerned about students' attitudes toward the whole schooling experience, their attitude toward *what you teach* may be your most important concern when they sit in your class. If you can't persuade them to like your subject(s), then your chances for persuading them to develop more positive attitudes toward learning and the schooling process are likely to be slim. So, let's return to the problem posed at the beginning of this section, now focusing on what you teach: How will you know when you have achieved your persuasive objective of influencing your students to have positive attitudes toward your subject(s)? Must you be able to say that every student leaves your class with an attitude that falls at point 5, 6, or 7 on the scale in order to claim success? What about students who already have positive attitudes when they enter your class? Do you exclude them from consideration?

To answer these questions, let's first consider the instance in which a teacher, Mr. Jones, infers that a particular student, George, has an extremely negative attitude toward Mr. Jones' course, Introductory French. Disregarding for the moment the techniques Mr. Jones may use to change George's attitude, consider the possible outcomes of his persuasive efforts.

Mr. Jones' efforts would be characterized as wildly successful if George became the outstanding student in Introductory French, was elected president of the French Club, and volunteered to work after school in the language lab without pay. In short, success would be total if George developed an extremely positive attitude. On the other hand, it is possible that Mr. Jones' attempts at persuasion might have a "boomerang" effect. The boomerang effect would occur if George developed an even more negative attitude. Such would be the result, for example, if he stopped coming to French class entirely. When a boomerang effect occurs, the persuasive attempt is unquestionably unsuccessful.

How likely is it that George will develop an extremely positive attitude toward French after just one course with Mr. Jones? Not very. Why? Because extreme changes in attitudes don't usually occur that quickly. George's very negative attitude is likely to have been acquired gradually as a result of many experiences with schools, particular teachers, parents, peers, and other important people in his life. It would hence be very unlikely to expect a complete turnabout in attitude position in a very short time. Does this mean, then, that Mr. Jones should simply write George off as a hopeless case? No, it doesn't.

Between the extremes of total conversion and the boomerang effect are several other possible outcomes. French may not become George's favorite subject, but he might increase his study time of the language from zero to three hours a week. He might turn in 25 percent of the homework

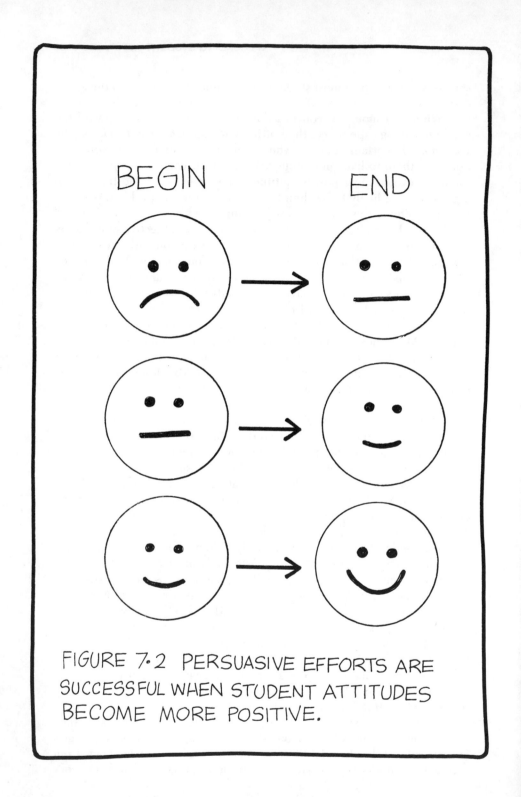

BEGIN   END

FIGURE 7·2 PERSUASIVE EFFORTS ARE SUCCESSFUL WHEN STUDENT ATTITUDES BECOME MORE POSITIVE.

assignments, up from his former average of 0 percent. He might come to class 60 percent rather than 30 percent of the time. Are these signs of persuasive success? You bet they are. *Conclusion:* If, as a result of Mr. Jones' efforts, George becomes in *any measure* more positive toward French, then we may say the persuasive attempt was successful.

Before finishing this section a word or two about the student who already has a positive attitude should be included. A student's attitude doesn't have to be negative to warrant your attention. For the student with a positive attitude, you should attempt to increase the strength or intensity of the attitude, that is, make it more positive. It is not often necessary, for instance, to persuade students who join the French Club to have positive attitudes toward French. It may be quite likely, however, that many of the club-sponsored functions are undertaken with the purpose of strengthening commitment to this view. In such instances, we say that persuasion has occurred if the learner increases his or her commitment to a position, and that persuasion has not occurred if the attitude is unchanged or becomes less positive.

If the preceding examples have been of value, you should now be able to say what persuasion is. We stated in Chapter 1 that communication was an event. Persuasion is also an event. Communication occurs when one person assigns meaning to the behavior of another. Persuasion is one specific outcome of communication. *Persuasion occurs when one person acts in ways which bring about an intended change in the attitude of another.* The emphasis in this definition is on the effect—the outcome—of interaction between two people. The outcome must be an intended change in attitude, for no matter what is said or done, if intended change does not occur, then there has been no persuasion.

What is the implication of this definition for you as a would-be persuader? Just this: No matter whether learners have a positive, neutral, or negative attitude when you first meet them, your objective is to persuade them to have a more positive attitude toward what you teach. If students are making more positive responses toward the subject matter when the term ends than when it began, you have succeeded (Mager, 1968).

The following principles should help to clarify the relationship of attitudes, persuasion, and your persuasive objective as a teacher. In the section that follows, we examine how that persuasive objective can be achieved.

PRINCIPLES 7.1

1. Students' attitudes affect how readily they learn and their willingness to use what has been learned.
2. Attitudes are internal states which represent evaluations of people, things, ideas, and events.

3. When students voluntarily put themselves in contact with certain subject matter, positive attitudes may be inferred. When students avoid contact with certain subject matter, negative attitudes may be inferred.
4. Whether a student has a positive, neutral, or negative attitude at the outset, your objective is to persuade him or her to have a more positive attitude toward what you teach.
5. If a student is making more positive responses toward the subject matter when the term ends than when it began, your persuasive efforts have been successful.

ACHIEVING INFLUENCE IN THE CLASSROOM

Because no one has yet found a totally reliable explanation of how humans influence one another, there are several competing theories and strategies of persuasion. We can't even begin to consider them all. Instead, we examine one strategy based on reinforcement theory, which has been demonstrated to be highly effective in a variety of settings and which has the added advantage of being easy to understand and use.

At the conclusion of the preceding section we said that persuasion occurs when one person acts in ways which bring about a change in the attitudes of another. *Learning* can also be defined as change—the somewhat permanent change that occurs when individuals interact with people, as well as with other aspects of their environment. Many of us typically think of learning as being limited to the cognitive skills required to read, spell, or do multiplication, or to the motor skills needed to ride a bike or throw a ball. Attitudes, however, are also human capabilities which develop in children in ways similar to cognitive and motor abilities. If we can view the changes in student attitudes you wish to bring about as learning, then it makes sense to look to principles of learning theory to determine how you might be the most successful in attaining your goal.

One of the most consistent findings of learning research is that people differ in the way they learn. Hence you can expect diverse responses from students to your persuasive efforts. Bettinghaus (1973) suggests two principles which help to account for such differences.

1. *Students differ in their ability to respond.* This principle recognizes that students differ in what they are capable of doing. Unlike college classes in which students are often very similar in ability, much greater ranges of ability typically exist at the elementary and secondary levels. What is important to remember is that *before* a student can respond in the way you want her to, it is necessary to make certain that she is assigning the meaning to your behavior that you intended. As indicated in Chapter 1, the pupil's physical and psychological condition, competence in the use of verbal and nonverbal codes, and numerous other variables affect her ability to interpret your messages as you intended.

2. *Students vary in their readiness to respond.* Rosenfeld and Civikly (1976, p. 33) state, "Biological rhythms affect our capacity to perceive, respond, and perform according to outside stimuli, and may help explain a good deal of our interpersonal behavior." Three of these biorhythms are our physical, sensitivity, and intellectual cycles which occur, respectively, in 23-day, 28-day, and 33-day cycles from birth. For the first 11½ days of our physical cycle we have abundant energy, during the next 11½ days our energy is reduced. For the first 14 days of the sensitivity cycle we are likely to be cheerful, but more irritable and depressed during the last 14 days. Finally, with respect to the intellectual cycle, the first 16½ days should be the most productive for studying and learning, while our ability to perform such tasks is lowered during the last 16½ days. In addition to these rather long cycles, each person can expect to hit "high" and "low" periods during each day in which his or her ability to learn, attention span, and so on, is greatest or least.

   The point here is that, even if all students were of equal ability, each would differ at any moment in the school day (week or month) in readiness to respond. Regrettably, even if you could determine each student's optimal periods for attending and learning, such information would be of little value unless instruction could be completely individualized. You must accept the fact you have little control over students' readiness to respond, although this variable has a great influence on your success at persuasion.

These two principles regarding differences in ability and readiness to respond should help you to understand better the responses students make to your persuasive attempts. Bettinghaus (1973) suggests that, when a persuader knows exactly what responses he or she wishes to obtain, the use of additional principles from learning theory is valuable in achieving the persuasive objective. Three such principles are considered here.

1. *Reward responses to establish them.* The cardinal assumption of the reinforcement theory of persuasion is that people are motivated to seek rewards. Like many of the other concepts you encounter in your study of communication and instruction, you are already familiar with how reinforcement works to affect how people behave. Although they may not have been aware of it, your parents used the principles of this theory to influence your behavior, even as an infant. When you performed a desirable action, such as eating your oatmeal, you were rewarded with chin chucking, smiles, and exclamations of "good!" This pattern was repeated thousands of times throughout your childhood: When you behaved in a desired fashion, you received rewards. The way in which these rewards worked to affect your behavior can be

explained in terms of these principles of reinforcement theory:

a. When behavior is rewarded, it tends to be repeated.

b. When behavior is not rewarded, it tends not to be repeated.

c. When rewards are provided for *new* behavior, that new behavior is likely to be repeated.

The implication of reinforcement theory for the persuader is that people will change their behavior in desired ways *if* they receive benefits for doing so.

Prior to giving rewards of course you must decide what rewards should be given. This is no easy task in that no single reward has the same effect on all students. For example, grades such as "A" and "B" (or their equivalent) have long been used by teachers to reward students. While such grades may function as powerful rewards for children from the competition-achievement-oriented middle class, they are often not meaningful consequences for pupils from other class origins. An important task, then, is to identify rewards which are sufficiently attractive to cause students to be willing to change their behavior in order to obtain them.

2. *The more often a response is rewarded, the more likely it is to become established.* A persuasive campaign to change students' attitudes to be more positive toward what you teach is not an undertaking begun and ended in the first two weeks of the term. Even if you are able to produce desired changes immediately, available research suggests that, without additional reinforcement, such changes will disappear and attitudes will return to their original positions. The implication is that, to maintain change, you must continue to reward.

3. *The shorter the time between the response and the reward, the more likely that the response will occur again.* Suppose, for example, that it is the third week of the term and Mary has yet to turn in any of the homework assignments. Today, however, as the students file from your class at the end of the period, Mary places the completed assignment on the pile with those of her classmates. Because you have little time to talk with her at the moment, you might make a mental note to write a special comment on her paper indicating how pleased you are that she attempted the assignment. The written comment is fine, but it will be at least 24 hours or longer before Mary receives it. While the written comment can still serve as a powerful reward, we also suggest that you speak with Mary *before* she leaves your classroom to praise her effort immediately.

The more closely the reward follows the response, the better. When there is a delay between the two events, the student will have made other responses, and the reward may come to be associated with responses other than the one you wished to increase.

Now, how do these learning principles apply to your development of a strategy to achieve your persuasive objective? Let's state your objective once again. It is to *increase the number of positive responses students make toward what you teach.* To use a reinforcement theory approach to persuasion, wait until the student makes a desired response. As shown in Table 7.1, such a response can range from such minimal behaviors as simply coming to class, to actions indicating increased interest, such as participating in nonrequired activities. When the student makes a desired response (whatever it might be), you act to provide a reward immediately. As noted earlier, to use reinforcement principles effectively, it is necessary that you identify and use rewards which work. In the following section some of the rewards available for use by teachers are examined.

Rewards

The various kinds of rewards which can be used by teachers can be sorted into several categories. The first category we consider has been called *tokens* by Dunkin and Biddle (1974). These are rewards whose value must be learned by students in the classroom context. Tokens take on value when they can be exchanged for something students desire. Tokens may be poker chips, gold stars, and the like. Although the use of tokens has received substantial attention in recent years, the practice of using them as rewards is quite old. Cureton (1971), for example, notes that in the 1880s medals were awarded to students. In some instances these medals could be exchanged for money (another token). In recent years, systems have been established in schools whereby students can exchange tokens for candy, toys, and even radios and television sets, although it is more typical to permit their exchange for some sought-after privilege such as free time or viewing movies.

Presuming that teachers are able to provide students with things they value in exchange for tokens earned, then the use of tokens as rewards has several advantages: (1) They can be awarded for whatever type of student response the teacher wishes to increase. (2) They can be given to students immediately after desired responses are made. (3) They provide students with the option of responding with no penalty for not responding. In this way the student's right to freedom of choice in behavior is maintained. (4) Finally, available research reveals that tokens are effective in increasing pupil involvement in the subject matter (Dunkin and Biddle, 1974).

Despite these advantages, there is a great obstacle to the use of tokens in traditional schools. Often, teachers may simply not have the needed resources to implement a token system effectively. With the exception of experimental programs, teachers will not have toys, money, clothing, and the like to distribute to students. In addition, in many traditional schools, teachers will not be able to structure the classroom and activities in such ways as to allow students access to movies, playground time, and other valued activities. This situation, more than any other, works effectively against the successful implementation of tokens as rewards.

A second major category of rewards is *teacher praise*. Unlike tokens, whose value must be learned by students in the classroom context, praise is frequently considered a reward which students learn to value long before coming to school (Dunkin and Biddle, 1974).

What constitutes teacher praise? Well, praise certainly consists of verbal responses. For example, when a student responds in some desired way, the teacher is likely to indicate approval by exclaiming "good!" Nonverbal actions accompany such verbal responses. Sometimes nonverbal acts alone convey approval. We considered several classes of such nonverbal behaviors in Chapter 5, but it may be helpful again to identify quickly some examples.

TABLE 7.2 SAMPLE NONVERBAL BEHAVIORS WHICH INDICATE APPROVAL

1. Body movement
   Placing index finger and thumb together in O.K. sign. Clapping. Nodding head up and down. Winking.
2. Facial expression
   Smiling.
3. Spatial relationships
   Approaching. Standing or sitting close. Turning head to face-to-face position.
4. Touch
   Patting, squeezing gently, holding, stroking.
5. Paralanguage
   Pitch, rate, and volume used together or singly to indicate approval.
6. Time
   Giving a student time to respond to a question. Giving students time to comment. Giving students time to interact individually or in small groups with the teacher.

We hasten to remind you of course that the meaning intended by a teacher or assigned by a student to any one or a combination of these acts is dependent upon the situation. Yet, when teachers respond in the ways identified above, most students, most of the time, interpret such acts as signs of praise.

What are the advantages of using praise as a reward? As with tokens, praise can be awarded for whatever type of student behavior the teacher wants to increase. It can be given immediately after desired responses are made, and there is no penalty to the student for not performing. Another advantage is that praise is readily available for use by all teachers at all grade levels in every type of instructional setting. Not only do teachers have an inexhaustible supply of this reward available, but the cost is right: Praise is absolutely free.

Significant as these advantages are, the greatest advantage of using praise, in our view, is that it allows the teacher to establish and maintain personal relationships with students, even in a class of 30. We noted in Chapter 1 that each pupil views his or her relationship with the teacher as interpersonal, one-to-one. To praise a student by word or nonverbal sign is to create an interpersonal bond between the two of you. To praise is to indicate that *you* are aware of *his or her* accomplishment as distinct from those of the other 29 children in the room. In addition, you can adapt praise to the individual needs of the student and situation (e.g., how much and how often) in a fashion not possible with tokens.

Having described in rather glowing terms the advantages of praise, we are obligated to identify some of the disadvantages, but also to suggest what you might do to overcome them.

First, you should recognize that in a multipupil classroom you can't reward every positive response a student makes toward what you teach. No matter how hard you try, you simply can't attend to each student all the time.

Second, many authorities argue that, to use praise with maximum effectiveness, you must do three things: (1) Work up an individual reward schedule for each student, observing and noting over time how different types of praise affect each learner. (2) Identify the minimal number of rewards each student needs and then follow a schedule to provide the minimum. (3) Develop an in-depth understanding of how a student has been praised in the past and adapt your praise accordingly.

Such procedures may be all well and good if you are working with a handful of students for the entire day. For a teacher with 35 students, however, let alone one who has six classes of 35 different learners, such practices simply aren't realistic.

Given these problems, is it even worth the effort to try and influence students with praise? Well, consider the alternative: For many teachers, no other rewards are available for use!

Despite these obstacles to using praise with maximum effectiveness, there are some positive aspects to think about. Even though you can't be aware of every positive response a student makes, you can praise many of the responses you do observe. Be mindful that, any time you notice a student doing something that indicates liking for what you teach, you have the opportunity to increase the likelihood that such a response will occur again.

Actions of praise need not be complex. A murmured "uh-huh," a smile, a nod of the head, or an O.K. sign take only a single second. Despite the ease with which teachers can provide praise, available evidence suggests that most don't take advantage of opportunities to do so,

FIGURE 7·3 TEACHERS HAVE AN INEXHAUSTIBLE SUPPLY OF PRAISE.

and that in typical classrooms praise is used sparingly. You can probably confirm this on the basis of your own experiences. How many teachers have you known who praised students (and particularly *you*) too much? Our guess is—not many.

The fact that many teachers don't use praise as much as they could suggests that they may be unaware of the way they respond to student behavior. We made the same point in Chapter 5. We suggested then that, whenever possible, you view videotape recordings of yourself to gain greater awareness of your nonverbal behavior. Now we suggest that you can also profit from viewing tapes of yourself in actual or simulated teaching situations to determine how often and how well you use praise.

To this point we have considered the types of messages which constitute teacher praise, and some of the advantages and disadvantages of using praise as a reward. No discussion of praise would be complete, however, without considering students' perceptions of teachers, for *the effect of teacher praise is dependent in large measure on such perceptions.*

Teacher Credibility

As mentioned earlier, it has often been assumed that children learn to seek praise through interactions with parents, hence that teacher praise is *always* a reward. In our opinion this view is not valid, because it assumes that the effects of praise are constant, regardless of the source. Even a casual examination of your everyday relations reveals that this is not the case. There are some people whose opinion of us is simply of no concern. Such is the case with persons we neither like nor respect. Such people can praise us to the heavens and we remain unaffected. There are other individuals, though, whose smile or single word of approval keeps us elated for hours.

Bidwell (1973) explains such effects by suggesting that *there is a general tendency to want to be liked and respected by those we like and respect, and to seek evidence of such sentiments.* We might predict then that, when a teacher is esteemed by students, they act in ways which cause the teacher to express esteem (e.g., praise) for them. When the teacher is not esteemed, however, he or she is not able to make use of praise to reward. It seems important then, to consider factors which affect such perceptions of teachers. We refer to such perceptions as *credibility.*

It is convenient to refer to the credibility a teacher acquires and possesses, but it is perhaps misleading because credibility does not reside in the teacher but rather in the minds of students. Like all other attitudes and beliefs, a teacher's credibility can be expected to vary from student to student. So also do students' images of their teachers differ from the teachers' own self-views. What a particular student thinks of you, then, may be entirely different from what others think, or from what you are really like. No matter, a student's impressions are accurate as far as he is concerned, and they influence your ability to persuade him. We cannot overemphasize how important it is that students have positive images of their teachers. As noted in Chapter 2, investigations of the process of persuasion have repeatedly shown that, to be successful, a would-be persuader must be perceived in positive ways by those he or she wishes to persuade.

Now let's consider the nature of the perceptions which compose teacher credibility. Before doing so, however, it is important to point out that the number and nature of such perceptions have not been precisely identified. Two studies (McGlone and Anderson, 1973; McCroskey, Holdridge, and Toomb, 1974) have focused specifically on the nature of teacher credibility, but because these studies were conducted in college classrooms, it is unknown how applicable the findings are to elementary, secondary, or special-education settings. Over the past several years, though, several dimensions of credibility have emerged as important for a variety of sources across a variety of contexts. McCroskey, Larson, and Knapp (1971) have identified competence, character, and intention as three important dimensions. We again take up the consideration of these which we began in Chapter 2.

> *Competence*   When students evaluate the competence of a teacher they decide if she is expert regarding the subject matter and, more generally, if she is a well-informed and intelligent person. At the high school level, where students may be quite sophisticated and the subject matter quite complex, the teacher's perceived competence in her specialty comes to serve as a primary basis for respect. In contrast, in the primary grades, the teacher may be considered an authority on everything by virtue of her status as an adult. Hence judgments of teacher competence are of little consequence at this level.
>
> *Character*   When students assess the competence of a teacher they consider his expertness in a field of study; when they evaluate his character, they judge his basic nature. Is he honest and fair? Can he be trusted not to reveal information given in confidence? Does he play favorites? Does he discriminate against students because of their race, religion, ethnic origin, or socioeconomic background? Is he ethical in his relations with students? Answers to questions such as these identify students' perceptions of a teacher's character.
>
> *Intention*   When students evaluate the intention of a teacher, they assess her motives. Is she truly concerned about their well-being, or does she simply go through the motions of teaching? At a more specific level, students may question the motives teachers have for

making certain assignments and ask, "Why do we have to do this? Is it really important, or just busywork?"

There is little evidence to suggest which dimension is most important for teachers, if any one can be singled out. McCroskey, Larson, and Knapp (1971) suggest that it is important for persuaders to be perceived favorably on all three dimensions. These authors further suggest that being perceived unfavorably on any *one* dimension might damage one's overall persuasive effectiveness. Consider, for example, a university professor who is very much involved in conducting research. Such a professor may be exceptionally knowledgeable about his field (competence), and very honest and ethical in dealings with others (character). Yet, if it is apparent to his students that he teaches classes simply because he can't avoid doing otherwise (intention), it would not be surprising to discover that students hold him in low regard as a teacher. It is essential then, for a teacher to be perceived in favorable ways on all three dimensions to maximize the chances of being successful in persuading students.

Initial and Derived Credibility.   We said earlier that credibility exists in the minds of students. What you may not recognize is that these perceptions can exist about you long before students sit in your classroom. Bidwell (1973) observes that most local schools are ranked by reputation in the community, and that simply by taking a position at a school, the school's reputation is transferred to the teacher. Hence, the higher the ranking of the school, the greater the competence students perceive you to possess, at least initially.

Another source of *initial credibility* (i.e., credibility existing before students interact with you) is the reputation you acquire as you teach in the same school or district over time. When a school has a small student body, for instance, you can expect new students to possess a fairly complete set of perceptions about your knowledge, teaching ability, personality, fairness, and so forth, acquired from "old hands" who have either studied with you or formed their impressions from the comments of others who have. When both the reputation of the school and the teacher are favorable, the teacher usually enjoys high initial credibility. In contrast, the unknown teacher assigned to a low-ranking school has to work purposefully to establish a favorable reputation.

Whether or not you possess a reputation at the beginning of the school year, one inevitably evolves as the term progresses. This is *derived credibility*. It is what learners think of you as a result of what you say and do in your daily interactions with them. While initial credibility is important, you should be more concerned with the ongoing impression you create. No matter how favorable your initial reputation, or that of your school, you cannot afford to sit back and rest on your laurels. Rather, you must continually strive to achieve and maintain high derived credibility, for it is this set of perceptions, which evolves on a continual basis, that most influences the outcome of your persuasive efforts.

A CONCLUDING NOTE

We conclude the chapter with this thought: Any time you are in the presence of a student, your responses indicate: "I approve of what you're doing," "I disapprove," or "I'm unaware." As stated in Chapter 1, whether you intend to have your behavior interpreted in these ways does not matter—students make such interpretations. If you do approve of a student's actions, try to let the student know it. Only a second is required to do so.

PRINCIPLES 7.2

1. Responses to your persuasive efforts vary because students differ in their ability and readiness to respond.
2. Persuasive strategy based on reinforcement uses these three principles: (1) Reward responses to establish them; (2) reward desired responses frequently; and (3) keep the time interval between the response and the reward brief.
3. Tokens are rewards whose value must be learned in the classroom context. The major disadvantage of using tokens as rewards is that exceptional resources are required.
4. Both verbal and nonverbal indications of approval constitute praise. Praise is a reward with high potential value, because it is readily available in all instructional settings.
5. Praise is underemployed as a reward by teachers.
6. The effectiveness of praise as a reward is dependent upon your credibility.
7. Your reputation and your school's reputation influence your initial credibility. Your derived credibility is determined by your interactions with students.

REFERENCES

Beisecker, T. D., and Parson, D. W. *The process of social influence.* Englewood Cliffs, N.J.: Prentice-Hall, 1972.

Bettinghaus, E. P. *Persuasive communication.* New York: Holt, Rinehart and Winston, 1973.

Bidwell, C. E. The social psychology of teaching. In R. M. W. Travers (Ed.), *Second handbook of research on teaching.* Skokie, Ill.: Rand McNally, 1973, pp. 413–449.

Cureton, L. W. The history of grading practices. *NCME Measurement in Education*, 1971, 2, 1–8.

Dunkin, M. J., and Biddle, B. J. *The study of teaching.* New York: Holt, Rinehart and Winston, 1974.

Gagné, R. M., and Briggs, L. J. *Principles of instructional design.* New York: Holt, Rinehart and Winston, 1974.

Karlins, M., and Abelson, H. I. *Persuasion.* New York: Springer, 1970.

McCroskey, J. C., Larson, C. E., and Knapp, M. L. *An introduction to interpersonal communication.* Englewood Cliffs, N.J.: Prentice-Hall, 1971.

McCroskey, J. C., Holdridge, W., and Toomb, J. K. An instrument for measuring the source credibility of basic speech communication instructors. *Speech Teacher,* 1974, **23,** 26–33.

McGlone, E. L., and Anderson, L. J. The dimensions of teacher credibility. *Speech Teacher,* 1973, **22,** 196–200.

Mager, R. F. *Developing attitude toward learning.* Belmont, Calif.: Fearon, 1968.

Rosenfeld, L. B., and Civikly, J. M. *With words unspoken.* New York: Holt, Rinehart and Winston, 1976.

Simons, H. W. *Persuasion: Understanding, practice, and analysis.* Reading, Mass.: Addison-Wesley, 1976.

Chapter 8
Attraction Systems in the
Classroom Group

OBJECTIVES

After reading this chapter, you should be able to:

1. define interpersonal attraction.
2. describe the relationship between communication and interpersonal attraction.
3. identify the characteristics of interpersonal attraction.
4. explain the relationship between attraction systems and the person perception process.
5. describe the ways individuals acquire impressions of one another.
6. define, verbally and by example, the basic model of interpersonal attraction (balance model).
7. explain the importance of information integration in attraction systems.
8. explain the role of relational messages of attraction in the classroom.
9. provide examples of positive and negative attraction cues.
10. define the concept of teacher immediacy.

11. describe the role of availability (propinquity) on determining attraction effects.
12. explain the relationship between physical characteristics (sex, attractiveness, and racial and ethnic characteristics) and the development of liking.
13. identify the functions of self-presentation in the development of liking.
14. identify and explain ingratiation tactics in the classroom.
15. explain the relationship between similarities (personality and attitudes) and the development of interpersonal attraction.
16. describe the relationship between interpersonal skills and effective teaching.
17. explain the relationship between attraction effects and student learning.

The poem was scrawled at the bottom of a teacher evaluation questionnaire, unsigned. It read:

Roses are red
Violets are blue
I love peanut butter
Good luck in the future!

The absence of literary style or originality did absolutely nothing to diminish the teacher's smile or sense of pleasure and satisfaction.

Each of us shares what Carnegie (1939, p. 137) has described as a "growing and unfaltering human hunger for appreciation," a sort of positive confirmation of our special worth and contribution to our fellows. It is precisely this impulse that poets, philosophers, and song writers have described for centuries. Thus, when you enter a classroom, both you and your students bring to the interaction the need to be liked, the desire to be reassured of one's individual capabilities and merits. If you question the accuracy of this statement, think about the first day you entered the classroom for this course. Probably the first questions you asked yourself included, "Will I like this teacher? Will I like the course? Will the teacher like *me*?" Such questions are inevitable.

Our experiences have taught us that it is impossible to participate in communication transactions without responding to others on an emotional level. Simply stated, we tend to either like or dislike individuals with whom we communicate. Quite often, our response occurs without immediate awareness. On other occasions, it may take place instantaneously and with dramatic force: "I cannot *stand* that man." Make no mistake, this response, at whatever level of intensity, will occur. It is for this reason

FIGURE 8·1 EACH OF US HAS A NEED TO BE LIKED.

that we have included a chapter on interpersonal attraction in a text on classroom communication. Our goal is not to guide you toward becoming a more "attractive" teacher. Rather, we feel it is extremely important that you become aware of interpersonal attraction as a variable which influences teacher-student relationships significantly and on many levels. We therefore examine attraction first as one critical element of the communication process and then explore the development and consequences of liking in classroom settings.

A MODEL OF THE ATTRACTION PROCESS

We have asserted that the forces of interpersonal attraction are inevitable whenever individuals come into contact with one another. What, then, are the characteristics of the process? We may begin by confusing you slightly when we say that attraction may be both a cause and an effect of communication. You may start a conversation with someone simply because they appear to be someone you'd like to know better. If this first encounter goes smoothly, you may have many talks with the person. On the other hand, someone who strikes you less forcefully initially may, as a result of frequent interactions, become one of your most valued friends or associates. Attraction can therefore develop preceding or following communication between two individuals. This is so because interpersonal attraction is primarily an evaluative perceptual response, specific to the individual. Stated another way, interpersonal attraction is the direct result of how another individual perceives us: whether we are likeable or repulsive, whether we are pleasant to be around or a real pain, and whether or not we make others feel positively about themselves, to mention a few typical perceptions. Thus, while you feel Professor James is an enormously attractive individual who teaches physics, your roommate may refer to him as "old resistible force" and drop his course. You, on the other hand, might change your major and request Professor James as your academic advisor. Two psychologists who have studied attraction extensively, Berscheid and Walster (1969), summarize the role of individual perceptions in interpersonal attraction in this way:

> We shall see that although the qualities and behavior of another play a large role in determining whether we will find him attractive, researchers have found that the eye of the beholder is as important as that which is beheld. One must refer to the qualities of the attracter to achieve predictive accuracy in interpersonal attraction. (p. 12)

As is the case with most aspects of the process of communication, attraction is a dynamic, rather than static, force. We are capable of being drawn to someone in one setting and repelled by the same individual in a different setting. You have probably known teachers who affected you in this puzzling way. While in graduate school, we once worked with a professor of international repute on a federally funded research project. We were quickly impressed not only by his competence, but also by his lack of pretentiousness, his cooperativeness, and his firm but friendly relationship with the project staff. When the fall semester rolled around, we registered for his seminar which, since the class met at 8:00 A.M., was no small reflection of our esteem for this professor. Predictably, the congenial and stimulating project director had vanished without a trace, replaced by a disorganized, faintly autocratic, and decidedly deadly pedant who droned on tediously every day. Outside the classroom, he was again more relaxed and open. The point to be made here is that settings, as well as the people who surround us, influence our behavior, hence others' perceptions of us.

Since feelings of attraction are highly individualized experiences, we should note that they are not necessarily reciprocal. Just as many other social behaviors are somewhat idiosyncratic by nature, so it is with attraction. You may recall an unrequited "crush" on a teacher or classmate that was as puzzling as it was painful. After all, you had done your part—you liked him—why didn't he like you? As we shall see somewhat later in this chapter, liking someone is often a powerful inducement for them to reciprocate, but it may not be sufficient. Unfortunately, the bases for interpersonal attraction are not so simple.

Although admittedly complex, interpersonal attraction appears to be a rather systematic process. That is, most of us have certain standards or guidelines which we use as the mental yardstick against which new people are measured. We can protest that this is hardly a humanistic way to behave, but such protestations are fairly hollow when we consider the realities of life in a busy, crowded world. Without standards against which to evaluate new stimuli, including people, our sanity would be threatened. Research (Berscheid and Walster, 1969; Kleinke, 1975; McCroskey, Larson, and Knapp, 1971) indicates that we are actually quite consistent in judgments of what constitutes "attractiveness" to us, whether in terms of physical characteristics, social behaviors, attitudes, or values. Think about the people you are attracted to. If your experience is like ours, you will find that they share many qualities.

Communication of course is the principle means through which interpersonal attraction is developed and maintained. Although attraction may be experienced without direct communication, as in a case of hero worship or the sort of interest we might feel toward Paul Newman or Farrah Fawcett-Majors, these instances of attraction are usually short-lived. In most cases, the attraction system is tied to the frequency and quality of the communication between people. One perspective which demonstrates the relationship between communication and attraction is provided by the *person perception process*.

As we noted in Chapter 5, our initial response to new people is largely based on their object characteristics: physical appearance cues, demeanor, and so on. At this point a surprising number of judgments about attitudes, occupation, life-style, and status are made. Some researchers (Kleinke, 1975; Warr and Knapper, 1968) suggest that preliminary decisions about further contact are made on the basis of this information. In short, we decide whether we like an individual enough to want to invest the time and energy required to know them better.

A second source of information we use in the early phases of the person perception process is observation of another's behavior. On the first day of class, most students carefully scrutinize the teacher's behavior to try to gauge his or her general disposition, orientation toward students, fair-mindedness, and a host of related issues. Of course, teachers assess new classes in much the same way. By the end of the first class meeting both teacher and students have formed impressions which include a like-dislike dimension. Students and teachers use these first impressions to make predictions about future behavior.

Given time and continued contact, attention shifts from object characteristics to personal characteristics. Through voluntary and inadvertent self-disclosure, students and teachers are able to combine these first impressions and observations into a series of judgments about one another as individuals. We should note, however, that these judgments are not necessarily accurate. As a teacher you may find yourself initially attracted to students whose behavior complies with your ideas about what "good" students do. Whether their ultimate performance in class bears out your initial judgment will remain to be seen, *but*, you can be certain that your attraction to them will make a difference.

Interest in determining how attraction systems are developed and maintained has stimulated a number of researchers to design models enabling us to predict the direction and intensity of attraction effects (Heider, 1944; Newcomb, 1953). Grouped loosely under the rubric *balance theory*, these models share several basic assumptions about the operations of human attraction systems.

Each acknowledges the critical role of frequent contact and communication in the formation of attraction. Similarly, attraction is viewed as an approach-avoidance behavior whereby we strive to maximize our rewards and minimize social punishment such as rejection, humiliation, or embarrassment. Finally these models all postulate a basic human need for consistency, hence the term "balance theory." Simply stated, the consistency argument is that we are psychologically comfortable only when our perceptions of ourselves and others are corroborated by observed behavior. Perhaps the following example, based on a famous and often cited one by Allport (1954) will demonstrate the consistency principle.

Two teachers at a large urban school are discussing their students over lunch.

MS. GOODBODY: The trouble with these rich kids is that they only hang out with their own kind.

MS. DEWRIGHT: But the volunteer list shows that our wealthy kids staff more of the community self-help programs more than any other group of students.

MS. GOODBODY: That just shows that they're trying to curry favor with the administration and get power. That's all those kids think of—money and power.

MS. DEWRIGHT: Oh, I don't know. There are probably fewer wealthy students holding elective office in classes or on the Student Council than any other group on campus.

MS. GOODBODY: That's my point precisely. They couldn't care less about responsibility. They would rather be cheerleaders and pom-pom girls.

Ms. Goodbody is clearly determined to maintain her negative evaluation of the "rich kids" in spite of any information to the contrary.

The basic balance model provides a bridge from the phases of the person perception process, the basis of interpersonal attraction systems, to a consideration of the factors which determine and/or maintain interpersonal attraction between students and teachers. The model developed originally by Heider (1944) and refined by Newcomb (1953, 1971) essentially stresses the role of information integration in the formation of positive or negative attitudes toward others. According to Fishbein and Azjen (1975), as we learn progressively more about another person we deal with the new information by trying to maintain a consistent image of that person. Thus, if we like or dislike someone, we will strive to find information which supports rather than contradicts that judgment.

The model describes relationships among three elements: (1) a particular individual, P, (2) another individual, O, and (3) an object, X. In terms of predicting attraction effects, we assume the view of P in the model and characterize the relationships among the three units as either positive (+) or negative (−). Attraction is predicted when two conditions are satisfied: The system must be balanced and communication has taken place. Balanced systems include those in which all three relationships are positive (P likes O, P likes X, and O likes X), or if any two relationships are negative and one is positive (P likes O, P dislikes X, and O dislikes X). All other combinations are considered imbalanced, hence less stable and less conducive to positive attraction effects. The following example should clarify the distinction we are trying to make. Ms. Banks (P) loves Chaucer (X) and likes her former student Ted (O). Ted, on the other hand, enjoyed English composition, but loathes Chaucer. Hence the system, depicted in Figure 8.2, is unbalanced.

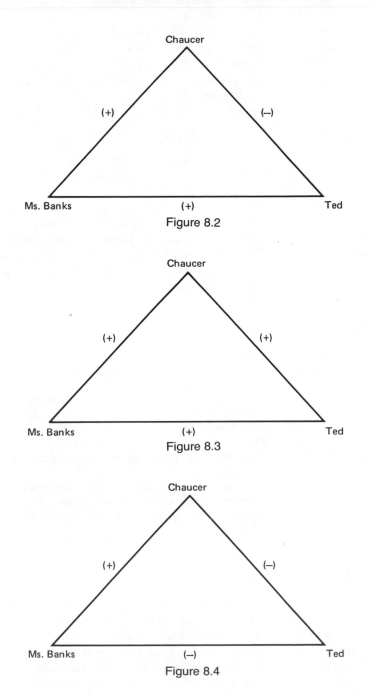

Figure 8.2

Figure 8.3

Figure 8.4

If, after a few classes, Ms. Banks is able to instill enough enthusiasm in Ted to change his negative response to Chaucer, the system will be balanced. (Figure 8.3). Should Ms. Banks hear Ted speak disparagingly of Chaucer and her course, her positive evaluation of Ted could shift, yielding a balanced state. (Figure 8.4).

You can easily recognize a number of factors which could affect the situation, such as the relative importance of the subject (X) to the two individuals in question, the nature of the relationship between the two individuals, and the frequency of communication between the two. In terms of predicting attraction, however, the model is particularly useful. We are not suggesting that you plan to sketch P—O—X diagrams for your students. Rather, we are encouraging you to consider the process underlying your attitudes toward them, collectively and as individuals.

The following principles concerning the nature of interpersonal attraction systems should suggest some immediate applications to communication in the classroom setting. In the ensuing section of the chapter we examine some common indicators of interpersonal attraction.

PRINCIPLES 8.1

1. Attraction effects are inevitable by-products of interpersonal communication.
2. Interpersonal attraction may be a causal factor for communication or may be a result of sustained communication over time.
3. Interpersonal attraction is a highly individualized, evaluative perceptual response that is dynamic, multidimensional, and may or may not be reciprocal.
4. Attraction systems typically develop through the person perception process.
5. Impressions that are the basis for attraction effects are formed through perceptions of another's appearance, behavior, and personal characteristics.
6. Models of the attraction process are based on the assumption that psychological states of balance or consistency are desirable.
7. States of balance are maintained through the process of information integration.

SIGNALS OF ATTRACTION

Lyricists of popular music over the decades have capitalized on the often elusive, ever-provocative means by which people betray their attraction toward one another. Regardless of whether your musical taste inclines you toward Beatles' music or the Rodgers and Hammerstein style, you are probably well aware of the varying cues which signify attraction or rejection. While you may have a strong intuitive appreciation of these culturally learned behaviors, we believe it will be useful to review briefly some signals of attraction which are frequently observed in classroom settings. You will recognize that these signals are specific examples of some of the concepts we discussed in Chapter 5. Keep in mind as you read this section, however, that nonverbal cues serve many classroom functions. The expression of liking is but one.

How can a teacher recognize liking on the part of students? The key is observation. Except in the early school years, most students are too restrained to declare their sentiments openly to a teacher; the risks of a rebuff or embarrassment are simply too great. As is the case in many other social settings, then, messages of liking and approval are frequently exchanged on a nonverbal level. Teachers, no less than students, reveal their attitudes in the unspoken dialogue of the classroom. These relational messages (Burgoon and Saine, 1978) typically express inclusion, the sense of involvement, affection, the sense of liking and approval, and control. For both teachers and students, relational cues form a vital link in classroom transactions. They permit the expression of personality, establish interpersonal relationships and, in large part, determine the atmosphere of the classroom.

One major relational cue that signals attraction is eye contact. Generally when we like someone or are attracted to them we are likely to look at them for longer periods of time, while we look less at those we dislike (Ellsworth and Ludwig 1972). Combined with a smile, eye contact is one of the most powerful signals of liking and approval. We should caution you, however, against overreliance on eye contact to determine whether your students are responding positively. Students, as you are well aware, realize that high levels of eye contact are requisite to the performance of their "good student" role. We believe that in classroom settings it is the prolonged, active avoidance of eye contact that is important. To be sure, almost all students look away from the teacher occasionally for a variety of reasons. The student whose eyes are rarely, or never directed toward you, though, may be expressing feelings that warrant your attention.

Similarly, distance or spatial cues convey liking and approval. Reports on classroom seating behavior (Rosenfeld and Civikly, 1976; Adams and Biddle, 1970) suggest that students who select seats at the front or near the center of the room typically have more positive attitudes about school, learning, *and* their teachers. It seems quite logical to infer that the same generalization might be made about teachers. Think about your own preferences for a moment. What is your impression of the teacher who greets you from across a wide expanse of desk, or who appears only as a disembodied head and upper torso from behind a rostrum? You may be amused to hear this, but we can recall a somewhat controversial discussion in our first teaching methods class concerning the appropriateness of sitting on a desk while you are teaching! (No. We were not in college in 1940.) Our experience suggests that teachers who increase what Mehrabian (1971) calls "immediacy" between themselves and their students are likely to be perceived as positive and likable by their students. Immediacy is increased by direct eye contact and closer physical distance. Of course, there are limits. Too much of either physical proximity or eye contact is likely to produce altogether different results.

Research from the helping professions—medicine, psychiatry, counseling—has revealed other relational cues which signal attraction and liking. Scheflen (1972), for instance, discovered that doctors and patients in clinical situations often give one another subtle attraction cues. These nonverbal cues, incidentally, appear in almost all settings, including the classroom. Because they parallel the behaviors seen in normal courtship, Scheflen labeled them "quasi-courtship behaviors." Apparently the occurrence of such cues does not necessarily mean that a student or teacher expects intimate involvement with the other. Rather, Scheflen argues that quasi-courtship behaviors are rewarding in and of themselves. There are basically three stages in quasi-courtship: courtship readiness, positional cues, and actions of appeal and invitation.

Courtship readiness refers to a range of conscious and unconscious actions which usually precede the actual encounter. A typical indicator of this phase is increased muscle tension, which results in better posture, and a generally more alert facial expression. Preening behaviors may occur, such as straightening clothes or arranging hair. These actions seem to signify a heightened awareness on the part of an individual.

Positional cues, including seating or standing position, forward leans, and general body orientation, appear to signal the degree to which two individuals are involved in an interaction. Generally speaking, the more direct the orientation, the greater the liking and approval expressed. Look around a classroom sometime. You may be surprised at the variation you see in terms of positional cues. Even in the somewhat restrictive confines of the traditional desk most students have to occupy, you can quickly notice that some students are even "mirroring" the positional cues of the teacher. Mirroring or matching the positional cues of the teacher is a common signal of attraction in classrooms. Thus the more casual teacher who sits atop a desk while teaching should not be surprised to see a classroom full of students lounging in their seats rather than sitting stiffly erect.

The final phase of quasi-courtship behavior, actions of appeal or invitation, includes a variety of behaviors which vary in terms of frequency and intensity. Maintaining eye contact longer than usual, fluttering eyelashes, or turning the wrists and palms outward are positive signals. Other examples are even slightly suggestive, such as unbuttoning extra buttons, or striking poses to capture and hold attention. We must reemphasize here that these behaviors occur for the most part unconsciously. Only rarely is there the intent for the exchange to go beyond even a flirtation level. It is not at all unusual for male students and female teachers, or female students and male teachers to fall unconsciously into quasi-courtship routines in the process of instruction. These behaviors, after all, are ingrained patterns of expressing liking. Hence it is highly unlikely that, when your teacher places her hands on her hips while emphasizing a statement, she is doing anything other than accenting her remarks.

Attraction signals in the classroom are not limited exclusively to nonverbal messages. In terms of verbal messages, however, it is usually not so much what is said, as how often or how intensely something is said. When students do not like a course or a teacher, they are not likely to express these sentiments verbally but simply to remain silent. In short, we all tend to talk more frequently, and probably at greater length, to those we like than to those about whom we feel neutral or actively dislike. In this way a curious sort of cycle often is set in motion. Those students who feel positively toward their teacher tend to speak up in class more often, remain after class to talk, and drop by the teacher's office to chat. Teachers of course respond to these students differently than to others. Over time, through this continued contact and mutual self-disclosure, the probabilities of interpersonal attraction are substantially increased. The potential problems for the teacher should be quite apparent to you; too often the silent student is inadvertently excluded, thereby decreasing the likelihood that his perceptions of the teacher, class, or even himself will be positive.

The series of studies reported by Brophy and Good (1974) that we introduced in Chapter 3 demonstrates this point vividly. Most of us who teach genuinely try to avoid the pitfalls of letting personal feelings override professional judgment. The fact remains, though, that we unconsciously reveal our appraisals of students both verbally and nonverbally. One of the ways in which we disclose our preferences, according to Brophy and Good, is in our questioning behavior: who is asked questions, how long are they allowed to speak, and how stringently are their answers evaluated. Students who are "good" in teachers' eyes tend to be called on more often, are allowed to speak longer, and, perhaps most importantly, are given more help from the teacher if their answer is not quite correct. Less favored students, if recognized at all, are likely to be simply corrected if their answer is wrong.

Do teachers intentionally exclude students they don't particularly like? We think not. Instead, we suggest that all teachers are unwittingly influenced by many subtle factors. It is altogether too easy to fall into a pattern of, for example, calling only on students we know will have read the assignment or, worse still, students whose opinions or ideas are similar to our own. Perhaps one of the most difficult challenges you have as a teacher is acceptance of an old classroom cliché: learning does not equal liking.

It is important at this juncture to restate our intent in this chapter. We are convinced that your effectiveness as a classroom teacher will be enhanced if you become more sensitive to the potential attraction signals you encounter in teaching situations. Others, such as Rogers (1973), might argue that we should all strive toward becoming facilitators in the classroom, in which case the foregoing section might be translated into a series of specific goals for you to achieve. We believe, however, that this decision is for you to make. As you read the following principles based on this section, remember that students and teachers are, above all else, individuals. Our descriptions in this section have been purposefully drawn in the broadest terms, for it is our firm belief that there is no single list of behaviors that identifies the "attractive" teacher.

PRINCIPLES 8.2

1. Students and teachers use nonverbal relational cues to express attraction in the classoom.
2. Relational messages establish relationships, permit expression of personality, and influence classroom climate.
3. Teachers who are immediate with students are perceived as positive and likable.
4. Teachers reveal their appraisals of students through the frequency and duration of their verbal interactions with them.

DEVELOPMENT OF LIKING IN THE CLASSROOM

We have examined the nature of attraction systems in the classroom and the attraction signals teachers and students exchange. We now consider some of the determinants of attraction in instructional settings. Although we treat each of several factors separately, you should realize that in most classroom situations it is likely that several of these factors operate simultaneously. In discussing the bases of interpersonal attraction we move from the external factors which have immediate effects on your perceptions of another to those more internal characteristics which tend to be revealed over time.

Availability of the Other

It should come as no great surprise to you that simple perceptual availability, in terms of physical propinquity (closeness), is the "almost sufficient condition" to cause interpersonal attraction between two individuals (McCroskey, Larson, and Knapp, 1971). Stated in the most basic way, the principle is: Other things held constant, the closer two people are geographically, the more likely it is that they will be attracted to each other. Numerous research studies have demonstrated that propinquity influences not only friendship choice but also mate selection, racial tolerance, and violent crime (Berscheid and Walster, 1969).

The number of classroom contact hours you spend with individual students depends on the level at which you teach. Variations in the amount of time spent in one another's presence doubtless influences perceptions and thus attraction effects. You may have had experiences which, like ours, illustrate the role of time and propinquity on student-teacher relationships. Night classes always present special problems for us, particularly in terms of becoming acquainted with students we see only once a week. Indeed, the first few class meetings always seem to be less enjoyable, as we struggle to maintain a consistent flow of information between the class and ourselves. Classes that we meet three or more times a week proceed far more smoothly. Obviously, frequency of contact is at least as important as the length of contact.

Propinquity is a potent contributor to attraction effects in the classroom. Do not assume, however, that merely sharing a classroom with students ensures that you will ultimately like them, or vice versa. Berscheid and Walster (1969) have suggested that it is more appropriate to think of propinquity as a general intensifier of sentiments, regardless of whether they are positive or negative. By implication, repulsion can flower as readily in close contact as attraction. The mildly annoying mannerisms of a teacher that are tolerable from a discreet distance may quickly become unbearable after daily exposure.

Propinquity affects interpersonal attraction primarily because closeness increases the amount of information we have about one another. While vicarious or even anticipated contact may enhance the possibility of interpersonal attraction (Berscheid, Boyle, and Darley, 1968), there is no substitute for direct experience. If you recall our model of interpersonal attraction, you will remember that the role of information integration was stressed as a critical aspect of the attraction system. What propinquity affords is the opportunity for students and teachers to gain information about and share experiences with one another. One of the most important things propinquity between student and teacher reveals is the type of rewards and punishments each may expect from the other. If we may be metaphorical, propinquity is the framework upon which the fabric of friendship is woven.

The last statement is not to be taken lightly. In the classroom setting, the greater information flow between student and teacher produced by propinquity should increase attraction rather than breed hostility. Although negative attraction effects remain possible, Newcomb (1956, p. 576) has posited that "when persons interact, the reward-punishment ratio is more often such as to be reinforcing rather than extinguishing. . . ." To the extent that students and teachers are interdependent parts of the instructional process, dependent on one another for rewards, Newcomb's statement seems quite reasonable. Even though the nature of teaching dictates that negative evaluations must be given, these can be

FIGURE 8·5   PROPINQUITY IS THE
FRAMEWORK UPON WHICH THE FABRIC
OF FRIENDSHIP IS WOVEN.

handled in ways that do not disrupt the balance of student-teacher relationships. As we discuss at some length in Chapter 9, it is possible, even imperative, for you as a teacher to learn to criticize a student's work without attacking his or her worth as an individual.

Finally, propinquity has a qualitative dimension which should not go unmentioned. Your availability to your students inside and outside class influences their attitudes toward you. The teacher who conveys a sense of impatience with students who want simply to chat for a few minutes may unintentionally create an atmosphere of nonimmediacy. While it is not necessary or desirable to be totally unselfish with your time, most students view their relationship with a teacher as essentially one-to-one in nature. Time invested in such relationships can yield dividends in the classroom.

Physical Characteristics of the Other

Availability of the other of course presumes that both teacher and student are aware of one another's physical appearance and basic characteristics. In assessing the role of physical characteristics in the development of liking, three factors emerge as potential influences: sex, attractiveness, and racial or ethnic characteristics. We briefly consider the impact of each of these variables.

If we asked you to predict the direction of any biases teachers have toward students on the basis of sex, what would you guess? Do female students really fare better in the classroom? Are teachers of one sex biased against students of the same sex? If you are like most of our students, you might tentatively answer "yes" to both questions. Conventional folk wisdom argues that girls are better students than boys, and that male teachers give more favorable treatment to female students just as female teachers give unfavorable treatment to male students. Intuition in this case, however, is a poor predictor.

Extensive research on the relationship between sex of teacher and sex of student conducted by Good, Sikes, and Brophy (1973) reveals that male and female teachers are actually quite similar in their treatment of students. In view of the controversy concerning the lack of male teachers in elementary schools this finding has interesting implications for hiring policies. As these researchers aptly note, the plight of the male student at the mercy of a female teacher may be grossly exaggerated.

There are, however, significant differences in the way male and female students are treated, at least in early school years. Boys tend to be more active and interact more frequently with teachers than girls, but they also receive more intense teacher affect. That is, boys tend to receive more positive *and* more negative contacts from teachers, and proportionately more of these contacts are negative. Girls receive fewer contacts, a higher percentage of which are positive.

Taken together, these findings suggest that, if indeed teachers are attracted to students of one sex or the other, their classroom interactions do not disclose such a preference. The Good, Sikes, and Brophy study clearly indicates that it is the sex of the student that influences, rather than any teacher characteristic. While male and female teachers differ in terms of teaching style, their treatment of students seems remarkably similar.

A second physical characteristic which has dramatic impact on virtually every aspect of social behavior, including the classroom, is physical attractiveness. Research data on the value of good looks in achieving academic and social success are consistent. From the early school years forward, physical beauty is equated with goodness and talent. A study by Clifford and Walster (1973), in which 400 elementary school teachers participated, illustrates the point graphically. Each teacher was provided with a summary record and photograph of a fifth-grade student. Records for all students were identical and purposefully constructed to appear above average. Photographs accompanying the school records were varied, so that some teachers judged students who were attractive and others judged unattractive students. Male and female teachers, evaluating identical records, concluded that attractive students had (among other things) significantly higher I.Q.'s, significantly better social relationships, and higher educational potential than students who were less attractive. Startling? Quite.

Similar findings exist for college students. Landy and Sigall (1974) report that, when asked to evaluate an essay which they thought was written by the woman whose picture was attached, male students rated the essay much more favorably when they thought it had been written by an attractive rather than by an unattractive woman. Even a poor essay attributed to an attractive woman was evaluated nearly as highly as a good essay allegedly written by an unattractive woman.

Several implications of these findings are worth mentioning. You saw in Chapter 2 the impact a teacher's judgments can have on a student's self-concept. What should concern us is the potential damage to a student's sense of personal identity and worth that can result from differential treatment. Dion and Berscheid (1974) posit a circular effect in the physical attractiveness situation: When unattractive children are perceived differently from attractive children, they are treated differently. Such treatment in turn makes them behave differently, leading to even greater perceptions of difference.

Happily, there are no data which suggest that the initial impact of physical attractiveness is carried over into long-term associations. It seems reasonable to expect that teachers and students overcome these attraction effects and deal with one another as individuals. We can make this statement with considerably more assurance as far as teachers are concerned, however, than in the case of students. Studies reviewed by Grash and Costin (1975) indicate that, in terms of teaching evaluations, attractive teachers fare no better than their less attractive peers. Evidence reported in Chapter 5 concerning the academic prospects of attractive versus unattractive students is less reassuring. Beauty may not be a prerequisite to success, but it clearly is a facilitating factor.

A final factor about which we know relatively little in the classroom setting is racial and ethnic characteristics. Unfortunately, the social implications surrounding the issue have been such that little systematic research has been aimed at determining the role of these characteristics in the development of student-teacher relationships. From the Coleman Report (1966) we know that racial minority students tend to perform at lower levels on standardized achievement tests than their nonminority peers. Volumes have been devoted to explaining the causes of and potential solutions to this problem, but few have looked at classroom effects per se.

Do teachers respond differently toward students on the basis of racial or ethnic background? We feel that it is inevitable that they do, although there are no data which suggest that the treatment is necessarily negative. As we discuss more fully in a later section of this chapter, we are all drawn to those whom we perceive as similar. Thus it does not seem unlikely that initial student-teacher attraction effects are increased by racial or ethnic similarity. Whether this means that black teachers evaluate black students differently is an open question.

Transracial communication, whether in the classroom or larger society, appears to present special difficulties. Smith (1973), Rich (1974), and others have suggested that such transactions are likely to produce a wide variety of effects on the perceptions of interactants. One of particular importance for academic settings is anxiety. If you have had the experience of entering a classroom and discovering that your instructor was of a racial or ethnic extraction other than your own, you can probably corroborate this. You may have wondered whether your apparent difference would be translated into a real deficit in your final grade. Teachers thrust into a classroom full of minority students for the first time frequently experience similar doubts about their ability to successfully relate to their students. Anxiety tends to inhibit rather than facilitate interpersonal communication. We must conclude then that racial and ethnic differences are not conducive to attraction, at least initially. As specified by our attraction model, however, we predict that the information and accumulated experiences resulting from interaction will be sufficient to overcome these effects.

Self-Presentation of the Other

Have you ever thought about the ease with which you apply labels to people? Or why a fairly nonsensical term such as "dork" is so immediately recognizable as a negative description of an individual? At least one reason underlying the popular usage of this and similar terms is that they express a truism about interpersonal attraction. There are certain immediately recognizable traits, some of which seem to mark an individual a "winner" and others that stamp one a "failure." Far from being inborn, these attributes are essentially a matter of an image presented for public consumption. All of us practice what Goffman (1959) has called "impression management" as a matter of course. We selectively present and withhold information about ourselves and our motives to secure rewards or avoid punishment. In this regard we briefly review the aspects of self-presentation related to being a winner in the instructional setting.

Role behavior is one of the principal ingredients of self-presentation. When we detect discrepancies in the role enactment of those around us, we usually devalue those individuals, hence feel less attracted to them. Positive attraction effects result from our perceptions of another's mastery of his or her role. For this reason, teachers are expected to be competent, composed, and compassionate in their dealings with students. Students? Well, students are expected to be, above all else, obedient. This presents some very real problems for some students, particularly boys in the early school years. Much of their socialization prior to the schooling experience has stressed autonomy, expression, and independence. These behaviors are most assuredly not positively regarded in the classroom, so boys receive more disapproval from teachers than girls (Brophy and Good, 1970). Indeed, researchers Good, Sikes, and Brophy (1973), and Jackson, Silberman, and Wolfson (1969) agree that the disproportionate amount of negative affect boys receive is attributable to the conflict between their early socialization and the school expectations which dictate another sort of performance altogether. Role socialization for male students appears to remain incomplete until the junior high or even high school level. We might infer from these studies that there is some basis for the assumption that boys like school less than girls.

Teachers' role demands are really no less stringent than students', particularly with regard to competence. There are, however, exceptions to this general rule which are intriguing. We might characterize this exception as the "pratfall theory of interpersonal attraction" (Aronson, Willerman, and Floyd, 1966). The basic premise of the minitheory is that competent individuals are frequently perceived as aloof and unapproachable and that an unexpected accident makes them seem more human, and thus more attractive. According to Aronson, Willerman, and Floyd (1966):

FIGURE 8·6 AN OCCASIONAL BLUNDER MAY MAKE YOU MORE ATTRACTIVE.

> A near perfect individual who shows that he is capable of an occasional blunder or pratfall may come to be regarded as more human and more approachable: consequently he will be liked better *because* of this pratfall . . . a mediocre person . . . will not undergo an increase in attractiveness. (p. 227)

This notion should reassure those of you who, like us, have a predilection for spilling coffee, dropping chalk, and other classroom mishaps.

The second aspect of self-presentation related to the development and maintenance of liking in the classroom concerns mutual esteem enhancement. Stated simply, the rule is that we tend to like individuals who express liking for us. Think for a moment about your own daily experiences. How much of your activity is directed toward obtaining the esteem of others? For most of us, social approval is a highly desired commodity. Like money, this approval is a valuable resource because it reinforces so many behaviors in a wide variety of contexts. Teachers and students alike modify their actions to achieve the approving glance, the smile, or the verbal pat on the back that constitute what we call the "narcotic of the classroom."

Given that all of us have esteem needs, it seems reasonable to predict that teachers and students whose interactions are positive in nature are more inclined to like rather than dislike each other. We are reminded of a scroll a colleague hung on his office door. It proclaimed in elaborate gothic lettering "Forsooth, young seekers of truth. Remember that teachers need love, too." Similarly, there is an abundance of literature demonstrating that student learning is enhanced by praise, particularly when this reinforcement comes from a highly esteemed teacher. While all students may not hold their teacher in high esteem, most teachers control the reward systems in the classroom. Students therefore seek positive rewards if for no other reason than to avoid social punishment. Students quickly learn that one way to increase positive rewards is to express liking for their teacher. Even the most forbidding instructor is often, as our students describe it, "given the treatment."

Both teachers and students engage in ingratiation tactics occasionally. There are a number of reasons for the less than perfect results that this interpersonal strategy yields. You may remember from Chapter 2 that, when you receive esteem that is not congruent with your own self-image, you probably respond negatively. A more general factor that determines our response is an awareness that liking may be offered to us for a variety of reasons quite unrelated to our own assets and abilities. In such instances the personal motivations of the other individual become a matter of concern. When an expression of esteem is judged, correctly or incorrectly, by the recipient as ingratiation, it is unlikely that esteem will be reciprocated. Thus the teacher who lavishes praise on a class immediately before course evaluations are to be completed may not obtain the anticipated results. Neither, incidentally, should the student who chooses the semester final exam date to tell the teacher that he or she is "the best teacher . . . " expect liking to be reciprocated. We cannot over-emphasize the importance of sincere, personalistic evaluations for the development and maintenance of positive attraction effects. Playing the ingratiation game may provide some short-term gains, but over time is likely to detract and disrupt student-teacher relationships.

Similarity of the Other

Probably no single factor is more important to the *maintenance* of inter-personal attraction than perceived similarities. When continued associa-tion and physical attractiveness have begun to pall, shared interests and attitudes appear to be the factors which sustain relationships. Numerous research studies have demonstrated the importance of similarities, real or merely perceived, in predicting attraction between spouses, peers, and co-workers (Byrne, 1971). Though substantially less abundant, studies of classroom interactions suggest much the same principle. Teachers and students are most attracted to one another when they recognize their common traits or behaviors.

There is a variety of explanations for the impact of similarity on the development of liking. In the first place, discovering that someone else shares your opinion is a form of social validation that most of us find highly reinforcing. So reinforcing is this type of similarity that we tend to generalize interpersonal similarities in a few areas to all areas. In terms of our model of attraction, we would predict that, the higher the proportion of agreements between a student and a teacher, the higher the level of attraction. Stated another way, those with whom we agree, we like, and those whom we like, we assume agree with us. There is even evidence that when we like someone we tend to overestimate the extent to which our attitudes and beliefs are shared (Byrne, 1971).

In much the same way, perceived similarities seem to increase the salience of interpersonal needs. Complementarity of need systems en-hances the potential attraction between two individuals when each per-ceives that his or her personal psychic needs may be satisfied through interaction with the other. Teachers and students frequently satisfy such mutual needs. On the broadest level, it has been argued that teachers are actually surrogate parents to students, gratifying similar needs *in loco parentis*. Regardless of whether this argument is accurate, there is a certain plausibility in the reasoning that perceived similarities of needs increase the level of rapport or empathy between individuals. This tends to enhance positive attraction effects.

Two areas of perceived similarities are presumed to be important in the development of liking in the instructional process. Educational re-searchers have focused their attention on the impact of similarities in personality traits and similarities in attitude. While the research on either topic is far from abundant, we may infer something of the effects of these variables on classroom interactions from these studies and related research on attraction in other interpersonal settings.

Research on the relationship between personality traits and interpersonal attraction has been most frequently investigated in engaged and married couples. The general conclusion to be drawn from these studies is that, the greater the similarity in the personalities of a couple, the greater the probability of a stable, happy relationship (Berscheid and Walster, 1969). In terms of student-teacher relationships, the relationship is far less clear. Costin and Grush (1973) found that students' perceptions of their teachers' personality traits correlated positively with their ratings of teacher skill. In a second, more carefully controlled study, the same authors determined that students' evaluations of teaching effectiveness were *not* affected by similarities in personality traits. In fact, the similarities in personality between the students and their teachers appeared to be rather negligible in determining students' affective responses to instruction (Grush and Costin, 1975).

Attitudinal similarity appears to be a more important factor in shaping student-teacher relationships than personality similarities or dissimilarities. Attraction theorist Byrne (1965, 1971) has explained the role of attitudinal similarity in the growth of liking between people as a simple matter of rewards and punishments. Discovering that another's likes or dislikes are similar to yours creates a bond between you. All of us, after all, prefer to be around people who share our views. Agreement therefore is reinforcing, and disagreement has negative reinforcement value. Applied to the classroom setting, this theory postulates that, the greater the number of agreements between a teacher and a student, the greater the perceived similarity in attitude, leading to greater liking.

Current research findings on the impact of similar attitudes in classroom settings support the direct relationship between attraction and similarity. A study conducted by Smith, Meadow, and Sisk (1970) revealed that, when asked to evaluate the performance of an individual on a learning task, a higher rating was given to the individual who was presented as similar to the evaluator than to one who was presented as dissimilar, even though the performances were identical. To those of you who may be entering the job market soon, the results of the following pair of studies should be of interest. A descriptive study conducted by Griffith and Jackson (1970) found that people making hiring decisions and salary recommendations on undergraduate research assistants based their decisions on the degree of similarity between the applicants' attitudes and their own, rather than on the basis of ability. Even more startling data come from a survey of school principals and hiring decisions. Merritt

(1970) discovered that principals preferred to hire teachers whose beliefs were similar to their own. Merritt's data suggest that, for these principals, belief similarity outweighed even the teachers' amount of experience as a determinant in the selection process.

Taken together, these studies reveal a hidden agenda of fairly substantial proportions. Does this mean that teaching success and good teacher-student relationships depend upon attitudinal similarity? We suspect not. These effects do, if unchecked, most assuredly occur, but we cannot endorse passive acceptance on your part. Neither do we recommend that you attempt to hide your identity. Rather, we suggest that you begin now to accept and increase your ability to appreciate dissimilarities in others. As we discuss this issue in some detail in Chapter 9, we leave you with this thought. Learning to appreciate dissimilarities may not be an easy task, but it is potentially one of the most self-actualizing challenges you will face in your teaching career.

Examining the development of liking in the instructional process has hopefully sensitized you to some of the subtle mechanisms operating on the affective level in the classroom. The following principles based on this section should suggest some significant questions to you. If we have anticipated accurately, you will find some answers in the following section.

PRINCIPLES 8.3

1. Propinquity tends to increase the probability of attraction between teachers and students by allowing them to gain information about and share experiences with one another.
2. Propinquity over time increases positive attraction effects regardless of initial impression.
3. Sex role behaviors influence the development of liking between teachers and students, particularly during early school years.
4. Contrary to folk psychology, male and female teachers do not appear to differ in their treatment of students.
5. Physical attractiveness in students is associated with positive attributions concerning intelligence, social class, and educational potential.
6. Racial and ethnic differences between teachers and students inhibit the development of attraction, at least initially.
7. Teachers and students regularly practice impression management as a means of obtaining social rewards.
8. Discrepancies in role performance diminish attraction effects.
9. Mutual esteem enhancement, if perceived as sincere, is conducive to interpersonal attraction.
10. Ingratiation, if recognized or suspected, diminishes attraction effects.
11. Perceived similarities are of paramount importance in maintaining interpersonal attraction effects, because similarity is a reinforcing event.
12. Similarities in personality appear to have negligible effects on attraction.

EFFECT OF ATTRACTION
ON STUDENT-TEACHER
RELATIONSHIPS

We have focused on four factors that have emerged from the literature on the development of liking in the instructional process: availability, physical characteristics, self-presentation, and interpersonal similarities. In considering each of these we have emphasized attraction as a process, a continuous and inevitable aspect of classroom communication. Let us now turn our attention to the products of attraction between teachers and students in terms of specific learning outcomes.

A basic assumption underlying our treatment of attraction systems in the classroom setting is that successful teaching requires skill in interpersonal communication. Stated another way, we believe there is a distinct and measurable difference between knowing a subject and teaching this subject to a group of students. Current research findings provide support for this belief. Teachers whose overall levels of interpersonal skills are high tend to be more effective in promoting positive instructional outcomes than those whose overall levels of interpersonal skill are low. This general conclusion applies to instruction at the elementary, junior high, high school, and college levels (Aspy, 1969, 1972; Boak and Conklin, 1975; Christensen, 1960; Hefele, 1971; Wagner and Mitchell, 1969). Positive learning outcomes in these studies usually refer to scores on achievement tests and/or measures of teaching effectiveness. The latter are of particular interest here because most student evaluations of instruction assess the level of attraction students have for their teachers. While we must guard against overgeneralizing findings from these studies, it seems reasonable to suggest that such interpersonal skills as empathy, rapport, and understanding are significant aspects of effective teaching.

Does interpersonal attraction between students and teachers facilitate learning? There is no simple answer to this question. A "sometimes yes, sometimes no" response is closer to the truth. Since relatively few studies have explored the relationship between liking and learning directly, we must be somewhat tentative. Two rather obvious factors to consider are teacher characteristics and student characteristics.

Attractive Teachers?

Think for a moment about the teacher you feel the most liking for. What makes this particular teacher distinctive? Is it good looks? Personal style? Professional expertise? A composite of all positive traits? Since you are a college student, it is most likely that the attraction you feel toward your favorite teacher is based on two of the four factors we've discussed in this chapter. A teacher's availability or physical characteristics appear to have far less impact on college students' liking for that teacher than factors of self-presentation and attitudinal similarities.

Consider teacher self-presentation. In terms of college student judgments of teaching effectiveness, there may be no more important factor influencing the development of liking. A teacher's mastery of the roles of subject matter expert, classroom facilitator, and evaluator is pivotal in shaping student response. Grush and Costin (1975) found that college students' evaluations of teaching effectiveness were most affected by students' estimates of a teacher's teaching skill. For these students, judgments of their teachers' personal attractiveness was of negligible importance. Professional expertise, then, appears to be one teacher characteristic that has positive effects.

Additionally, we may expect attitudinal similarities between teachers and students to enhance learning. To the extent that students perceive teachers as fundamentally similar to themselves in attitudes toward subject matter, values, and so on, liking and learning tend to progress side by side. You probably feel more attracted to teachers in your major department for this reason. You share an interest in and commitment to a particular subject matter. Although you may like other teachers in different fields, you have doubtless experienced problems in relating to and/or learning from teachers in courses you abhorred. Studies reported by Hamlish and Gaier (1954), Sapolsky (1960), and Dilendik (1975) reveal a positive relationship between teacher-student similarity and learning, in terms of retention, task performance, and course grades. Knowing that their teacher shares their attitudes appears to make students more receptive to learning.

Based on the foregoing discussion of attitudinal similarities and self-presentation in the liking-learning relationship, you may be plotting strategies for subtly conveying to your students that you are one professional expert who really shares their view of life in the larger sense. Before you complete this particular script, we must offer a cautionary note. It is entirely possible for the level of student-teacher and student-student attraction to be high, with *no* accompanying increase in learning. Turner and Thompson (1974) investigated the relationship between learning gains and student evaluations of teaching effectiveness. Student ratings of graduate teaching assistants in introductory college courses were compared with student test scores on course examinations over a two-year period. The results? Learning gains were consistently *negatively* correlated with ratings of teaching effectiveness. In short, the teachers whose ratings were highest were the ones whose students' performance was poorest on tests, and vice versa.

Taken together, the findings on attraction effects and learning suggest two implications. It seems readily apparent that attraction in the classroom cannot determine the amount of learning that will take place. It is but a single factor in a series of complex communication events. We might say that, while different levels of attraction between teachers and students are inevitable, their effects are variable.

A second implication involves the bases of attraction we have discussed—availability, physical characteristics, self-presentation, and attitudinal similarities. Teacher attractiveness, like credibility, is a multidimensional phenomenon which resides in the minds of students. Different students respond to different dimensions, based upon their unique needs or expectations. The relative importance of any single factor varies according to the total classroom context. You as a college student are probably most influenced by your professors' self-presentation in terms of interpersonal attraction. Perceived similarities are also important. The availability and physical appearance dimensions may facilitate the development of liking, but they probably do not predominate. Unless, of course, your math professor could double for Robert Redford and his office door is always open. . . .

Attracted Students

Our discussion of the relationship between student-teacher attraction and learning outcomes must also consider the specific characteristics of students which affect the relationship. We have noted throughout the chapter that the liking experience is a highly individualized one. Rest assured that no one who teaches is universally deemed attractive on any or all dimensions we've discussed. Nonetheless, there is one student characteristic of particular relevance to the influence of attraction on learning.

The age or academic level of students does not dictate the *likelihood* of attraction occurring between student and teacher. Rather, students' age or academic level seems to intensify or devalue the *importance* of attraction effects on learning. For the *schoolchild*, it seems especially critical that the student-teacher attraction effects be positive if learning is to proceed at an optimal pace. Elementary school students often rhapsodize about their favorite teachers. When they do so, it is likely that they are more receptive to the instruction the teacher provides. Shared feelings of liking between the elementary student and teacher are a powerful motivational force. The impact of teacher praise and attention on childrens' self-concepts as students, discussed in Chapter 2, can profoundly shape their immediate learning and subsequent responses to the schooling experience.

For high school and college students, on the other hand, motivation may be more internalized or dependent on sources other than the teacher. Peer opinion or family pressures may be more salient to students at these levels. Consequently, the impact of attraction effects may be somewhat diminished. What is intriguing about this shift is that the influence of attraction effects is reduced, but *only* as far as learning outcomes are concerned. Shared liking between teacher and student at this level is a pervasive force affecting students' attitudes toward self, subject matter, and the entire schooling experience. Good and Brophy (1973) summarize the paradox succinctly:

> In general, it appears that teacher behavior which facilitates student learning and that which optimizes student attitudes largely overlap at the preschool and early elementary school levels. However, as students get older and become more unique and differential in their personalities, interests, and learning styles, affective teacher variables assume increasingly greater importance in determining teacher effects on students, and the kind of teaching behavior that maximizes student learning shows less overlap (and often direct contradiction) with teacher behavior that promotes positive student attitudes. (p. 82)

A Matter of Balance and Proportion

Now that we've explored some of the sources, signals, and effects of attraction on student-teacher transactions, you may be muttering to yourself, "They can like me and learn more, or like me and learn less. What am I supposed to do anyway?" Some reassuring words follow. You know that learning is not the only important instructional outcome influenced by shared attraction between teacher and student. We concede that it would be something of an understatement to observe that interpersonal attraction is related to the affective outcomes of instruction. The point has been made directly as well as by implication throughout the chapter. A related point, however, warrants final emphasis. We have attempted in this chapter to acquaint you with a different perspective for viewing student-teacher relationships. Interpersonal attraction, like teacher expectations, contributes greatly to a hidden "affective curriculum" that pervades and influences the entire instructional process. The implications for teacher awareness and behavioral change are profound.

We want to stress the need for an appropriate balance between awareness and change. Like most teachers, you want your students to like you. Liking your students, collectively and as individuals, is an equally desirable goal. Much of the material in this chapter was discussed to illustrate the inevitability of attraction effects in the classroom group. Your awareness of these principles should enhance development of liking between you and your students. Nonetheless, your concern with attraction effects should not obscure your primary classroom goal, the promotion of learning. Teaching, as one of our colleagues often remarks, is not the surest route to popularity. We agree. Sacrificing teaching goals to achieve your students' liking is not the sort of change we recommend. Rather, we suggest that you accept the fact that some of your students will like you, others may dislike you, and many will not feel strongly in either direction. Do what you can to facilitate liking, within reason. Directing your energy toward making yourself into a likable teacher for each unique classroom group should be a secondary consideration.

The type of change we advocate will result from your attention to the attraction signals you convey to students. Some of your students are more attractive to you than others. It takes real effort on your part to avoid treating these students differently from those you like less. Learn to think of teaching effectiveness in terms of your ability to aid every student's learning, regardless of your personal preferences. Changing the tendency to deal with students according to your likes and dislikes is not always easy. Equitable treatment for all students, however, is the hallmark of a professional teacher.

PRINCIPLES 8.4

1. Teachers with highly developed interpersonal communication skills facilitate positive instructional outcomes.
2. Students may respond to one dimension of a teacher's overall attractiveness more than others as a function of the total classroom context.
3. The impact of attraction effects on learning is partially determined by the academic level of the student.
4. Attraction between teachers and students influences students' affective development as well as learning outcomes.

REFERENCES

Adams, R. and Biddle, B. *Realities of teaching: Explorations with videotape.* New York: Holt, Rinehart and Winston, 1970.

Allport, G. *The nature of prejudice.* Reading, Mass.: Addison-Wesley, 1954.

Aronson, E., Willerman, B., and Floyd, J. The effect of a pratfall on increasing interpersonal attractiveness. *Psychonomic Science,* 1966, **4,** 227–228.

Aspy, D. The effect of teacher-offered conditions of empathy, positive regard and congruence upon student achievement. *Florida Journal of Educational Research,* 1969, **11,** 39–48.

Aspy, D. *Toward a technology for humanizing education.* Champaign, Ill.: Research Press, 1972.

Berscheid, E., Boyle, D., and Darley, J. Effects of forced association upon voluntary choice to associate. *Journal of Personality and Social Psychology,* 1968, **8,** 13–19.

Berscheid, E., and Walster, E. *Interpersonal attraction.* Reading, Mass.: Addison-Wesley, 1969.

Boak, R., and Conklin, R. The effect of teachers' levels of interpersonal skills on junior high school students' achievement and anxiety. *American Educational Research Journal,* 1975, **12,** 537–549.

Brophy, J., and Good, T. *Teacher-student relationships: Causes and consequences.* New York: Holt, Rinehart and Winston, 1974.

Brophy, J. and Good, T. Teachers communication of differential expectations for children's classroom performance: Some behavioral data. *Journal of Educational Psychology*, 1970, **61**, 365–374.

Burgoon, J., and Saine, T. *The unspoken dialogue.* Boston: Houghton Mifflin, 1978.

Byrne, D. *An introduction to personality: A research approach.* Englewood Cliffs, N.J.: Prentice-Hall, 1965.

Byrne, D. *The attraction paradigm.* New York: Academic Press, 1971.

Carnegie, D. *How to win friends and influence people.* New York: Simon & Schuster, 1937.

Christensen, C. M. Relationships between pupil achievement, pupil affect-need, teacher warmth, and teacher permissiveness. *Journal of Educational Psychology*, 1960, **51**, 169–174.

Clifford, M., and Walster, E. The effects of physical attractiveness on teacher expectation. *Sociology of Education*, 1973, **46**, 248–258.

Coleman, J. et al. Equality of educational opportunity. Washington, D.C.: U.S. Government Printing Office, 1966.

Costin, F., and Grush, J. Personality correlates of teacher-student behavior in the college classroom. *Journal of Educational Psychology*, 1973, **65**, 410–444.

Dilendik, J. Teacher-student attitude similarity and information retention. *American Educational Research Journal*, 1975, **12**, 405–414.

Dion, K., and Berscheid, E. Physical attractiveness and peer perception among children. *Sociometry*, 1974, **37**, 1–12.

Ellsworth, P., and Ludwig, L. Visual behavior in social interaction. *Journal of Communication*, 1972, **22**, 375–403.

Fishbein, M., and Azjen, I. *Belief, attitude, intention, and behavior: An introduction to theory and research.* Reading, Mass.: Addison-Wesley, 1975.

Goffman, E. *Presentation of self in everyday life.* Garden City, N.Y.: Doubleday, 1959.

Good, T., and Brophy, J. *Looking in classrooms.* New York: Harper & Row, 1973.

Good, T., Sikes, J., and Brophy, J. Effects of teacher sex and student sex on classroom interaction. *Journal of Educational Psychology*, 1973, **65**, 74–87.

Griffitt, W., and Jackson, T. The influence of ability and nonability information on personnel selection decisions. *Psychological Reports*, 1970, **27**, 959–962.

Grush, J., and Costin, F. The student as consumer of the teaching process. *American Educational Research Journal*, 1975, **12**, 55–66.

Hamlish, E., and Gaier, E. Teacher-student personality similarity and marks. *School Review*, 1954, **62**, 265–273.

Hefele, T. The effects of systematic human relations training upon student achievement. *Journal of Research and Development in Education*, 1971, **4**, 52–69.

Heider, F., Social perception and phenomenal causality. *Psychological Review*, 1944, **51**, 358–374.

Jackson, P., Silberman, M., and Wolfson, B. Signs of personal involvement in teachers' descriptions of their students. *Journal of Educational Psychology*, 1969, **60**, 22–27.

Kleinke, C. *First impressions: The psychology of encountering others.* Englewood Cliffs, N.J.: Prentice-Hall, 1975.

Landy, D., and Sigall, H. Beauty is talent: Task evaluation as a function of the performer's physical attractiveness. *Journal of Personality and Social Psychology,* 1974, **29,** 299–304.

McCroskey, J., Larson, K., and Knapp, M. *An introduction to interpersonal communication.* Englewood Cliffs, N.J.: Prentice-Hall, 1971.

Mehrabian, A. *Silent Messages.* Belmont, Calif.: Wadsworth, 1971.

Merritt, D. The relationship between qualifications and attitudes in a teacher selection situation. Ph.D. dissertation, Syracuse University, 1970. Reported in Byrne, D. *The attraction paradigm.* New York: Academic Press, 1971.

Newcomb, T. An approach to the study of communicative acts. *Psychological Review,* 1953, **60,** 393–404.

Newcomb, T. The prediction of interpersonal attraction. *American Psychologist,* 1956, **11,** 575–586.

Newcomb, T. *The acquaintance process.* New York: Holt, Rinehart and Winston, 1971.

Rich, A. *Interracial communication.* New York: Harper & Row, 1974.

Rogers, C. The interpersonal relationship in the facilitation of learning. In D. Avila, A. Combs, and W. Purkey (Eds.) *The helping relationship sourcebook.* Boston: Allyn & Bacon, 1973, 214–233.

Rosenfeld, L., and Civikly, J. *With words unspoken: The nonverbal experience.* New York: Holt, Rinehart and Winston, 1976.

Sapolsky, A. Effect of interpersonal relationships upon verbal conditioning. *Journal of Abnormal and Social Psychology,* 1960, **60,** 241–246.

Scheflen, A. *Body language and the social order.* Englewood Cliffs, N.J.: Prentice-Hall, 1972.

Smith, A. *Transracial communication.* Englewood Cliffs, N.J.: Prentice-Hall, 1973.

Smith, R., Meadow, B., and Sisk, T. Attitude similarity, interpersonal attraction, and evaluative social perception. *Psychonomic Science,* 1970, **18,** 226–227.

Turner, R., and Thompson, R. Relationships between college student ratings of instructors and residual learning. Paper presented at the annual meeting of the American Educational Research Association, Chicago, 1974.

Wagner, H. and Mitchell, K. Relationship between perceived instructors accurate empathy, warmth, and genuineness and college achievement. University of Arkansas, 1969. Reported in Boak and Conklin, *American Educational Research Journal,* 1975, **12,** 537–549.

Warr, P., and Knapper, C. *The perception of people and events.* New York: Wiley, 1968.

Chapter 9
The Social Environment of the Classroom

OBJECTIVES

After reading this chapter you should be able to:

1. define social environment.
2. identify the basic properties of social environment.
3. compare and contrast the operations and effects of physical and social environments.
4. discuss the effects of teaching style on classroom social environments.
5. identify characteristics of direct and indirect teaching styles.
6. describe the components of teacher style that are most conducive to positive social environments.
7. discuss the limitations of a pupil-talk-oriented teaching style.
8. identify the bases of a teacher's social power in the classroom.
9. identify strategies of coercion commonly observed in classrooms.
10. describe the elements of a behavior modification approach to classroom discipline.
11. describe the effects of student characteristics (conformity, apprehension, alienation) on classroom social environment.

12. identify strategies teachers use to overcome the impact of conformity on classroom transactions.
13. identify strategies teachers might use to assist students affected by apprehension or alienation.
14. provide examples of the ways teachers can facilitate the development of trust in the classroom.
15. define empathic ability and discuss its contribution to student-teacher relationships.
16. discuss the contribution of a teacher's listening behavior to the classroom social environment.
17. identify the characteristics of discriminative listening.

It was, all in all, a luxurious morning; the weather was exceedingly fine for early May. There was a pristine quality in the air that promised only good things. The woman watching the sun warm the bricks of the administration building just opposite shifted her attention back to her students, bent in varying degrees of intensity over a final examination. Surveying the class thus absorbed made the teacher reflective. "How did I do," she wondered. "What was the quality of their experience in our class?"

It is not particularly unusual for teachers to engage in this form of self-questioning. More often than not, however, the question joins the list of assorted imponderables each of us muses over on occasion. It is one thing to estimate the amount of learning that has taken place in a class and quite another to assess the social effects. Does this make the teacher's behavior in our example seem romantic or self-indulgent? We think not. Rather, her concern signals an awareness of classroom dynamics that echoes one of our basic contentions about instruction. The instructional process is essentially a *social* process in which teachers and learners communicate within a context. The terms in this principle of immediate concern to us are "social" and "context."

In earlier chapters we examined the instructional process in terms of the major participants, the symbol systems used, goals, and outcomes, continually stressing the interdependence and mutual influence of these factors. We now direct our attention to the sum of these parts: the social environment. We do so for a number of reasons. Each class inevitably produces a social environment which affects learning and/or teaching efforts. For this reason alone, it is desirable that your awareness and understanding of classroom social environments be heightened. Moreover, we believe that educators are too often preoccupied with what Getzels (1968) calls the *effectiveness* of an instructional system (success in achieving learning goals) as opposed to the *efficiency* (satisfaction of members) of the system. Let us buttress this value judgment with another, stronger one. We agree that promoting student mastery of subject matter is a major responsibility of teachers. We do not agree, however, that such outcomes are the only important consequences of instruction. As a teacher, your expertise in a subject matter and teaching skills are really prerequisites to your teaching performance. In your classroom we anticipate that you will find, as we have, that the most challenging problems emerge from breakdowns in the social system of the classroom. Resolution of these problems requires understanding of the effects of the classroom social environment on student and teacher behavior.

We won't pretend to make you a systems analyst through reading this chapter, but we believe that you will find the information has superior "survival value." First, we review the social environment concept. Then we highlight some characteristics of students and teachers which influence the development of a social environment.

PERSPECTIVES ON SOCIAL ENVIRONMENT

You are probably accustomed to thinking of the environment in purely physical terms: something tangible like giant redwoods or other natural resources to be conserved and protected. Physical environments may be shaped and influenced to accommodate our basic survival needs or to satisfy our aesthetic values. On the other hand, our behavior is shaped and influenced by the environment. This conception of physical environment, discussed fully in Chapter 6, is also useful in analyzing the social environment. The notable distinction between the two environments is that resources in the social environment tend to be more psychic than physical. Functionally, however, the difference is negligible. The rewards of social relationships (friendship, feelings of self-worth, respect) are no less real because they are intangible.

Similarly, each of us has a symbiotic relationship with our environments. We shape our social environment through selecting our friends, accepting or rejecting group memberships, and the like. When choice is not possible, however, the individuals we are thrust into contact with affect our behavior as inexorably as any physical phenomenon. There is a final distinction that can be drawn between the two types of environments, which has critical implications for classroom process. Physical environments, especially those associated with education, are designed for durability. Most physical settings in which instruction takes place are created on the assumption that they will serve the needs and purposes of teachers and students for many years. It is not surprising then that there is often little room for individual change and expression in these environments. Social environments, however, are composed of individuals and their relationships. For this reason they are fluid rather than static. As such, they are amenable to control and positive change.

The notion that classrooms and their occupants generate unique social environments is hardly new. We know, for example, a great deal about the social milieu of education in ancient Greece from Plato's dialogues. Nineteenth-century British classrooms are vividly described in Charles Dickens' *Hard Times* and *David Copperfield,* and scathingly satirized in Lewis Carroll's *Alice in Wonderland.* Contemporary treatments such as Kozol's *Death at an Early Age* present a startlingly bleak picture of life in American classrooms. The major problem? A desensitized, uncaring social environment which stifles rather than stimulates students (Kozol, 1967).

Whenever groups of individuals are assembled, there are many dimensions of experience for the group as a whole, as well as for individual members. Just as most groups have tasks to complete, so too do individuals have social and emotional needs which are affected by the group experience. Students and teachers within classrooms are no different. Learning is the dominant task of the classroom group, but have you ever considered the social-emotional dimension of your experience? Think about the class you have enjoyed most in the last year. What made it especially good? Was it the amount of new information you gained or was it perhaps something less directly measurable? If your experience is like that of most, your answer is probably "both." It is not uncommon to find that students seem to learn more, or at least learn more easily, in classes they enjoy. If you've had this experience, then you have a basis for understanding your response to the social environment.

Over the last two decades, it has become commonplace to speak of the social-emotional dimension of classroom experience in terms of "climate" or "atmosphere." Educational researchers have determined that positive classroom climates are more desirable than those which are negative. On this point there is consensus. Less apparent, however, is agreement on what actually constitutes a positive classroom social environment. Some authorities (Flanders, 1963, 1970) view teacher behavior as the principal determinant. Others (Schmuck and Schmuck, 1975; Friedrich, Galvin, and Book, 1976) stress a process orientation in which students and teachers alike influence the development and maintenance of the social environment. Moreover, there are differences among authorities concerning the number and types of factors which characterize positive or negative classroom climates. Hence it is difficult to make a summary definition of social environment. Nonetheless, we can identify at least two general properties of the concept, which may provide us with an acceptable definition.

Social environments of learning describe and reflect the emotional experiences of the participants in a given educational event. Think about

FIGURE 9·1 SOCIAL ENVIRONMENTS ARE COMPOSED OF INDIVIDUALS AND THEIR RELATIONSHIPS.

the various classes you are currently attending. You can probably characterize the feeling tones associated with these classes quite easily. Some classes may be formal and serene, while others may be unpredictable, active, or even explosive. In one class, you may feel secure, alert, and involved. In another you may experience only feelings of anxiety, frustration, or resentment. In a like manner, teachers can usually label the feelings they experience in the various classes they teach. What determines the direction and intensity of these feelings? The answer is at once simple and complex, because we are dealing with the interpersonal relationships between teacher and students as well as those between students. Therefore each individual's perception of self, others, class structure and subject matter, and the schooling experience influences one's affective state. The full range of human needs, expectations, motives, and values are brought into play in determining the emotional response each of us has toward a classroom situation.

The second property of social environments concerns the process nature of communication and instruction. Simply stated, we are referring to the constant interplay of the elements of a communication event. You know that on some days your ability to respond is lower than on others and that your moods may vary widely within the course of a single hour. What seems amusing during one class meeting may become irritating during another. Fluctuations in social environment may thus result from internal shifts in mood or interest of either student or teacher.

External factors of course create changes also. One familiar juncture of classroom life at which such changes may occur is when tests are given. Have you not been appalled and outraged on occasion to witness the metamorphosis of your previously reasonable, equitable, and congenial Professor Jones into a dogmatic, arbitrary, ill-tempered, and decidedly tyrannical despot? Sound familiar? Possibly a matter of tricky multiple-choice questions that Professor Jones (AKA "The Great Pretender") insists "discriminate adequately at the appropriate level of difficulty." All well and good, but you *know* that question 34 has at least three correct answers among the five possible. Meanwhile, Professor Jones is probably entertaining some fairly colorful speculations about your behavior, too. Our point is simply this: Social environment is a dynamic element of classroom life in which shifts in direction and intensity of feelings are inevitable.

The social environment, then, may be defined as the level and quality of emotional involvement experienced by the classroom group. It evolves through the dynamic processes of classroom interactions, involving interpersonal relationships at several levels: teacher-class (group), teacher-student, student-class (group), and student-student. It influences and is influenced by the task goals (learning) of the classroom. Finally, the social environment is manifested through the styles of relating used by members of the classroom group.

PRINCIPLES 9.1

1. Every classroom group generates a unique social environment.
2. The social environment is defined by the affective outcomes of instruction but influences the cognitive (learning) outcomes as well.
3. A classroom social environment is a dynamic outgrowth of the communication exchanges between and among members of the classroom group.

TEACHER IMPACT ON SOCIAL ENVIRONMENT

In this section we summarize the findings from decades of research aimed at identifying the characteristics of efficient and effective teaching. Moreover, we are concerned specifically with the impact of various teacher behaviors on the social environment for learning. Our analysis is intended less as an attempt to identify specific discrete behaviors that you should apply in your classrooms than as an objective interpretation of available findings. Hopefully, this analysis will enable you to make a reasoned decision about classroom management techniques based on your own and your students' needs.

We insert this disclaimer because we firmly agree with critics who assert that too much of the literature on the theory and practice of instruction is founded on equal parts of myth, generalization, and well-intended but ill-defined perceptions of how things "ought to be." After 75 years of sustained research, few genuinely authoritative statements relating teacher characteristics to pupil performance exist. Why? Quite simply, the answer lies in individual differences. Methodological errors, the absence of grounded theory, and a variety of other problems characterize the research. None of these deficits, however, has so drastic an impact on the utility of these findings as the compelling reality of teachers and students as unique, individual participants in the learning environment. Knowing that you are deeply concerned about maximizing your effectiveness as a teacher only emphasizes the importance of these qualifying statements in our approach. You know that we are wary of labels and their implications, so we must stress a critical point. *The principles we identify are not absolutes.* Rather, they are most appropriately viewed as generalizations. The applicability of these principles is subject to any number of personal and situational constraints. Your informed judgment will be an essential ingredient in determining the optimal strategy for you. With this admonition in mind, we proceed to probe two areas of teacher behavior we consider important to the development of classroom social environments: teaching style and discipline.

Teaching Style

The role of the teacher in determining social atmosphere has long been recognized as a dominant and pervasive one. No other individual has more power, decision-making options, and opportunities for interaction in the classroom group. If whimsy were appropriate, we could easily offer you a set of adjective pairs, direct you to select the ones which were most appealing to you, provide composite descriptions associated with each, and send you on your way. The choices available? Approaching it cafeteria style, you can presumably choose to be traditional or progressive, open or closed, custodial or humanistic, reactive or proactive, student-centered or teacher-centered, direct or indirect, impulsive or reflective, convergent or divergent, formal or informal, dominant or integrative, and/or democratic or authoritarian. This listing, admittedly not an exhaustive one, is not included to overwhelm or amuse you. We hope, instead, that it will heighten your awareness of the diversity of teacher traits or behaviors that have been investigated and the problems involved in creating a profile of ideal behavior. Moreover, we suspect that, if you reread our list, you will be struck by the degree to which many of the labels appear to be synonomous and are laden with emotive significance. Is there any real question in your mind which of the paired adjectives describes the "ought to be" state of affairs we alluded to earlier?

Early studies of teaching style attempted to apply findings from small-group leadership research in educational settings. The prototype for these investigations was the classic Lewin, Lippitt, and White (1939) study. They investigated the effects of three styles of adult leaders— authoritarian, democratic, and laissez-faire—on the efficiency and effectiveness of teams of boys doing construction projects at a summer camp. Authoritarian leaders took personal control, made all the decisions, and assumed responsibility for the project. Democratic leaders assumed responsibility but sought active involvement from the boys by seeking their ideas, stimulating them toward self-direction and stressing group consensus on proposed actions. Laissez-faire leaders did nothing. They avoided leadership, refusing to provide structure, information, or advice.

Results of the study indicated that authoritarian and democratic leadership styles produced substantially superior products than the laissez-faire style. Boys directed by authoritarian leaders produced the best projects, but observers noted that their efforts were conducted in an environment riddled with anxiety, tension, and frequent outbursts of hostility, arguments, and fights. Boys under democratic leaders were only slightly less efficient than those in the authoritarian-led groups. The researchers contended that the slight difference between the two groups' performances was attributable to the greater amount of time required to arrive at a group consensus before proceeding. Unlike the other group, these boys appeared to work together harmoniously. Furthermore, they were capable of sustaining a cooperative effort even in the absence of their leader. The group led by the laissez-faire style accomplished almost none of its tasks. Still, the boys appeared to have a good time, despite the confusion and lack of coordination that surrounded their efforts.

FIGURE 9·2. THERE ARE MANY CHOICES FOR TEACHING STYLE.

Educators were immediately aware of the potential implications for teachers' leadership styles in the classroom. Results from a number of early studies comparing democratic and authoritarian teaching styles summarized by Anderson (1959) revealed that there was indeed support for the assumption that the two styles produced different learning outcomes. Inconsistency, however, marked the findings with regard to which style produced the most learning.

Of greater relevance to our discussion of social environments are the findings on students' preferences for two leadership styles. On this matter there was much higher agreement among the findings. Teachers with democratic styles were perceived more positively by their students. Similarly, the classrooms of the democratic teachers were found to have much more positive social environments than those of authoritarian teachers. Students seemed to be more actively involved, more cooperative, and less frustrated.

Dozens of studies followed these early findings. Those associated with the general concept of teacher-student interaction analysis originated by Flanders (1963, 1970) have generated the most consistent findings across student populations, educational level, and teachers. Flanders' analysis leads to a characterization of teaching style along a continuum from teacher "directness" to "indirectness." Teachers who have a direct style tend to lecture, give directions, and criticize student performance. These teachers are frequently referred to as those who engage in a lot of "teacher talk." The category descriptions in Table 9.1 provide examples of the types of comments associated with this style. Indirect teachers, by contrast, are those who tend to accept feelings, provide praise and encouragement, and use students' ideas frequently.

Findings reviewed by Flanders (1970) and Rosenshine and Furst (1971) generally support the contention that indirect teacher behaviors facilitate student learning when measured by achievement tests. As you might infer from inspection of Table 9.1, indirect teachers were considerably more effective in generating a positive social environment than their counterparts with direct teaching styles. Indirect teachers made greater use of "pupil talk" which appeared to enhance student involvement, independent activity, and feelings of satisfaction toward school and schoolwork. Arguing the merits of indirect teaching, Flanders notes that the frequency of teachers' statements making use of ideas expressed by students is directly related to the average class scores on attitude scales of teacher attractiveness and liking the class, and to average achievement scores for the class as a whole (Flanders, 1970).

When considering the development of social environments, two other characteristics of teacher performance become important. Teacher warmth and teacher enthusiasm facilitate students' feelings of self-worth and positive social climates and promote student learning as well. In-

Table 9.1   FLANDERS' INTERACTION ANALYSIS CATEGORIES (FIAC)

	Response	1. Accepts feeling. Accepts and clarifies an attitude or the feeling tone of a pupil in a nonthreatening manner. Feelings may be positive or negative. Predicting and recalling feelings are included. 2. Praises or encourages. Praises or encourages pupil action or behavior. Jokes that release tension, but not all at the expense of another individual; nodding head, or saying "um hm?" or "go on" are included. 3. Accepts or uses ideas of pupils. Clarifying, building, or developing ideas suggested by a pupil. Teacher extensions of pupil ideas are included but as the teacher brings more of his own ideas into play, shift to category five.
Teacher talk		4. Asks questions. Asking a question about content or procedure, based on teacher ideas, with the intent that a pupil will answer.
	Initiation	5. Lecturing. Giving facts or opinions about content or procedures; expressing his own ideas, giving his own explanation, or citing an authority other than a pupil. 6. Giving directions. Directions, commands, or orders to which a pupil is expected to comply. 7. Criticizing or justifying authority. Statements intended to change pupil behavior from non-acceptable pattern; bawling someone out; stating why the teacher is doing what he is doing; extreme self-reliance.
	Response	8. Pupil-talk—response. Talk by pupils in response to teacher. Teacher initiates the contact or solicits pupil statement or structures the situation. Freedom to express own ideas is limited.
Pupil talk	Initiation	9. Pupil-talk—initiation. Talk by pupils which they imitate. Expressing own ideas; initiating a new topic; freedom to develop opinions and a line of thought, like asking thoughtful questions; going beyond the existing structure.
Silence		10. Silence or confusion. Pauses, short periods of silence and periods of confusion in which communication cannot be understood by the observer.

SOURCE: From Flanders, N. A. *Analyzing Teaching Behavior.* Reading, Mass.: Addison-Wesley, 1970. © 1970, Addison-Wesley. Reprinted by permission.

terestingly, the elements which create student perceptions of a teacher as warm are quite similar to those which characterize the indirect teaching style, including frequent use of praise and student ideas, and development of personal relationships with students. Enthusiasm is expressed largely through a teacher's presentation style, incorporating verbal and nonverbal cues associated with liveliness, interest, and involvement.

Taken together, these findings invite you to conclude that an indirect teaching style, combined with enthusiasm, is ideal. We agree, but with some distinct reservations. Brophy and Good (1974) have noted a disturbing trend in the literature on teaching which equates teacher talk on the Flanders scale with teacher domination of the classroom. Accompanying this impression is the exceedingly shaky inference that the social environment of a classroom is positive *only* when the ratio of pupil talk is high. We find this assumption, which has achieved some popularity, totally unwarranted and in fact rather dangerous. Consider what your reaction would be if this notion were extended to the logical extreme. You enter class on the first day and find an instructor who is willing to structure the class almost solely on the basis of what happens to be brought up by you or your classmates on that and subsequent days the class meets. You may think that sounds just fine now. Certain teaching strategies, particularly those which emphasize student self-paced or independent learning, operate in this manner. If, however, neither the subject matter nor the teaching strategy warrants this style, you might find yourself saying, "Hey, what's he doing here, leading discussions or teaching us something?" That may sound harsh, but it reveals a serious point about teaching style and teaching substance that we must emphasize. Teaching, regardless of what the subject matter is, necessarily involves some informational exchange among students and teachers. Hopefully, the teacher has the larger share of the information, and this means that teacher talk should predominate. In our eagerness to establish good social environments we cannot lose sight of our primary responsibility—optimizing learning gains in students. While we certainly believe that the social environment affects the learning of your students, we do not recommend that you sacrifice substance to achieve style.

Similarly, there are limitations on these elements of teacher style attributable to differences in the subject matter you teach. Can you imagine trying to teach physics through group discussion? Ridiculous, right? There are many subject matter areas which are best taught by the teacher and not with the often unwieldy technique of trying to involve everyone. The time for bringing the lecture method up from disrepute is long overdue. The defensiveness with which this instructional method is treated in many teaching methods textbooks is both distasteful and misleading. The bulk of research literature comparing various teaching methods clearly indicates that, at worst, the much maligned lecture is no less effective than most of the methods with which it is compared.

As supporting evidence for this argument we refer you to Chapter 8 in which we reported findings that the most effective teachers are those that students judge as dominant. You may be certain that your students will disagree with the behaviors that are characteristic of direct teaching, but these are an integral and vital part of instruction. We see no rationale for excluding any of them because they might increase the incidence of conflict. Remember that you must derive the teaching style that is functional for you, your students, and your subject matter. Slavish adherence to any single style is an error.

Discipline

Few topics are more surrounded by confusion and emotionalism than the question of discipline in contemporary classrooms. The question of corporal punishment, for example, seems to be continuously debated in PTA groups as well as in courtrooms. We do not intend to deal with this issue but focus instead on the business of handling deviance in the classroom. We also attempt to identify how some of the ways that teachers keep students "on task" affect the social environment. At the outset, we confirm what you already know: There are no methods of discipline that create good feelings. None of us really enjoys the prospect or process of discipline, regardless of our status as student or teacher. Nonetheless, dealing with deviant behavior is a problem that confronts every teacher. We therefore briefly consider some of the methods that you should definitely *avoid* to create an optimal environment for learning.

In an earlier chapter, we identified power discrepancies between teachers and students as a potential source of conflict. Discipline is the exercise of a teacher's power, and the strategies of discipline chosen determine much about the social climate for the classroom group. You can turn your classroom into a jungle in which nothing short of whips and tranquilizer guns can maintain a semblance of order. At the other extreme, you may make yourself one great voice above a sullen silence. We frankly do not know a great deal about the value of various disciplinary measures, because they have been examined as part of the total mosaic of teacher-student relationships rather than studied in isolation. We can, however, make some inferences from what is known about the uses of power in the classroom and in other settings.

French and Raven (1959) identified five types of power: *Expert power* is attributed on the basis of the knowledge a person is perceived to have. *Legitimate power* is attributed on the basis of the role or the perceived "right" to influence. *Reward power* is assigned on the basis of an individual's control of rewards. *Referent power* is attributed on the basis of a group's identification with a person as their leader. *Coercive power* is attributed on the basis of a person's ability to inflict punishment.

The ideal teaching power probably stems from referent and expert power. Realistically, however, we would probably be more accurate if we chose legitimate, reward, and coercive power to describe life in most classrooms. By virtue of their position, most teachers have legitimate power and reward power. Coercion seems to be a disciplinary strategy which has survived largely because it is somewhat effective and certainly the most easily applied. Its impact on interpersonal relationships among teachers and students is another story altogether.

Coercion in the classroom may occur on a number of levels. These range from subtle forms of trickery and intellectual game playing to physical threat. Strom (1973) has delineated several of these techniques. One familiar strategem is the omnipotence-omniscience routine. The teacher's self-presentation indicates the depth of her power over the student through the information she possesses about him and the entire world of knowledge. Veiled or explicit references to a student's personal file, what other teachers are saying or have said about him, and a series of similar bluffs are used to keep the student fully aware of his inferior status. Such ploys quiet overt expressions of disagreement, but at what price? Omniscient strategies begin with the fallacious assumption that there are right answers for every question—and who knows them all? Right. Teacher does. A colleague of ours refers to this form of coercion as "speaking with the assurance that the stonecutters are hovering nearby, chisels ready to etch the final truths in granite as they trip from the teacher's lips." You've seen this show before; the complex language that completely clouds the question, or that hoariest of old chestnuts, "Why, you're right Hector, I was wondering if anyone was really listening." One of the exercises we recommend teachers employ to combat this impulse is writing, "I am not infallible nor should I be," on the chalkboard 100 times, at least once a week.

A related strategy Strom (1973) calls the "big lie," a time-honored method for undermining confidence and inducing submission, particularly when the lie contains just enough truth to make it believable. Remember your first-grade teacher's most awesome threat? We do, and vividly: "If you children do not finish your lunch, you will have it fried for breakfast tomorrow." Now, that should *not* have worked at all because our mothers wouldn't even eat in the school cafeteria, much less come by to pick up the scraps. Quite often, the "big lie" creeps into a teacher's repertoire because it reflects genuine intentions and is exaggerated for purposes of emphasis. Regardless of intent, the continued use of threats is a negative practice with few happy consequences. If overused, threats lose credibility, leading to a wildly ascending spiral of progressively greater threats. In the end, everyone has lost.

A final coercive strategy we find particularly insidious is the friendly enemy game, designed to be played one-on-one with the purpose of undermining a student's sense of security. In essence, the game involves a two-step influence in which the student is subtly made to believe (1) that everyone in the environment is against her, and (2) that the teacher is her only friend. Skilled players can sometimes achieve this with entire classes, setting one group against another or one class against the larger school system. Manipulative strategies should not be confused with motivational techniques. The implications of leading an errant student to believe you are her last and only resort are too serious to risk and, to our way of thinking, far more damaging than any classroom misbehavior could warrant.

Other techniques of discipline, studied extensively by Kounin (1970) and his associates, have focused on the effectiveness of "desist tactics." These are actions teachers take to stop deviant behavior once it has started. Kounin's research dealt almost exclusively with elementary school students. Behavior patterns established in early school years, however, are probably stable enough to warrant some generalization to all levels of education. You may not act out your impulse to leave your seat and go over to talk to your best friend in the classroom today, but the tendency toward inattention may remain. In any case, Kounin's work revealed that none of the desist tactics were related to teacher behaviors which were effective in promoting student work involvement. Morrison (1974), among others, confirmed the general finding that specific teacher attempts to stop deviant behavior had no effect on the amount of deviant or productive behaviors in the class.

Given these findings, what approach can be relied upon for a reasonable mixture of control and concern? A number of options exist, beginning with the most vital resource at your disposal as a teacher: awareness and understanding of your students as a group unlike any other. Equally important is a clearly defined set of expectations which is fully and frankly communicated to students, not in terms of threats and punishments, but simply in terms of the consequences you feel are most significant for your class as a group. Given the opportunity to share some responsibility in shaping this set of expectations can create a sense of involvement for students that is never achieved otherwise. Then, be prepared for deviant behavior, because it will occur unfailingly. We suggest that you abandon the "survival orientation" to discipline, which stipulates that deviance be confronted as it happens on a moment-to-moment basis, and apply the principles of behavior modification. Calling attention to deviant behavior through disciplinary moves, according to this approach, may serve only to create conflicts and reinforce the behavior. A more productive strategy is to ignore the deviant behavior and reinforce only desired behavior. An increasing amount of evidence suggests that, as teachers apply this principle through the contingent use of praise and attention, deviant behavior decreases. Over time this leads to more positive social environments.

STUDENT IMPACT ON SOCIAL ENVIRONMENT

Although teachers are the acknowledged pacesetters in establishing a social environment, the success or failure of their attempts is at least partially determined by their students. For the most part, the group characteristics of a particular class are likely to interact with teacher characteristics in shaping a social environment. The blend of personality, behavioral, and situational factors that each class brings into play is staggering. Two student-related phenomena that are particularly important are conformity and anxiety or alienation.

Conformity

Throughout this chapter we have stressed the notion of a class as a social unit rather than a collection of individuals. This emphasis may seem contradictory to our basic contention that teaching is an interpersonal communication event. Well, it isn't, and it is. This simply means that, although teaching is interpersonal in nature, every class assumes a character that is greater than the sum of its individual members, a "groupness" that influences a teacher's behavior and is logically distinct from the effects of individual members. Regardless of whether the class comes to perceive themselves as a group or not, teachers invariably view their classes as groups with specific characteristics and respond to them accordingly. This of course influences the development of affective relations among all parties present.

One of the overriding influences that warrant the designation "group" for a class is conformity. Over time (less time required than you might predict), a class develops certain informal norms, roles, and status hierarchies that may be influenced by teacher behavior but may also differ markedly from the teacher's conception. The old "teacher's pet" phenomenon may illustrate the idea for you. In the teacher's eyes, the chosen one is at the top of the status hierarchy in the class. In the students' view, the teacher's pet may be the least esteemed person in the class. When students conform to standards of behavior that differ from the teacher's and the system's, the prospects for the social environment are not happy.

Peer influence on student behavior is one of the most significant realities of classroom life. Once a child enters school, she begins to spend more time with individuals her own age than she does with adults. This pattern remains throughout the schooling years and adulthood. Wright (1967) reports that the difference in favor of peers emerges early. The typical 8-year-old spends 40 percent of her time with peers and 20 percent with teachers and parents. By age 16, approximately 80 percent of her time is spent with peers compared to less than 20 percent in adult company. Given these data the argument for a pervasive peer culture affecting in-class behavior seems indisputable.

Jackson (1960) was among the first to examine systematically the powerful role of students' influence on student life in education. Conformity is the price of admission to peer culture. It is a price most students are eager to pay for the rewards of acceptance and affiliation. These motives, powerful throughout life, are singularly forceful to students because they are afforded so little individual autonomy and power. The security afforded by group membership provides both solace and the sense of strength that comes through mutual identification.

We are all familiar with the manifestations of conformity that seem amusing from the comfortable distance of the immediate past. Consider dress norms. Remember the agony involved in convincing your parents that *nobody* would be caught dead dressed in _____? Much less laughable are studies demonstrating the degree to which peer norms change students' college aspirations, self-concepts, and personal value systems. Moreover, the conformity of students to peer standards plays a critical role in their academic performance.

Problems arise when norms for the student population and the norms of teachers are incongruent. When this situation develops in a classroom, conflicts are likely to occur frequently and intensely. Usually, direct tactics on the teacher's part only serve to create an outside threat to the cohesiveness of the group. Since this strategy maximizes differences between norms, rather than emphasizing similarities, it has a low probability of success. Effecting positive change toward congruency between peer and teacher norms is perhaps best accomplished through a more indirect approach.

We know that conformity has its basis in modeling, the observation and imitation of an esteemed individual's behavior. Students high in conformity are also likely to prefer structured, well-defined environments. An optimal strategy therefore includes an assessment of the dominant members (opinion leaders) of the peer group, since their behavior is likely to influence the rest of the group. Shared leadership and decision-making responsibilities could be delegated to these students to encourage fuller group participation. A vivid case in point occurred during the tense period following the initiation of a federally ordered busing program in Louisville, Kentucky, in 1975. After several anxious weeks, punctuated by outbreaks of violence between black and white students, it became apparent to opinion leaders within both student groups that continued

FIGURE 9·3 CONFORMITY IS THE PRICE OF ADMISSION TO PEER CULTURE.

hostility was undesirable. In a short time, violence in the schools decreased sharply, although the parents of the students continued their campaigns of hostility and harassment unabated in the streets surrounding the schools.

Less dramatic are numerous instances teachers share with us concerning their way of dealing with disruptive "ringleaders" in the classroom. One colleague, an elementary school principal, reports that the time-honored strategy of appointing these leaders to positions as hallway, playground, or crosswalk monitors is as effective in 1977 as it ever was. Rules are observed, apparently without the damaging effects of teacher threats and student rebellions.

Sharing leadership of course is not the ultimate panacea. Do not expect major shifts immediately. You should instead adhere to a reasonably tightly structured teaching and classroom management strategy which will reduce the ambiguity that drives students to seek peer opinion for confirmation. Above all, remember that groups define social reality for their members. Verbal broadsides on the incongruent norms of your class only polarize their position.

Apprehension and Alienation

Our decision to consider apprehensive and alienated students together is purely arbitrary. The two problems are not synonomous, although the conforming student, the apprehensive student, and the alienated student share similar problems and frequently behave comparably. Generally the student who is apprehensive about learning and the school environment, like the conforming student, responds best in learning gains and affective outcomes to more directed, structured teaching styles.

Apprehension

Communication apprehension, a term used to describe the experience of the individual who suffers anxiety concerning communicative (teaching-learning) events, appears to differentiate among students with regard to various aspects of classroom life. McCroskey (1977) summarizes research suggesting that high communication apprehension is likely to affect student performance adversely in all academic settings that require active communication between teacher and student or student and student. The impact of communication apprehension on teacher expectations for student performances is largely negative, leading to a host of possible negative outcomes for the student (Smythe and Powers, 1978).

Given the foregoing statements, you can imagine the potential effects of communication apprehension on classroom social environments. The problem is rather cyclic in operation. Apprehensive students actively avoid communication, and their withdrawal heightens the probability that their performance will be negatively evaluated by peers and teachers alike. Attempts to force involvement on apprehensive students tend to aggravate the condition by increasing the students' desire to withdraw. Too often, teachers and peers respond to the apprehensive student's reluctance to participate in the classroom group with impatience, frustration, or even scorn. A destructive pattern for the apprehensive student and the tenor of classroom life is all too quickly established.

Not much is known concerning how or why students become apprehensive. Some authors advance the idea that early socialization experiences in the home as well as the school environment foster development of the problem. Remember our discussion in Chapter 5 on student self-presentation? At that point we identified silence as the basic behavior expected of students. Perhaps some students internalize this aspect of classroom life so thoroughly that it permeates their entire lives. Other perspectives suggest communication apprehension is a personality trait or a product of continued association with other apprehensive individuals (teachers, too).

Regardless of its origins, communication apprehension can become a disruptive factor in classroom life. Consider the impact of an apprehensive teacher combined with apprehensive students on the social environment. The potential for developing a healthy exchange of feelings, or even minimal relating between teacher and student or student and student, is virtually nil. We would also anticipate that negative effects on learning might occur.

While the apprehensive student is not hard to recognize in the classroom, dealing with the problem in a supportive, effective way is substantially more difficult. The student who is apprehensive about talking avoids talking in class as vigorously as you might avoid thrusting your hand into a box of live white rats. Where possible, intervention strategies such as counseling by trained personnel should be undertaken. While systematic desensitization programs have proved effective in reducing apprehension for certain age groups (McCroskey, 1972), and are fairly simple to learn and administer, too many teachers are unqualified or unable to offer such treatment to their students. Bear in mind also that as a teacher you may pose a considerable threat to the anxious student.

Equally undesirable strategies include hectoring the student or, worse still, ignoring the problem altogether. No student should be bullied into participation "for his or her own good." The potential damage to self-esteem is too real. On the other hand, allowing apprehensive students to withdraw completely consigns them to what we call the "more of less" classroom life: less attention, less involvement, less satisfaction. Perhaps the best prescription we can offer is one discussed in Chapter 6. The power of teacher praise, when sincerely given to reward performance, can effect a change in the apprehensive student's behavior. Making communication a rewarding rather than a painful event for these students increases the chance that their perceptions of the risks and threats involved in communicating will moderate. Be realistic. The student who has been sitting in your classroom for a solid month without uttering a solitary word has probably spent a number of years acquiring that pattern. You cannot expect to create a talking wonder, but positive gains are possible. Moreover, the reduction in tension for your apprehensive students, the classroom group, and yourself can only accelerate the development of positive social environments.

Alienation

As an aspect of student life and academic performance, alienation is a problem of indeterminate proportions. High attrition rates in secondary schools, colleges, and universities are widely cited as evidence of a spiraling increase in the number of students that have physically or psychologically withdrawn from the classroom. There are, however, few accurate statistics available. Alienation may be thought of in one sense as the logical outcome of the powerlessness characterizing the student role. We know a young man who enrolled in a class we taught as graduate students and impressed us by his intelligence, insight, and perseverance. His academic promise was reflected in his performance over the first two years of college, but in his junior year he began to change. At first he seemed only more reserved and calm, which we attributed to maturation, but as the year wore on, it became increasingly apparent that our former student was experiencing some deep changes in outlook. He became cynical about the motives and intentions of everyone associated with education (ourselves included). As his grades began to suffer from his excessive absenteeism, he blamed his professors for discriminating against him. He became more and more like a character in a J. D. Salinger novel, until one day he was gone, "drained," he said, "by a parasitic, unfeeling, and inhumane bureaucracy."

Alienation among students is at once a cause and an effect of poor social environments for learning. Like the conforming and the apprehensive student, the original problem lies in the student's concern with his potential to achieve in academic settings. His response differs in that he becomes disaffected, indifferent to whether or not his performance conforms to his own or the system's definition of success. Whereas many communication-apprehensive students actually want to change in terms of their ability to communicate, the alienated student neither desires nor seeks such change. More often than not, alienated students physically absent themselves from the school environment. If attendance is forced upon them, whether by legal or parental constraint, they are likely to psychically "drop out." In either case, these alienated students are difficult to reach. In a sense, this creates more serious problems in environmental maintenance for the teacher and classroom group. The apprehensive student avoids the kinds of communicative exchanges that are essential to social environments. The alienated student flatly rejects not only communication, but the entire group as well. As you no doubt know from your own experience, there are few things more quelling than total rejection.

Studies reported by Van der Berg (1976) suggest that the problem lies in the discrepancy between the orientation students bring to the classroom and the system they encounter there. Particularly acute are the discrepancies for students who have a high orientation toward interpersonal relationships. These students bring to their encounters with teachers a strong need for personal confirmation, closeness, or understanding. Finding this need unsatisfied, they become alienated from both their teachers and the entire educational process. These observations indicate the importance of a positive social environment in the prevention of alienation.

The implications of student anxiety and alienation for social environments seem to be twofold. Neither characteristic is one which the typical classroom teacher is likely to be able to deal with on a treatment level. Indeed, Jackson (1973) concedes that there is no established treatment for alienated students. Given that as much as 25 percent of the population suffers from communication apprehension, however, it is highly likely that you will encounter these students in your classrooms. Our current understanding of these problems suggests that anxious and alienated students suffer from a low tolerance for ambiguity. Clarity, then, in terms of expectations, criteria for evaluation, student role, and the meaning of academic success are essential to the development of positive learning experiences for these students. What seems apparent is that they have endured a history of punishment in academic learning encounters that they neither understood nor overcame. Explicit, direct instruction advanced in a positive, supportive social system will not necessarily overcome years of frustration, but might facilitate their movement toward greater self-respect and liking.

These characteristics of teachers and students are not the sole influences in the classroom social environment, but each aspect discussed in the foregoing sections is likely to influence every classroom to an appreciable extent. We have summarized some of the principles from this section as follows.

PRINCIPLES 9.2

1. The influence of teaching style on classroom social environment appears to revolve around the concept of teacher control; the more control exerted, the less positive the environment.

2. Indirect teaching styles, characterized by high levels of pupil talk seem to produce greater student satisfaction. This style, however, is not always appropriate or desirable for learning goals.
3. Teachers whose style is characterized by warmth and enthusiasm appear to promote learning gains and positive social environments.
4. Conflicts frequently arise over a teacher's exercise of power in terms of discipline.
5. Coercive discipline strategies are conducive to negative social environments.
6. Desist tactics as discipline strategies appear relatively ineffective in promoting learning or positive social environments.
7. Behavior modification techniques appear to be an effective means of maintaining discipline without negative effects on the social environment.
8. Incongruent teacher and class goals or values negatively affect student-teacher relationships.
9. Students may conform to group norms that are disruptive to instruction as a result of peer pressure, anxiety, or the need to reduce uncertainty about their personal goals or merit.
10. Apprehensive and alienated students tend to reject either teacher norms or group classroom norms as an expression of their withdrawal from group membership, dissatisfaction, or fear concerning any aspect of the learning situation.
11. Many teachers are not qualified to deal with anxious or alienated students on a treatment level. Instead, teaching strategies stressing clarity and structure may be effective in dealing with the conforming, anxious, or alienated classroom group.

TOWARD POSITIVE SOCIAL ENVIRONMENTS FOR LEARNING

Throughout this chapter we have attempted to demonstrate how the teacher in our opening example could begin to answer her question about the quality of her students' experience in the class they shared. In the process we have raised problems for which there are no wholly satisfactory solutions. Now we want to share our philosophy with you about developing positive social environments.

Your primary responsibility in the classroom is to promote learning gains in your students. You knew before you read this text, however, that there is much more to successful teaching. Our goal from the outset has been to assist you in your efforts to become a maximally effective member of the instructional group. Your awareness of the implications of social environments for learning increases your chances of achieving that level of effectiveness. In your daily encounters with students your behavior determines much about the quality of the learning experience for them. The following behaviors describe a realistic yet humanistic set of attributes that should characterize your relationships with students. Developing these attributes does not, unfortunately, guarantee a healthy, positive social environment. But, like mother's chicken soup, it can't hurt.

Trust

Virtually every description of the competent teacher emphasizes the necessity for establishing trust in relations with students. Certainly your credibility as a teacher depends on the level of trust students place in your abilities. Their feelings about the educational setting are similarly influenced. Rogers (1973) argues that trust determines the extent to which you will be able to affect any change, cognitive or affective, in your students.

Developing trust in classroom settings cannot be expected to take place without effort on your part. Unless you are teaching kindergarten, your students bring to your interactions a history of relationships with teachers. These expectations combined with their initial impressions of you shape their responses. Therefore you should work toward establishing trust early on as an integral element of your classroom environment. Some specific suggestions for developing trust stress acceptance, consistency, and honesty in your interactions with students. We consider each of these briefly.

In Chapter 2 the significance of teacher appraisals in shaping students' perceptions of their personal worth was emphasized. Your willingness to provide *unconditional acceptance* of your students as individuals sharply affects their willingness to trust you. Let your students see from the outset that, regardless of their personal and/or academic characteristics, you acknowledge their unique individuality and grant them the regard for feelings and dignity that you expect from them.

Similarly, you should strive for consistency in your encounters with students. All of us have bad days, but a switch from Mary Poppins to a feminine version of Attila the Hun is not conducive to forming trusting relationships. No rigidity is implied here, but your students should be able to rely on you to avoid sudden changes in the standards you've established. Saying one thing and doing another creates mistrust and misunderstanding if it becomes a pattern. This statement applies as well to relationships as it does to rules. A willing confidant one day, who becomes an aloof superior the next, is not likely to inspire much confidence. Finally, consistency implies equitable treatment for students. Permitting your expectations for a student to dictate his or her classroom experiences, or engaging in the old teacher's pet routine are destructive practices. It requires real effort on your part to avoid them.

Honesty is essential to the establishment of trust on two levels. First, candid feedback is vital to effective instruction. Skip the sugar-coating treatment and phrase your evaluations in simple, nonjudgmental language. Straight talk breeds respect, even when the news is bad. On

FIGURE 9·4 TREAT ALL STUDENTS
FAIRLY AND AVOID TEACHERS' PETS.

another, more important level, honesty involves risk taking. Letting your students see who you are may cost you a little power, but you've lots to spare, and the dividends in trust and liking are potentially high. When you err, admit it and leave it behind you. Above all, don't pretend to be someone you are not. You've more than enough to do without having to orchestrate a command performance for every class. There's nothing more destructive to trust than dishonesty.

Empathy

The ability to comprehend fully the feelings, experiences, and perceptions of another describes empathic ability. All of us possess this ability in some degree. This special sensitivity enables you to understand the subjective world of others, to "stand in their shoes" as the old saying goes. Rogers (1973), Bochner and Kelley (1974), and Barbour and Goldberg (1974) indicate that empathic skill distinguishes the most effective teachers, although there is considerable disagreement on whether or not empathy can be learned. Implications for teacher-student relationships are obvious. The more empathic you are, the more likely you are to communicate accurately with your students, thereby avoiding the misperceptions that lead to frequent conflicts.

Research on empathic individuals reveals that these people are oriented toward others and are likely to ask questions about others' thoughts and feelings. These findings suggest that, if you are not by your own estimate a particularly sensitive or empathic person, you can compensate by actively seeking the information the empathic person senses. Take the time to ask about your students' feelings and reactions. Accept the information without judgment. Such actions contribute to a positive social environment, simply because you openly demonstrate your interest in your students' feelings. Moreover, taking the time to learn about their reactions improves communication and thereby reduces the frequency of conflicts.

Listening

Too often we tend to dismiss listening as an issue requiring our attention and effort. The fact remains, however, that most of us are less practiced in listening than in any of our basic communication skills. We tend to confuse hearing (the reception or recognition of auditory cues) with listening. To be sure, listening requires that we hear, but also that we attend to, understand, and retain aural messages (Barker, 1971).

In many situations, we listen passively without any real sense of involvement in a conversation or expenditure of energy. Such passive listening leads to hazy impressions and misperceptions. In contrast, when we actively listen, we focus our attention fully on a conversation. We involve ourselves totally in terms of our attitudes, beliefs, and emotions. Most of us need to practice active listening more often than we do, and for teachers it is extremely important. Why? You know by now that classroom messages include far more than academic information. Students' answers to questions may be correct or incorrect, but if you feel that your listening responsibilities end with that distinction, think again. In Chapters 2 and 8, we discussed the ways students acquire self-concepts or express liking through classroom messages. Regrettably, some teachers ignore these messages and, by not listening, create negative social environments.

A colleague of ours relates an experience that demonstrates our point quite well. In his first teaching position, he decided that class time should be devoted to learning. Thus when students raised questions he considered irrelevant to the topic for the day, he either ignored the comment or steered the class back to the assigned discussion. In a short time, his students stopped expressing opinions. A bit later, they stopped asking questions altogether. As our friend puts it, "It was ironic. It took several days of solid silence from my students to teach me that I had not been listening."

The type of listening that is more productive for members of the classroom group is what Barker (1971) calls discriminative listening. Specifically, *discriminative listening* is aimed at understanding and remembering. It includes a variety of skills, such as understanding a speaker's intent, and attention to detail. Four levels of listening are involved in this process, which Barker labels attentive, retentive, reflective, and reactive.

Attentive listening is aptly described by the old classroom adage, "Pay attention." Attending to a message, as we noted in Chapter 3, is the most basic step in the communication process. Attentive listening therefore is only the first step in discriminative listening. *Retentive* listening entails attentive listening with an additional effort to recall a speaker's message. A common example from every teacher's experience is learning students' names in a new class. Without conscious effort to remember which name goes with which face, the task is almost impossible.

Reflective listening is primarily evaluative. Here the teacher not only attends and retains but also interprets a message. When you listen reflectively, you assess a message in terms of its total context. Inferences about the speaker's mood and motives or the importance of the message are common examples. We suspect many disruptions of classroom communication may be attributed to the failure of members to practice reflective listening. When meaning is attributed to messages that are only heard, rather than listened to, the result is usually misunderstanding.

Reactive listening is the final and perhaps most critical level of discriminative listening. As the label suggests, this is the stage in which verbal and nonverbal feedback signal to a speaker the listener's evaluative response to his or her message. Of course, we all react to messages sometimes without listening discriminatively. The distinction lies in the three stages of the process preceding a reaction. If a teacher has attended to, retained, and reflected on a student's message, his or her response will indicate reactive listening. This does not mean that you should plan your responses while a student is speaking. That would preclude listening. Rest assured that the reactive level will emerge naturally if you attend, retain, and reflect as you listen.

By now you are probably thinking that discriminative listening is an unattainable goal, given the number of messages occurring during a single class. You are correct. No one can practice discriminative listening at all times. This fact, however, does not diminish its importance in setting a social environment. Two observations seem warranted. Listening is a part of the total communication process. Therefore shifts in the level of listening from active to passive are inevitable. It is not so critical that you always listen discriminatively as it is that you recognize the times when the situation requires this level of involvement. We suggest that you be guided by the general principle that every student deserves listening on your part.

A second point is that your listening ability is largely conditioned by your listening habits. Most of us have rather lazy habits, but these are not permanent. Thus you can change poor listening habits and develop skills of discriminative listening. You will find that with a sustained effort you can effect this sort of change independently. We believe you will find that the dividends of improved communication and social environment justify the investment of your time and energy.

PRINCIPLES 9.3

1. Trust develops as a function of the quality of communication between teacher and student; the level of trust affects both affective and cognitive outcomes of instruction.
2. Teachers who are capable of empathizing with students are especially effective in promoting learning and minimizing student-teacher conflicts.
3. Active listening facilitates accurate communication between teacher and student.
4. Listening skills are learned. Teachers should practice discriminative listening to facilitate a positive social environment.

REFERENCES

Anderson, R. Learning in discussions: A resume of the authoritarian-democratic studies. *Harvard Educational Review*, 1959, **29**, 201–215.

Barbour, A., and Goldberg, A. *Interpersonal communication: Teaching strategies and resources.* New York: ERIC/RCS Speech Communication Module, 1974.

Barker, L. *Listening behavior.* Englewood Cliffs, N.J.: Prentice-Hall, 1971.

Bochner, A., and Kelly, C. Interpersonal competence: Rationale, philosophy, and implementation of a conceptual framework. *Speech Teacher,* 1974, **23**, 279–301.

Brophy, J., and Good, T. *Teacher-student relationships: Causes and consequences.* New York: Holt, Rinehart and Winston, 1974.

Deutsch, M. Conflicts: Productive and destructive. *Journal of Social Issues,* 1969, **25**, 7–41.

Dunkin, M., and Biddle, B. *The study of teaching.* New York: Holt, Rinehart and Winston, 1974.

Flanders, N. Teacher influence in the classroom. In A. A. Bellack (Ed.), *Theory and research in teaching.* New York: Bureau of Publications, Teachers College, Columbia University, 1963, 37–52.

Flanders, N. *Analyzing teacher behavior.* Reading, Mass.: Addison-Wesley, 1970.

French, J., and Raven, B. The bases of social power. In D. Cartwright (Ed.), *Studies in social power.* Ann Arbor, Mich.: Institute for Social Research, 1959, 150–167.

Friedrich, G., Galvin, K., and Book, C. *Growing together: Classroom communication.* Columbus, Ohio: Merrill, 1976.

Getzels, J. A social psychology of education. In G. Lindzey and E. Aronson (Eds.), *The handbook of social psychology,* Vol. 5. Reading, Mass.: Addison-Wesley, 1969, 459–537.

Jackson, J. Structural characteristics of norms. In N. Henry (Ed.), *The dynamics of instructional groups,* Part 2. Chicago, Ill.: National Society for the Study of Education, 1960.

Jackson, P. Alienation in the classroom. In R. Strom and P. Torrance (Eds.), *Education for affective achievement.* Skokie, Ill.: Rand McNally, 1973, 122–135.

Kozol, J. *Death at an early age.* Boston, Mass.: Houghton Mifflin, 1967.

Kounin, J. *Discipline and group management in classrooms.* New York: Holt, Rinehart and Winston, 1970.

Lewin, K., Lippitt, R., and White, R. Patterns of aggressive behavior in experimentally created "social climates." *Journal of Social Psychology,* 1939, **10**, 271–299.

McCroskey, J. C. The implementation of a large scale program of systematic desensitization for communication apprehension. *Speech Teacher,* 1972, **21**, 255–264.

McCroskey, J. C. Classroom consequences of communication apprehension. *Communication Education,* 1977, **26**, 27–34.

Morrison, T. Control as an aspect of group leadership in the classroom: A review of research. *Journal of Education,* 1974, **156**, 38–64.

Rogers, C. The interpersonal relationship in the facilitation of learning. In D. Avila, A. Combs, W. Purkey (Eds.), *The helping relationship sourcebook.* Boston: Allyn & Bacon, 1973, 214–233.

Rosenshine, B., and Furst, N. Research on teacher performance criteria. In B. Smith (Ed.), *Research in teacher education: A symposium.* Englewood Cliffs, N.J.: Prentice-Hall, 1971.

Schmuck, R., and Schmuck, P. *Group processes in the classroom*. Dubuque, Iowa: Brown, 1975.

Smythe, M.-J., and Powers, W. G. When Galatea is apprehensive: The effect of communication apprehension on teacher expectations. *The Communication Yearbook*, Vol. II, 1978.

Strom, R. Reversing coercive strategies. In R. Strom and P. Torrance (Eds.), *Education for affective achievement*. Skokie, Ill.: Rand McNally, 1973, 281–290.

Van der Berg, S. Student alienation: Orientation toward and perceptions of aspects of educational social structures. *Urban Education*, 1975, **10**, 262–279.

Wright, H. *Recording and analyzing child behavior*. New York: Harper & Row, 1967.

Chapter 10
Conflict in the Classroom Group

OBJECTIVES

After reading this chapter, you should be able to:

1. define, verbally and by example, conflict.
2. describe typical teacher reactions to classroom conflicts.
3. discuss the relationship between communication and conflict.
4. identify and discuss the bases of classroom conflicts.
5. identify the positive contributions of conflict to classroom life.
6. identify and distinguish between the levels of conflict experienced by the classroom group.
7. describe common forms of conflict experienced by the classroom group.
8. describe some common myths and misconceptions concerning the nature of conflict.
9. discuss the functions of classroom conflicts.
10. describe the potential consequences of classroom conflicts.
11. discuss the relationship between conflict and the social environment.
12. identify appropriate methods for managing classroom conflicts.

Freedom was the issue, then, and still is. In some cities they cane students into submission; in many places, they slap, shake, and shove them. In many more, teachers subdue kids with threats, sarcasm, and ridicule. Like beatings with a blackjack, these techniques crush but leave no marks the eye can see. (Borton, 1970, pp. 151–152)

Conflict. For most of us, the term evokes very distinct negative feelings: recollections of shrill accusations, angry faces, events, and individuals out of control. Perceptions of conflict as a destructive force in interpersonal and group relationships or as a symptom of some dysfunction within a social system have rendered most of us to the status of victim in conflict situations, trapped between a powerful impulse to release our frustrations fully and an equally profound desire to retreat until the storm subsides. Teachers of course are largely denied both options when conflicts arise in the classroom. Idealized role prescriptions dictate that we assume the mantle of the stoic, staunch, and steadfast in the face of classroom insurrections. This role model is probably preferable to the cane-wielding, absolute authority figure of old who brooked no hint of disagreement or disobedience from students. Neither strategy, however, reflects a very enlightened approach to conflict. Since many teachers report that dealing with conflict is a source of anxiety, and conflict is an inevitable aspect of classroom life, we believe a clearer understanding of this issue will assist you.

THE NATURE OF CONFLICT

Conflict is one of the many products of every human social system. Numerous authors have noted that complex organizations are in a very basic sense created for the purpose of generating conflict. We believe this statement applies equally well to classrooms. Learning, after all, involves change, and any change meets with resistance, which implies conflict. We are less interested in cognitive conflict, though, than in social conflict and its effects on classrooms. Deutsch (1969) defines social conflict as follows:

A conflict exists whenever incompatible activities occur.... Conflicts may arise from differences in interests, desires, or values... or from scarcity of some resource such as money, time, space, position... or it may reflect a rivalry in which one person tries to outdo or undo the other. (pp. 7–8)

In the classroom, as in other settings, incompatible activities usually arise from differences between individuals' pursuit of some goal. For example, a teacher often establishes goals or objectives for a class period, such as the completion of five group reports. If only two of the groups scheduled to present their reports are prepared, the members of the remaining three groups might resort to delaying tactics to prevent the teacher from discovering their procrastination. So they raise questions, provoke disagreements, contest any point made by anyone, until everyone's patience is ragged. Meanwhile, the teacher grows increasingly frustrated as the carefully planned schedule of events crumbles. Time, that valuable classroom commodity, has in the teacher's eyes been squandered on irrelevant chatter. The teacher's goal, completing the assigned reports, and the students' goal, avoiding their presentation, are clearly incompatible. As the class proceeds, both the teacher and students engage in a variety of tactics designed to achieve their disparate goals. The stage for a full-scale conflict is thus set.

The foregoing definition and example provide immediate insight into our initial contention regarding the nature of conflict in the classroom. It is impossible to assemble 20 to 30 people for any length of time without the occurrence of incompatible activities. In fact, they probably happen daily. Certain aspects of the social system within classrooms are particularly influential in creating situations that invite conflict. In the ensuing section we discuss some of the more obvious of these aspects. Each is a potential cause of conflict within the classroom group.

BASES OF CLASSROOM CONFLICT

Conflict theorists are in agreement on the elements involved in interpersonal struggles. These include an awareness of conflict between individuals, the perception of incompatible goals or scarce rewards, and a sense of personal interdependence (Frost and Wilmot, 1978). These elements characterize all conflicts. Other factors assume importance as a function of particular communication settings. For classrooms, you may be able to think of numerous factors that cause conflicts between teacher and student(s) or student and student. Four factors are especially significant.

Me, Thee, and Them

The first, and probably most important basis for classroom conflict lies in the individual differences of members of the classroom group. Each participant, including the teacher, brings to the system differing expectations, attitudes, value orientations, and needs. Moreover, individuals vary widely in academic and interpersonal ability levels, which leads to a potent, utterly unpredictable mixture of people whose initial problem is to arrive at some means of coexistence. Inevitably, struggles develop in these early stages of group life. Members learn much about one another, including differences in personal conflict styles. Some are likely to be assertive, others accommodating, and some are collaborators and compromisers. Most classroom groups are a mixture, although we've all experienced classes in which one style or another predominated. One college professor we know became so exasperated with his Political Science class's unwillingness to debate controversial issues that he finally felt compelled to bait them. During one trying class session, he informed his students rather vehemently that they were living proof of C. S. Lewis' statement that the task of the modern educator is not so much to clear away jungles as it is to irrigate deserts. He reports that the students took the implication that their minds were as arid as the Sahara with heroic calm. Some diligently recorded the statement in their notebooks. Others simply regarded him with benign tolerance. This class was, to say the least, accommodating in the face of their teacher's invitation to dispute.

Factors other than personal conflict styles are related to the incidence of classroom strife. Conflicts frequently arise early in the development of classroom social systems as students and teachers jockey for control. Friedrich, Galvin, and Book (1976) describe Coffman's (1973) study investigating the incidence of student challenge behavior. The study sheds some light on the relationship between individual characteristics and conflicts. Female teachers were challenged significantly more often by their students than male teachers. Interestingly enough, the teacher's level of experience also made a difference in the number of challenges launched by students. The more experienced teachers actually received *more* challenges than their less experienced colleagues. Friedrich, Galvin, and Book suggest that this finding might be explained in terms of the more experienced teachers' superior ability to accept and deal with the conflicts. We advance an alternative explanation related to another factor, power, that is a basic cause of conflict in the classroom.

I'm in Charge . . . Right?

Conflict theory specifies felt or actual discrepancies in power relationships among members of a group as a major source of intragroup conflicts (Frank, 1973). You will recognize immediately that the discrepancy in power between students and teachers is substantial in most classrooms. A teacher's power is established and reinforced through all the major components of the educational system, as well as the larger society. Power is manifested through a variety of behaviors, including decision making with regard to classroom activities, stipulation of evaluation standards and, most significantly, assignment of grades. Students, by contrast, have almost no socially sanctioned power. Thus the finding that the students in Coffman's study challenged the experienced teachers more frequently than the less experienced teachers seems to us to be a reflection of the students' perceptions of the experienced teachers' assumption of control. We further suspect that students are more likely to identify with younger, less experienced teachers whose grasp of power in the classroom is less assured, hence less threatening.

We can hardly overstate the importance of power discrepancies in shaping the frequency and intensity of classroom conflicts. It is this imbalance in personal and academic power more than any other we discuss that dictates the inevitability of friction between students and teachers. Even when classroom decision making is shared by allowing students to determine what sorts of projects they will complete or the format for testing, the teacher still retains the ultimate power of the final grade. However stable our self-concept, most of us have an inherent fear of being evaluated. This anxiety promotes feelings of suspicion and resentment toward the individual who evaluates us.

Because the teacher is viewed as the representative of the larger social system of the school, students are likely to perceive that they can expect no recourse from a higher authority, a perception which magnifies the teacher's power in their minds. It is hardly surprising that these felt discrepancies on the part of students, when combined with the apparent discrepancies already described, surface in conflicts. Thus comments such as "What? You're going to give *how many* tests," accompanied by muttered remarks such as "What does he want—blood?," become a constant litany of classrooms.

I'd Really Rather Not . . .

A third factor affects the incidence of classroom struggles as directly as individual differences or power discrepancies. It is the nonvoluntary membership status of the participants (Frank, 1973). Count the number of classes you can easily recall that you had to force yourself to attend. Oh sure, you managed to survive the experience, but were you maybe a bit less tolerant, or quicker to find fault with the objectives, procedures, or outcomes of classroom events? Probably so. Unfortunately, every class we have ever seen has included some individuals who were present under duress. Whether because of legal restraints that enforce attendance in our secondary schools, or the requirements of a college student's program, nonvoluntary membership in a classroom group negatively affects social perceptions of self, others, and subject matter. This in turn increases the probability of conflict.

Teachers, we should note, are no less likely to be nonvoluntary members than are students. On the college level, required basic courses provide classic examples of unwilling participation by all parties. Our colleagues confirm our conclusion that there's no more dreaded teaching assignment than the basic course filled with graduating seniors who've postponed taking the course (hoping to the last for a change in the requirement) as long as they could.

Few of us react with good will to any restrictions on our exercise of personal choice. Nonvoluntary membership can be stressful on interpersonal relationships, particularly when said membership is a daily occur-

FIGURE 10.1 POWER DIFFERENCES ARE SOURCES OF CONFLICT.

rence spread over a period of months or an entire school year. It is not surprising therefore that the tensions produced by this situation often erupt into open conflict. Students who are unwilling participants in classroom life usually manifest their feelings through assuming the status of nonperson, withdrawing from the classroom group as completely as possible. If their personal conflict style is more assertive, they may evolve into students who challenge every decision and never miss an opportunity to express negative sentiments about any aspect of classroom life. Teacher withdrawal of course is no less easily recognized. As we discussed in Chapter 3, teachers can signal their expectations for their classes through both verbal and nonverbal signals. The teacher who rarely smiles or looks at students during class and responds to questions as rarely or brusquely as possible reveals an attitude that debilitates class morale and breeds resentment.

The High Price of Winning

The definition of social conflict quoted earlier reveals a final source of strife in educational settings. Our culture has ingrained competitive orientations in almost all students. For a variety of reasons, including tradition, this tendency is reinforced by most teachers. Good grades are the scarce and valuable commodity that students most frequently compete for. Frank (1973) has summarized a number of studies dealing with the effects of grading practices on student morale and classroom relationships that reflect a truth each of us has experienced in one way or another. Grades or their equivalents are necessary to the educational process as we know it. The pursuit of good grades, though, produces a host of undesirable social consequences. Rigorous grading standards, regardless of whether they are appropriately derived and applied, intensify potential conflict situations by making that particular scarce and valuable commodity increasingly difficult to attain. The natural competitive impulse students bring to the classroom, then, becomes a contributing factor in the development of conflicts between teacher and student or student and student.

In most classrooms, students are encouraged to compete with one another for scores on tests, special awards and scholarships, and favorable responses from teachers. In short, they compete for opportunities to confirm their worth as individuals in the school setting. Cooperation, on the other hand, is stressed only in special instances. Our purpose here is not to moralize, but to summarize what is known about the effects of these differing orientations on student performance and sense of personal well-being. We could easily cite a dozen studies which demonstrate the value of competitive learning environments. A like number argue that cooperative environments are superior, although they require greater amounts of time and energy. In point of fact, the question of which environment is the most effective in terms of accomplishing educational goals is unresolved.

Proponents of competitive learning environments base their arguments on two major claims. First, competition has long been viewed as a motivational device. Most of us *are* avid competitors on one level or another. Advocates of cooperative learning situations, in which participants work at their own pace or are not subjected to comparison with others, disagree, asserting that students should develop internal motivation if learning is to be meaningful and lasting (Dowell, 1974). Second, it is argued that competitive environments serve as preparation for life in the "real world." Proponents argue that, if students do not experience and learn to cope in competitive situations, they will be less effective participants in society. This claim is predictably countered with the argument that cooperation is an equally valuable and practical skill for students to master as a part of their preparation for realities beyond the classroom.

While data on learning outcomes from the two environments are inconclusive, the social-psychological implications are substantially less so. Most authorities agree that competition has negative effects on social relationships. How do you feel about your classmate who "set the curve" on the midterm in this class? Ever stop to wonder why we have so many negative labels to saddle these people with, or why the "gentleman's C" has had such a long and distinguished history? There is little doubt in our minds that the anxiety and self-doubt created by competitive learning environments provide a superb breeding ground for hostility and destructive interpersonal relationships between students. Deutsch (1969) has identified three outcomes of competition which suggest its disruptive effects.

1. *The quantity and quality of communication between competitors is reduced.* What happens to the development of any relationship when communication falters? The incidence of misperception and misunderstanding is accelerated. The potential for trust and rapport is diminished.

2. *Competition emphasizes a win-lose approach to problem solving.* Well, that's the name of the game, isn't it? The late Vince Lombardi's philosophy may be super (excuse the pun) for football, but as an interpersonal strategy there are few that are less desirable. When students believe, and you may be sure they do, that the only way they can win is through their peers' losses, Pollyanna herself could not expect to avoid social strife.

3. *Competition fosters suspicion and hostility.* When competition is intense or prolonged, the usually accepted rules of conduct and morality which shape your behavior toward others like yourself

become less applicable. Similarities between yourself and the other are diminished, and differences exaggerated. This relaxation of rules begets behavior toward a competitor which would be considered unspeakable if directed toward oneself. Nowhere is this statement more vividly demonstrated than in news accounts of students willfully and maliciously sabotaging one another's laboratory projects to ensure themselves a better chance for admission to medical school.

We won't mislead you. There is realistically little prospect for change in the norm dictating that students compete with one another. Moreover, this is probably not so grisly a prospect as it may sound. We believe that some competition facilitates performance without provoking open hostility in the classroom. The real issue for you is determining the optimal level. Our advice is to accept the reality without fatalism; teachers cannot overcome one of our culture's deeply held truths. Remember, however, that each class you teach comes together and creates a unique history in which you actively participate (Friedrich, Galvin, and Book, 1976). You, and your students, will have to identify the level of competition you can tolerate.

Myths and Misconceptions About Classroom Conflicts

These four factors, individual differences, power discrepancies, nonvoluntary membership, and competitive orientation, are present in every classroom. This does not mean, however, that each classroom is a seething hotbed of conflict. The "monster" class is as much a myth as the ideal classroom in which dissension never occurs. Rather, we might view these four bases as a set of constants, any one of which is sufficient to generate conflicts of varying intensity and duration. The relative importance of any one factor is determined by the unique identity of each class. You may have been in classes, for example, in which the level of competition was so high that you could hardly focus on learning because you were so preoccupied with wondering whether you were doing as well as your closest competitor. In our teaching careers, we have seen one or another of these factors provide experiences just as unpleasant as that one may have been for you. Paradoxically, we have also seen all of these factors present without creating serious problems.

The latter statement leads us to a second common misconception teachers relate to us concerning conflict. Too often, we mistakenly assume that conflict is a totally negative force, with far more liabilities than assets for learning and social relationships. Coser (1956) was the first scholar to explore the positive aspects of conflict for society. His basic argument stresses the necessity for conflict if society is to achieve desired changes.

Obviously, Coser's analysis applies equally well to classroom settings. Conflicts provide a variety of benefits to the classroom group that total harmony prohibits. Conflict, however unpleasant in process, always signals that the parties involved are evolving toward some new level. Can you think of a better description of learning or growth in interpersonal relationships?

A final myth concerning conflict warrants special emphasis. Too often we hear or see conflict described as a "communication breakdown." This term, like "credibility gap," is a relic of the tumultous period of the late 1960s and early 1970s when talking and writing about communication became fashionable. It is an omnibus term and frequently misapplied, as is the case with "interpersonal conflict" (Miller and Simons, 1974). We submit that it is shortsighted to assume that any or all conflicts mean that communication has failed or is faulty. Actually, conflict represents a distinct type of communication. As you know very well, parties to a struggle often have no difficulty whatever expressing themselves. That's an important point to remember when you find yourself in the throes of a struggle with your students. Conflict is sometimes the only avenue through which certain ideals, sentiments, or values can be expressed.

Reeducating ourselves about conflict is no easy task. Most of us are so well enculturated with our society's misconceptions on the subject that we are trapped by our own habits. Our students almost invariably tell us two things about their experiences with conflict. One is startling. Few students can describe a conflict they have enjoyed. Too, they report feeling frustration at their inability to respond with flexibility to even the threat of a conflict. As one expressed it,

> Everytime we get into it, I promise myself that next time around I'm going to play it different. Instead of losing it and starting to cry, I'm going to say what I feel. Well, so far, next time hasn't come and I'm munching Gelusil.

With these ideas in mind, we review the principles we've discussed about the nature and bases of conflicts between students and teachers. Then, we turn our attention to the types and uses of classroom disputes.

PRINCIPLES 10.1

1. Conflicts arise as a function of communication processes operating in social systems. In early stages of group life, conflicts serve definitional functions. Later, conflicts serve a variety of functions.
2. Individual differences among classroom group members produce conflicts as a result of varying conflict styles, goals, and value systems.
3. Power discrepancies are probably the single most influential factor contributing to the development of conflicts between teachers and students.
4. Nonvoluntary membership in the classroom enhances the likelihood of conflicts between teachers and students.

5. Competition for grades and classroom rewards fosters conflicts between students.
6. Contrary to popular thought, classroom conflicts are neither totally negative forces nor instances of failures in communication.

CONFLICT: FORMS AND FUNCTIONS

Our discussion of conflict thus far has focused on illustrating the factors which make conflict an inevitable element of classroom life. Your understanding would be incomplete if we did not consider the forms and functions of conflict. Our first observation must be a rather obvious one. Conflicts arise as a function of the total communication process. The misperceptions and inaccuracies that occur whenever meaning is assigned to behavior are the stuff of which conflicts are made; *but*, communication is also the key to the resolution of controversies. A little later in the chapter we examine this topic in some depth. For now, let's focus on the types of conflicts commonly found in the classroom and the functions they serve.

The Shape of Things to Come: Forms of Conflict

Although the scholarly literature is replete with descriptions of various types of conflict, it is not our purpose to review all of them for you. We cannot hope to provide an exhaustive listing, but there are four conflict forms we believe have special relevance to classrooms. These are Deutsch's (1969) manifest and underlying conflict and Miller and Steinberg's (1975) affective and substantive conflict typology. The former distinction is useful because it deals with the levels on which conflicts occur. The latter distinguishes conflicts on the basis of content and social motivations.

Manifest Conflicts. You have no difficulty recognizing manifest conflicts. These struggles are usually quite overt in nature. Subtlety in verbal and nonverbal cues is most assuredly not present. Parties in the dispute are usually quite aware of one another's position on the issue in question. Familiar examples from the classroom include dissension over procedural matters. "How-to-do-it" conflicts are among the most common in the classroom. Whether the question is when to schedule an hourly exam or the number of class days left before spring recess, you can count on varying opinions. One of the great mysteries we've observed over the years is how a class of 30 students can provide 60 opinions on any subject.

Manifest conflicts are no less real because they are so apparent. They may be related to almost any topic and range in intensity from a fleeting exclamation to a sustained struggle lasting for days. The scope of the conflict is governed by a variety of factors, including the specific issue in contention. The course of manifest conflicts, or any conflict for that matter, is influenced most by the conflict styles of the participants (Frost and Wilmot, 1978). Since they tend to be "up front," though, manifest conflicts are easily confronted.

Underlying Conflicts. Speaking metaphorically, a manifest conflict between teacher and student may be only the tip of the iceberg. Lurking beneath the surface, complete with jagged edges, lies an underlying conflict of indeterminate proportions. What we are saying is that manifest conflicts can occur without underlying conflicts, but an underlying conflict presupposes a manifest dispute. It is important to note that the issues involved in these two levels of conflict are usually different. Consider the following scenario.

Ms. Bredwell and Jamie are arguing about the relative weight given to group and individual projects in determining final grades. Jamie is expressing his concern, rather heatedly, that group projects are unfair. He argues that they force individuals to rely on potentially unreliable peers to achieve a satisfactory grade. Despite Ms. Bredwell's reassurance that group projects constitute a minor portion of the final grade, he remains unconvinced and displeased. The manifest conflict over grading systems is a readily apparent and familiar theme of teacher-student disagreements. According to Deutsch (1969), however, Jamie's behavior may suggest that the manifest conflict is symptomatic of an underlying conflict. Jamie's stubborn rejection of the grading system *may* be due to his stated reasons or may reflect an anxiety about his ability to perform in a group. Instead of a defense of the grading practices, Jamie might want reassurance that he can do as well in the group project as anyone else.

Now, there's really no way we've discovered for you to become the psychic who can discern a student's true motives on the basis of a single conversation. Our point is that manifest conflicts may not always be what they appear. Students, for a variety of personal and/or normative reasons, may not be totally candid. Your intuition may be necessary to bring the real issue out into the open. Manifest conflicts are seldom fully resolved until the underlying conflict has been exposed and dealt with. One signal that you need to start probing is the reoccurrence of conflicts on the same topic.

We include this treatment of the levels of conflict to sensitize you to one of the most common problems teachers and students experience when disputes arise. Expressing the real issues is often difficult. When the struggle is expressed first by a student, the power discrepancy in favor of the teacher can be a sure deterrent to openness. We discuss the techniques you may apply to this problem in a later section dealing with conflict management.

Affective Conflicts. Although the term "affect" is synonomous with "emotion," the sort of conflict we are describing does not refer exclusively to disputes in which people express emotions. That is, affective conflicts are not defined by flushed faces, raised voices, or temper tantrums. These struggles often proceed with behaviors as controlled as you might observe in any other communication event. It is the content and/or cause of the conflict that determines its label, not the behaviors which accompany it.

Affective struggles are, however, emotionally involving for the individuals concerned. How often has the teacher who gave you this reading assignment made you feel resentful, hurt, or embarrassed? Do your personal communication styles mesh or are they a mismatch? Does your teacher's teaching style conform to your expectations, or violate them? These are but a few of the potential areas in which you and your teacher can experience an affective conflict. Of course, we could just as easily reverse the questions and apply them to a teacher.

Most affective conflicts, then, are founded on individual differences and are likely to be fueled by our awareness that a student or teacher's attitudes or values disagree with ours. Ironically, these conflicts are likely to blossom in a classroom which has the characteristics of a positive social environment described in Chapter 9. Sound contradictory? Remember that the communication behaviors that determine the quality of classroom life are also those which display differences between people. Sometimes student and teacher self-disclosure can reveal disparities that can grow and flourish into bitter disputes.

Our own experiences with affective classroom conflicts agree with those reported by our colleagues and teachers at all levels. The single most frequent cause for these conflicts seems to be perceptions of inappropriate treatment. Part of the "emotional baggage" we all carry with us from one situation to the next is a well-defined set of expectations about the way we want to be treated. When these expectations are violated, it is both unsettling and irritating. Consistent violations yield one of three outcomes. We may choose to withdraw physically or psychologically from the source of the violation. Students can usually exercise this option by dropping a class if they dislike the treatment they receive from a teacher. Teachers of course are denied this option and must find some means of dealing with classes that won't talk, talk too much, or yawn openly and often in their faces.

A second option we can exercise when faced with perceived mistreatment is to change our self-concept or self-esteem. We may (and often do) scrutinize our behavior for clues that explain the unexpected treatment. Major change, however, is fairly unlikely. You are not likely to begin thinking of yourself as an imbecile because you have a teacher who behaves as if you are. Again, the teacher's experience differs. You may remember from our discussion in Chapter 2 that the strength of an appraisal in shaping self-concept is related to the number of times the appraisal is confirmed. If you doubt that 30 students in apparent agreement about your deficiencies as a teacher can affect your self-concept, you are in for a surprise when you start teaching.

Finally, you may simply endure the violations as best you can. This state of affairs is the prime breeding ground for affective conflicts between teachers and students. Each successive repetition of perceived mistreatment feeds feelings of frustration and resentment. These feelings ultimately find an outlet. Do we need to tell you which of these three options is most likely to occur?

Substantive Conflict. Since the classroom is a realm in which ideas and issues are major concerns, disputes over their content are inevitable. We are not merely referring to the intellectual disagreements that most teachers and students experience as an integral part of the learning process. Substantive conflicts can emerge from the mock debates that teachers or students sometimes stage, but the type of struggle we are describing is most often experienced when incompatible goals or discrepancies between words and deeds are involved.

At the beginning of this chapter, we used an example of a teacher whose goal for a class session was incompatible with the goal shared by a majority of the class. The conflict described in the example was substantive and could have escalated into a damaging episode for all parties. While affective disputes in the classroom impact negatively on the social environment, dissension on substantive matters strikes at the core of the process. Repeated conflicts of this type can seriously impede learning. For this reason, it is essential that you recognize and resolve substantive conflicts with dispatch.

Goal setting for the classroom group is widely acknowledged as the prerogative of the teacher. Moreover, teachers tend to guard this privilege rather jealously. It is probably more a matter of convenience than selfishness. Decision making in a small group is often unwieldy. Add 20 more people to the process, and you have real problems. In any case, the goals teachers establish for their classes are usually met with varying degrees of approval by the students. Most of us will never see the class that is in total agreement with us on this question, so the potential for substantive conflict is almost always present.

We should note that many students, particularly those at the elementary and secondary level, are not unduly concerned about influencing the goals teachers set for their classes. You are willing to concede that your teachers' expertise in a field enables them to set learning goals for your class. This does not mean, however, that substantive disputes are less likely to occur. Instead, these conflicts emerge from questions of how goals are to be achieved. If you loathe writing term papers, for instance, and your teacher announces that two-thirds of the final grade will be determined on the basis of five short papers, you may well feel the impulse to protest. Struggles like this one are more than a contest of wills. Teachers believe that they are best qualified to assess student progress toward the achievement of course goals. Students rightfully think that they are in a position to evaluate their level of mastery. And so it goes.

Substantive conflicts also emerge when students and teachers detect discrepancies in one another's actions and words. We call this the principles-practice dilemma, and it invariably affects the classroom group. All of us have certain principles which we use to justify our decisions. Problems develop when we attempt to apply these principles in a situation as dynamic and varied as the classroom. A typical example that affects many classroom groups is the oft-repeated myth of uniform treatment for all students. If you still believe that it is possible for you to treat each of your students identically, and equitably, we suggest a review of Chapters 3 and 8. You cannot, and your students perceive this quickly.

Another instance of contradictory principles and practices that provokes conflict between student and teacher is what one of our students calls "the tyranny of the normal curve." This conflict can begin on the first day a class meets. When teachers introduce their course to students, it is more or less predictable that grades will be mentioned. The contradiction appears when the teacher states that every student has a chance to earn an "A" for their course grade. Sounds innocent enough, right? One student submits that, if a teacher "curves" test scores to assign grades, it is impossible from the outset for all students to earn "A's," regardless of their mastery of course material. The process of scaling scores dictates what percentage of students will receive certain grades. He's correct, and never fails to call his teacher's attention to this discrepancy. It is not our purpose to argue the merits of grading systems here. We simply think that the student's behavior is a vivid illustration of the degree to which students perceive and respond to contradictory teacher behaviors. The reverse is equally true, and this can lead to intense interpersonal struggles.

The foregoing analysis of the forms of conflict is admittedly incomplete. We have attempted to alert you to the types we believe are typical of most classroom situations. As is true in any descriptive analysis of communication behaviors, however, we have presented only the outline. Just as you probably thought of other examples while you read ours, so too will you and your students script new variations.

What's Happening Here?: Functions of Conflict

By describing conflict earlier in this chapter as a specific type of communication behavior, we implied that people might use conflict systematically. We submit that all of us intentionally create or participate in conflicts for a variety of reasons. Three of these reasons find frequent application in classrooms. Each of the three functions that follow may be fulfilled by conflicts of varying intensity. It is important to note also that a single instance of conflict may serve more than a single function.

Conflicts for Clarification. Whenever teachers and students are together, they behave like any other task-oriented group in certain ways. Some members are on-task, while others are not. Individuals jockey for power and control, hurl challenges, or beat hasty retreats. Random activity occurs as frequently as that which is purposeful. In short, a lot of different activities are simultaneously ongoing at any specific moment. Therefore it is logical to assume that a certain degree of ambiguity pervades every classroom encounter. Conflict provides one useful means of maintaining this ambiguity at a level that is tolerable to all parties (Coser, 1956).

The need to reduce ambiguity shared by members of the classroom group is not to be underestimated. Because their performance is evaluated more explicitly, students feel this pressure rather keenly. In his provocative analysis of school life, Glasser (1969) refers to a "certainty principle" that is an outgrowth of our system of education. His contention is that our schools teach students to seek closure or definition to the point that closure in a situation becomes a desirable end in itself. By implication, Glasser suggests that, for many students, any answer which resolves ambiguity is preferable to continued ambiguity. The correctness or desirability of the answer are beside the point. If you question Glasser's analysis, review your own behavior the last time one of your teachers gave you a totally open-ended assignment or withheld feedback on your performance. You are the rare individual if the suspense of not knowing did not affect you. When the level of ambiguity surrounding any aspect of group life reaches an unacceptable level, conflict is a likely way to clarify the situation.

Similarly, students engage in a variety of reality-testing activities designed to clarify their understanding of their relationship to a teacher, the acceptable limits of classroom behavior, and so on. A key aspect of classroom life that is clarified, sometimes repeatedly, through conflicts is role behavior. The study by Coffman (1973) of student challenges to their teacher illustrates this clarification function well. What some teachers consider presumptive behavior on the part of their students is probably no more than an effort to identify the boundaries. Such conflicts, however minor, can be equally useful for teachers, because they clarify the existing power structure and reaffirm the rules of conduct.

Instrumental Conflicts. The most systematic use of conflict is found in instances in which individuals create a struggle to achieve a highly specific group or personal goal. This function of conflict, according to Deutsch

(1969), is a calculated attempt to seize control of a situation. There is little room for spontaneity or improvisation, and timing is a factor of paramount importance. Sounds like an ambush, doesn't it? Actually, that is not a bad analogy, because the chances for success in instrumental conflicts are enhanced if the opposing faction is unsuspecting.

The study of the ways in which people use instrumental conflicts to achieve their goals contributed to the rise of game theory approaches to human communication. Berne's *Games People Play*, an enormously popular book, describes in detail the infinite and complex variety of scripts people create and perform. While examples of these games are found in classrooms, we are more concerned with the purposes served by these conflicts than with their psychodynamic aspects.

Perhaps the most obvious reason students and teachers use instrumental conflicts is to simply "get their own way." While the young school child might throw a temper tantrum to overcome a teacher's resistance, older students are usually more subtle. Bluffs, implied threats, and intimidation are standard tactics. When was the last time that you cooperated, actively or tacitly, with a group of students to persuade a teacher to abandon a class project that you did not want to have to do? What tactics were employed? Intimidation is sometimes useful, for even the most imperturbable teacher can be swayed by the unrelenting protest of an entire class. Misrepresentation seems to be the staple of instrumental conflicts, particularly if the goal is to delay, rather than destroy, an assignment. We are continually amazed at our own unerring ability to select the identical day of the semester that our colleagues in at least five other departments have selected for an hourly examination. Coincidence? The laws of probability suggest otherwise.

Lest you infer that we view all instrumental conflicts as shady operations, consider instances in which learning is the goal of the individual. Teachers often play a devil's advocate role, purposefully arguing the least popular side of an issue with their class to promote a full analysis of the question. Similarly, students frequently stage instrumental conflicts when tests are returned and discussed by preparing defenses for the answers they chose. We had several classes with a fellow graduate student who was a master of this technique. As often as not, however, his goal was neither intimidation of the instructor nor winning the argument. Following one particularly lengthy dispute, he smiled and said, "I'd been wondering about the strength of that distinction for a while now. Just wondered what you thought it meant." Graceful losing? Perhaps, but we agree that our peer's account of his motives was completely straightforward. Instrumental conflicts provide a medium through which problems can be aired and solutions tested. In this sense, Deutsch (1969) asserts that such conflicts are at the base of positive personal and social change.

Expressive Conflicts. Researchers Dunkin and Biddle (1974) conducted lengthy observations of classroom behavior and concluded that there was a remarkable consistency with regard to the structure and predictability of the interactions that took place. One element of classroom interchange that is unique in each classroom group is the style of expressive conflicts. Since these conflicts are used primarily to project personality, release tension, or describe feelings, they are as varied and unpredictable as summer lightning.

One of the most intriguing examples of expressive conflicts we have seen is a ritual called "the dozens" (Kochman, 1971). Played by black students, "the dozens" is a game of progressive insults. The object is to insult your opponent more forcefully, colorfully, and wittily than he or she has insulted you. It is a form of one-upmanship that is singularly expressive.

When compared with the other functions of conflicts in the classroom group, expressive conflicts differ in several ways. Expressive conflicts tend to be an outgrowth of the social networks of the classroom. On a student-student level, they are a part of the classroom group's style of relating, among themselves and toward outsiders. A cohesive group engages in comparatively high levels of expressive conflict, apparently for the enjoyment value it provides. Mock disputes are enacted, and these performances seem to unify the group in much the same way that "inside jokes" operate.

Your willingness and ability to share expressive conflict with your students impacts many aspects of your classroom life. The social environment is particularly affected. Expressive disputes seem to function as relational messages which can build or reinforce perceptions of solidarity and liking within the classroom group without suppressing the free expression of feelings. As such, expressive conflict can be a powerful asset in achieving an optimal environment for learning.

By now we may have given you the impression that you can expect almost daily occurrences of conflicts which threaten to disrupt or destroy your relationship with your students. A final observation may reassure you. Many of the conflicts you experience with students are spontaneous, fleeting outbursts. Such eruptions reduce tensions, allow individuals to air their problems and feelings, and prevent stagnation. Viewed realistically, these struggles are essential to a healthy social environment. You may never learn to enjoy the groans and complaints that accompany your announcement of your favorite assignment, but you can recognize the conflict for what it is, as well as for what it signifies. It is feedback which gives you vital information about your students' feelings and responses and aids your understanding of them as individuals. Its occurrence signals that the communication channels are open, and if you can avoid overreacting to statements such as, "This test stinks!" you can turn the "duelogue" of the classroom into a dialogue.

CLASSROOM CONSEQUENCES OF CONFLICT

Any discussion of conflict provokes the question of how much controversy is desirable or tolerable before the social fabric of the classroom is strained beyond repair. Available literature offers no set formula. So, we cannot cheerfully prescribe two conflicts weekly for a happy, healthy classroom group. We offer instead a qualitative distinction between the typical outcomes of conflict, which should suggest some implications for the quantitative question.

Constructive Consequences

When conflicts arise, it is sometimes difficult to see any positive outcomes, particularly when the dispute has been carried on before an audience of 25 or 30 students. Coser (1956) was the first to contend that, in spite of their unpleasant process characteristics, conflicts yield many valuable products. Aside from the previously noted benefits of tension release, solution testing, and clarification, conflicts can also reveal strengths and weaknesses, prevent inequitable power plays, and promote new social networks. In short, conflicts can act as a vital check-and-balance system that protects rather than threatens the social environment for learning.

Realizing that conflict has potentially positive effects is no guarantee that these will emerge. That takes effort and planning on your part. The first step in the right direction requires that we be able to recognize a constructive outcome. Generally speaking, conflicts have constructive consequences when all parties receive some measure of satisfaction from any decisions, and a subjective impression that their efforts were productive (Deutsch, 1969). An example may illustrate the point.

One professor whose teaching philosophy we respect has developed a policy for dealing with arguments over examination questions that illustrates Deutsch's (1969) definition very neatly. When exams are returned and answers debated, he always yields at least one question to the students' interpretation. His rationale for this concession is that, while his tests are carefully developed, there is no way to create a test that is free of ambiguity. Hence every test has some shaky items, and these he readily exchanges for the positive effects the strategy yields.

Dysfunctional Consequences

Most of us have experienced the vague, but disquieting feelings following a conflict that suggest all is not well. Hostilities may have ceased, winners and losers may have been established, but a tangible aura of tension remains. This "fallout" from interpersonal disputes may not totally disrupt activities, but it produces a variety of side effects, most of which are negative. These dysfunctional consequences usually affect classroom groups in two ways.

First, dysfunctional outcomes do just enough damage to all parties to reduce the efficiency of the entire system. Communication becomes strained and awkward. Tasks are less easily accomplished, and agreements are made grudgingly rather than with genuine commitment.

The second way classroom groups are affected is in terms of effectiveness, or the level of satisfaction experienced through group membership. Dysfunctional outcomes diminish to some extent the social rewards students and teachers derive from their classroom relationships. When the facilitating aspects of group interactions are reduced, there are predictably poor effects on the social environment and learning.

Dysfunctional conflicts emerge from a win-lose orientation toward conflict. When teachers and students accept this orientation, a certain number of dysfunctional consequences become unavoidable. You may have experienced the kinds of consequences we've been describing if you have been on the losing end of a dispute concerning some aspect of classroom life with one of your teachers. If so, then you probably already realize that the problem with dysfunctional consequences is that they keep recurring. The win-lose orientation toward conflicts initiates a vicious circle. Each dispute resolved in this way leaves in its wake an unexpressed underlying conflict that will inexorably evolve into an overt one. Over time, the toll can prove heavy.

Destructive Consequences

The major characteristic of destructive conflicts is that they seem to follow a stubbornly upward spiral. Parties to the conflict seem unable or unwilling to choose other options for dealing with the dissension. So the dispute escalates, and destructive consequences accrue to everyone.

As one of our students once put it, "I can tell when a conflict is destructive well enough. It's when I feel like a loser even if I win." This statement is accurate. Destructive conflicts have no winners, because there are rarely solutions to these episodes. Instead, the struggle goes on until one person drops out. The outcomes? Dissatisfaction, distorted images of self, misperception of others, and resentment, to name a few.

Destructive consequences of conflict constitute a severe threat to the functioning of classroom groups. The emotional debris left in their wake is potentially too stressful for the social environment to withstand. When students and teachers are compelled to cope with these kinds of outcomes, it is also likely that the coping effort will absorb the time and energy required to achieve classroom learning goals.

Realistically, there may be no way totally to eliminate destructive conflicts and their consequences from your classroom. Some people, including teachers and students each of us has known, relish conflict in and of itself, regardless of the consequences. The frequency of conflicts, however, should be a matter of concern. Whenever conflict becomes the dominant characteristic of classroom interactions, a serious assessment of the situation is clearly indicated.

PRINCIPLES 10.2

1. Manifest conflicts may actually reflect underlying conflicts that students or teachers are unable to state directly.
2. Affective conflicts result when expectations for interpersonal relationships are violated.
3. Substantive conflicts emerge as a result of perceptions of inconsistent behaviors or incompatible goals within the classroom group.
4. Conflicts serve a clarification function for members of the classroom group by reducing ambiguities and defining relationships.
5. Instrumental conflicts between students and teachers are usually aimed at the achievement of specific personal or group goals.
6. Expressive conflicts act as vital escape valves for the accumulated tensions and pressures of classroom life.
7. The unique history and character of a classroom group is the most significant factor in determining whether conflicts have constructive, dysfunctional, or destructive consequences.

CONFLICT MANAGEMENT

Many modes of conflict resolution have been proposed in the literature. They range from arbitration to inquiry to therapy. Some of course are obviously less suitable for day-to-day classroom life than others. You are hardly able to send your entire class in for intensive psychotherapy. Furthermore, many of you find yourselves in school systems that don't have guidance counselors. To our way of thinking, it really shouldn't matter one way or the other. In your classroom, you are the principal arbitrator, as well as a frequent (hopefully not constant) party involved in the conflicts. Your choices, according to Frost and Wilmot (1978), are fairly clear. Four choices are available as your response to the conflict situation. You may choose to avoid or ignore the event. You may maintain the conflict at its present level. You may elect to escalate the conflict, or you may attempt to reduce the level of conflict. Needless to say, the choice you make will have a variety of implications for the quality of life in your classroom.

Given the special constraints of the classroom setting discussed earlier in this chapter, there is one option of the four that we do not recommend. It is difficult to imagine a classroom situation in which conflict escalation would be appropriate. We submit that there is too much risk involved, in terms of your students, to warrant that strategic choice. If a conflict between you and a student needs escalation, let it be on a one-to-one basis, outside the classroom.

We assume in this section that most of you are primarily interested in conflict reduction, as a means of preventing dysfunctional or destructive consequences for your classroom group. To manage classroom conflicts with any semblance of fairness and objectivity requires some sort of systematic plan. We offer the following blueprint for conflict resolution as just that—an outline of an approach we have found useful. You and your students will have to negotiate the specific details.

Positive Confrontation

Much like "conflict," the term "confrontation" reeks of things unpleasant. Most of us prefer a more circuitous route to harmony than something as direct as confrontation seems to imply. Nonetheless, the fact remains that our shrinking attitudes probably only aggravate conflicts. Galtung (1973) is one of the many educators who argue that we have been victimized by our cultural norms—compelled to swallow our feelings and suppress their expression until hostility, verbal abuse, or even physical violence erupts. Supporting this notion is the feudal structure of most classrooms, wherein the teacher is the sole authority in all disputes. Lacking the wisdom of Solomon, is it any wonder that such a power distribution is as draining for teachers as it is demoralizing for students?

A more realistic approach calls for different tactics altogether. Some alternative between becoming the totally harassed teacher and the utterly immovable force is desirable. A good beginning point lies in the acknowledgment of conflict as an inevitable, potentially valuable aspect of classroom life. Many destructive conflicts arise from teachers' inability or reluctance to admit that a problem exists. This is a rather disastrous signal of upcoming events for teachers and students alike. Lack of preparation almost certainly ensures a negative outcome to conflicts.

Confronting students positively involves a direct and open response to the immediate situation. No formulas apply to all conflicts, so your initial concern must be with identifying the source of the dispute. Uncovering basic issues is harder than you might think. The presence of other students, time pressures, and the impulse to simply ignore the problem can be powerful deterrents. Or you may find yourself tempted to master verbal karate and demolish your fractious students with a "put-down." You may buy some time by ignoring the issue or counterattacking, but the problem will probably only recur.

How to proceed? State your feelings about the specific event in question. Use self-descriptive, nonjudgmental language. It is sufficient to say, "When you interrupt me while I am speaking, I resent it." Clouding the issue with accusations and negative descriptions ("That was certainly a dumb, irresponsible thing for you to do.") only increases divisiveness. Owning your feelings objectively is not only more accurate communication, but also enables your students to respond less defensively than might otherwise be possible. Look again at our two sample sentences. The first is an example of an owning feelings dialogue, while the second perhaps describes the way too many of us respond to repeated interruptions. Which statement would you find most irritating or difficult to respond to calmly?

A second useful practice in conflict management is restatement. Too often, we leap feet first into a heated dispute without bothering to first determine our adversary's position, with predictably poor results. Taking the time to reiterate a student's objection, or requesting that he or she restate your own position to your *mutual* satisfaction is especially effective. Through restatement, both parties have a fuller opportunity to reflect on one another's feelings, maintain even tempers, or even offer solutions.

Furthermore, restatement reduces the possibility that you will mistake a purely expressive conflict for an attack on your competence or character. Students and teachers alike are guilty of bickering occasionally over trivial matters. Airing these disputes through restatement often reveals the empty argument for what it is with no losses or negative feelings on either individual's shoulders.

Finally, be assertive and encourage your students to be. A clear statement of your demands for the situation clarifies your position and enables your students to respond with equal candor. Stating and then restating one another's demands opens the door to mutual understanding and acceptance. Above all, remember that this strategy requires practice and patience. Over time, however, we think you will find it an effective means of disarming destructive conflicts and promoting constructive classroom goals. Once the problem has been confronted and the positions of all participants determined, the process of negotiation can begin.

Negotiation

While the previous recommendations apply to the initial stages of a conflict, we now propose a communication strategy you are likely to find indispensable in coping with conflict on an everyday basis. When controversies arise, a satisfactory method of dealing with the problem must be available. Your improvisations are useful, but also somewhat unreliable. If your experience runs similar to ours, you typically think, "Why didn't I say... ," several hours after the fact, rather than at the moment you needed the soothing word, appropriate disclaimer, or whatever. Neither are the two common reactions, anger and flight, very effective

FIGURE 10.2 RESTATING ONE ANOTHER'S DEMANDS MAY RESULT IN UNDERSTANDING AND ACCEPTANCE.

means of managing conflicts. This is especially applicable to teachers. To our knowledge, neither shouting nor running from the room has ever been identified as an ideal means of establishing a working relationship with a group of students.

Studies on conflict resolution strategies reveal that a host of options has been successfully exploited in a variety of contexts. One strategy in particular seems to be effective in all settings. You may recall that we mentioned some time ago that communication is at once a cause and a cure for conflicts. Adding a few qualifiers may illustrate our point. Careless communication is a frequent cause of classroom conflicts. Controlled communication is perhaps the most viable means of conflict resolution available. The negotiation plan we favor is valuable in any conflict situation but is of special relevance to those instances in which the dispute is between you and the entire classroom group. McCroskey and Wheeless (1976) have identified some guidelines for negotiations that apply well to educational settings:

1. Communication should be directed toward restoring trust. There is some evidence to suggest that reinstated communication in the absence of trust is not very useful.
2. Communication should focus on common goals. From our previous discussion of factors related to norms and power we would expect common goals to have an effect.
3. Communication should focus on other areas of similarity and agreement such as common attitudes, beliefs, and values.
4. Communication should be as positive and reinforcing as possible. This is particularly true of self-disclosures in conflict situations. Care should be given to positive and reinforcing disclosures.
5. Expressions of cooperation and compliance in areas indirectly related to the dispute should be sought.
6. Past behaviors indicating positive orientations should be discussed. (p. 257)

Keeping the communication channels open between all members of the classroom group is essential. This principle applies whether communication is being used in the process of compromise and bargaining to resolve conflicts or merely in the day-by-day exchange of the classroom. Healthy, positive social environments can neither develop nor survive without communication.

PRINCIPLES 10.3

1. Inadequate preparation for classroom conflicts is a common problem among teachers; the problem usually results in poor or inconsistent conflict management strategies.
2. Many teachers fail to recognize and exploit the potential benefits of classroom conflicts.

3. Positive confrontation techniques appear to be effective for teachers at all educational levels in dealing with conflicts.
4. Negotiation strategies which implement communication designed to restore trust, stress common goals, and accept disclosure are the most productive in classroom conflict management.
5. Conflict is a distinct aspect of classroom communication processes. Thus a systematic plan for conflict management rather than a series of conflict resolution tactics is likely to be the most productive for classroom life.

REFERENCES

Borton, T. *Reach, touch, and teach.* New York: McGraw-Hill, 1970.
Coffman, S. An investigation of teacher response to aggressive verbal student behavior. Purdue University, 1973. Reported in Friedrich, G., Galvin, K., and Book, C. *Growing together: Classroom communication.* Columbus, Ohio: Merrill, 1976.
Coser, L. *The functions of social conflict.* New York: Free Press, 1956.
Deutsch, M. Conflicts: Productive and destructive. *The Journal of Social Issues,* 1969, **25,** 7–41. © 1969. Materials on p. 246 reprinted by permission.
Dowell, C. The effect of a competitive and cooperative environment on the comprehension of a cognitive task. *Journal of Educational Research,* 1974–1975, **68,** 274–276.
Dunkin, M. and Biddle, B. *The study of teaching.* New York: Holt, Rinehart and Winston, 1974.
Frank, A. Conflict in the classroom. In F. Jandt (Ed.), *Conflict resolution through communication.* New York: Harper & Row, 1973, 240–310.
Friedrich, G., Galvin, K., and Book, C. *Growing together: Classroom communication.* Columbus, Ohio: Merrill, 1976.
Frost, J. H. and Wilmot, W. W. *Interpersonal conflict.* Dubuque, Iowa: Brown, 1978.
Galtung, J. Conflict as a way of life. In R. Strom and P. Torrance (Eds.), *Education for affective achievement.* Skokie, Ill.: Rand McNally, 1973, 47–53.
Glasser, W. *Schools without failure.* New York: Harper & Row, 1969.
Kochman, T. Rapping in the ghetto. In Barker, L. L. and Kibler, R. J. (Eds.) *Speech communication behavior.* Englewood Cliffs, N. J.: Prentice-Hall, 1971, 321–335.
McCroskey, J., and Wheeless, L. *Introduction to human communication.* Boston: Allyn & Bacon, 1976.
Miller, G. R., and Simons, H. W. *Perspectives on communication in social conflict.* Englewood Cliffs, N.J.: Prentice-Hall, 1974.
Miller, G. R., and Steinberg, M. *Between people: A new analysis of interpersonal communication.* Chicago: Science Research Associates, 1975.

Index

Destructive consequences of conflict, 264–265

Deutsch, M., 246, 252, 255, 256, 260, 261, 263

Deviant behavior, 229–230. *See also* Conflict in classrooms

Devito, J. A., 33

Dickens, Charles, 218

Dilendik, J., 209

Dion, K., 200

Direct teaching, 224–225, 227

Discipline, 227–230

Discriminative listening, 241–242

Double-bind messages, 124

Double negative, 90

Dowell, C., 252

Dress, 121

Dunkin, M. J., 175, 176, 262

Dysfunctional consequences of conflict, 263–264

Ekman, P., 110, 113, 114

Ellsworth, P., 193

Emblems, 113, 114

Emmert, P., 28

Empathy, 240

Esteem needs, 204

Evaluation

difference between student self-view and teacher, 41–42

number and consistency of appraisals, 44

Expectations, 15, 46–73, 251

as belief systems, 57–62

perception, nature of, 49–57

Pygmalion effect, 62–67, 70–71

signals of, 68–70

Expert power, 227, 228

Exposure, selective, 52

Expressive conflicts, 262

Eye contact, 129, 193, 194

Face Language (Whiteside), 111

Fast, J., 111

Feedback, 130–131

Fishbein, M., 51, 58, 59, 60, 190

Fitts, W. H., 31

Flanders, N., 218, 224–226

Floyd, J., 202, 204

Frank, A., 4, 248, 249, 251

Frank, L., 118–119

Franzolino, P., 147, 151

Freedman, J. L., 145

French, J., 227

French, R., 134

Friedrich, G. W., 159, 218, 248, 253

Friesen, W., 110, 113, 114

Frost, J. H., 247, 265

Functions of pragmatics, 97, 99–100

Furniture, in classrooms, 141

Furst, N., 224

Gagné, R. M., 163, 166

Gaier, E., 209

Galloway, C., 130, 131

Galtung, J., 266

Galvin, K. M., 159, 218, 248, 253

Games People Play (Berne), 261

Gergen, K. J., 12, 27, 41, 42, 44

Getzels, J., 216

Gingold, 146

Glasser, W., 260

Goffman, E., 128, 202

Goldberg, A., 240

Good, T. L., 62–64, 66–70, 72, 195, 199, 200, 202, 211, 226

Grade point average (GPA), 30, 31

Grading systems, 251, 259

Grant, B., 129

Griffith, W., 145, 146, 206

Grush, J., 201, 206, 209

Hall, E., 111, 114

Hamlish, E., 209

Haney, W. V., 55

Hansen, J. C., 23

Haptics, 116–117

Hard Times (Dickens), 218

Harrison, R., 122

Hedonism, 51

Hefele, T., 208

Heider, F., 189, 190

Hennings, D., 129

Holdridge, W., 180

Homonyms, 91–92

Honesty, 238, 240

Hopper, Robert, 75n, 87, 92

Human perception. *See* Perception

Illustrators, 113, 114

Imagining, 99

Immediacy, 193

Impersonal communication, 40

Impression management, 202

Indirect teaching, 224–226

Individual differences, classroom conflict and, 247–248

Inferential beliefs, 59–60

Influence. *See* Persuasion, influencing student attitudes and

Informational beliefs, 60–61

Information processing, perception as, 51–52

Informing, 97

Ingratiation, 204–205

78   79   80   81   82   9   8   7   6   5   4   3   2   1